D0117397

FUNNY

FOUNTAINHEAD PRESS V SERIES

Edited by
Catherine Cucinella

FOUNTAINHEAD
PRESS

Our green initiatives include:

Electronic Products
We deliver products in non-paper form whenever possible. This includes pdf downloadables, flash drives, and CDs.

Electronic Samples
We use Xample, a new electronic sampling system. Instructor samples are sent via a personalized Web page that links to pdf downloads.

FSC Certified Printers
All of our printers are certified by the Forest Service Council, which promotes environmentally and socially responsible management of the world's forests. This program allows consumer groups, individual consumers, and businesses to work together hand-in-hand to promote responsible use of the world's forests as a renewable and sustainable resource.

Recycled Paper
Most of our products are printed on a minimum of 30% post-consumer waste recycled paper.

Support of Green Causes
When we do print, we donate a portion of our revenue to green causes. Listed below are a few of the organizations that have received donations from Fountainhead Press. We welcome your feedback and suggestions for contributions, as we are always searching for worthy initiatives.
Rainforest 2 Reef
Environmental Working Group

Cover Image: © Graphicstock images

Design by Susan Moore

Books may be purchased for educational purposes.

For information, please call or write:

1-800-586-0330

Fountainhead Press
Southlake, TX 76092

Web site: www.fountainheadpress.com
E-mail: customerservice@fountainheadpress.com

First Edition

ISBN: 978-1-59871-801-0

Printed in the United States of America

INTRODUCTION TO THE FOUNTAINHEAD PRESS V SERIES

By Brooke Rollins and Lee Bauknight
Series Editors

The *Fountainhead Press V Series* is a signature collection of single-topic readers that offer a unique look at some of today's most pressing issues. Designed to give writing students a more nuanced introduction to public discourse—on the environment, on food, and on digital life, to name a few of the topics—the books feature writing, research, and invention prompts that can be adapted to nearly any kind of college writing class. Each *V Series* textbook focuses on a single issue and includes multi-genre and multimodal readings and assignments that move the discourse beyond the most familiar patterns of debate—patterns usually fettered by entrenched positions and often obsessed with "winning."

The ultimate goal of the series is to help writing students—who tend to hover on the periphery of public discourse—think, explore, find their voices, and skillfully compose texts in a variety of media and genres. Not only do the books help students think about compelling issues and how they might address them, they also give students the practice they need to develop their research, rhetorical, and writing skills. Together, the readings, prompts, and longer assignments show students how to add their voices to the conversations about these issues in meaningful and productive ways.

With enough readings and composing tasks to sustain an entire quarter or semester, and inexpensive enough to be used in combination with other rhetorics and readers, the *Fountainhead Press V Series* provides instructors with the flexibility to build the writing courses they want and need to teach. An instructor interested in deeply exploring environmental issues, for example, could design a semester- or quarter-long course using *Green*, the first of the *V Series* texts. At the same time, an instructor who wanted to teach discrete units on different issues could use two or more of the *V Series* books. In either case, the texts would give students ample opportunity—and a variety of ways—to engage with the issues at hand.

The *V Series* uses the term "composition" in its broadest sense. Of course, the textbooks provide students plenty of opportunities to write, but they also include assignments that take students beyond the page. Books in the series encourage students to explore other modes of communication by prompting them: to design websites, to produce videos, posters, and presentations; to conduct primary and secondary research; and to develop projects with community partners that might incorporate any number of these skills. Ultimately, we have designed the *Fountainhead Press V Series* to work for teachers and students. With their carefully chosen readings, built-in flexibility, and sound rhetorical grounding, the *V Series* books would be a dynamic and user-friendly addition to any writing class.

TABLE OF CONTENTS

INTRODUCTION: THE FUNNY THING ABOUT HUMOR IS THAT IT IS REALLY REALLY IMPORTANT!

By Catherine Cucinella

How many times have you laughed today? Research shows that the average adult laughs fifteen times each day, and in a 2013 survey, thirty-seven percent of men and fifty-eight percent of women identified a sense of humor as a "must have" in a relationship (Abbey). We encounter some aspect of humor everyday—on Facebook, Instagram, Twitter, Pinterest, in trending memes and GIFs, in advertising, on television, and in our use of emoticons and emoji. If humor is all around us, understanding its significance in our lives becomes a worthy quest.

A variety of disciplines study humor—psychology, biology, philosophy, sociology, anthropology, communication, and literature. Some scholars conduct research into the place of humor in our relationships. Others study the link between humor and bullying. Some humor scholars look for its evolutionary origins in an effort to identify humor's function in human survival. Many researchers and health practitioners claim that humor possesses a variety of health benefits. For example, laughing involves the diaphragm and abdominal, respiratory, facial, leg, and back muscles—hence the expressions, "laughed until it hurt," "side-splitting laughter," and "laughed our butts off" (Brain). However, studies done to validate the claims that humor and laughter can have a positive effect on immunity, pain tolerance, blood pressure, illness symptoms, and longevity are, in general, neither consistent nor conclusive. Work in clinical psychology does reveal that humor can potentially benefit one's sense of well-being and mental health (Martin 331, 270). Many who study the topic argue humor bridges cultural divides. Others, however, insist humor's reliance on stereotyping often perpetuates racism, sexism, and classism. Although these groups of scholars express opposing views about the effects of certain kinds of humor, they acknowledge its power to persuade or influence our thinking. These various disciplines and scholars employ different approaches and often stress the different aspects and effects of humor; however, they all assume that humor involves a degree of creativity and the capacity for conceptual understanding and conceptual shifts. Furthermore, many scholars argue that humor is a uniquely human characteristic. As you can see, humor is a relevant topic of study because of its significant role in the following three areas: identity (ontology), culture, and knowledge or meaning-making (epistemology).

What do I mean when I say that humor, or what we find funny, is connected to who we are, to our culture or society, and to what or how we know things? First, I proceed on the assumption that most of us agree that identity, culture, and knowledge are connected (at least, on some level, the culture and society in which we live, and the stuff we know, and how we make sense of things does influence our sense of self). Second, on the most basic level, I mean that what we find funny and how we use humor reflect and shape our identity. Third, because it generates from and means something within specific cultures and societies, humor reveals what a culture or society values. What a twenty-something-year-old Chinese American female living in San Jose, California finds funny might not tickle the funny bone of a twenty-something-year-old female living in Bangalore, India. In addition to this larger cultural aspect, our more immediate social environments influence what we find funny, and humor often serves a social purpose. We use humor to connect with people or to ridicule and exclude individuals, to smooth over awkward moments, or to diffuse a volatile situation. Fourth, because using and getting humor very often rely on stereotypes and on our prior knowledge, humor often influences our perspectives on people different from us and on political and social issues. In other words, what we laugh at can construct our knowledge of our world.

The articles, stories, studies, blogs, satires, and reports that comprise *Funny* complicate rather than simplify what humor is, how it works, and its place in our lives. These readings invite you to examine humor and laughter through diverse lenses and to think critically about the value, politics, and ethics of humor. As you read and write about this topic, you will necessarily have to grapple with issues of race, sexuality, class, exclusion, and inclusion, and perhaps religion, politics, free speech, nationalism, and health—all of which tie to identity, culture, and knowledge. Thus, becoming aware of the many aspects of humor opens exciting and provocative pathways of critical inquiry.

HUMOR, CULTURE, AND THE INTERNET

Today humor proliferates as the Internet has become the medium, par excellence, for creating and disseminating humor, as well as changing the cultural landscape of humor. The Internet meme phenomenon is only one example of social media's influence on what we deem funny. Although not a required characteristic, humor is often present in memes. A meme can suggest an "inside joke," and once the meme "goes viral," the circle of insiders who get the joke enlarges, thus expanding what individuals consider funny. Because cultural ideas and cultural humor are important characteristics of memes, they transmit both, a transmission that can potentially enhance cross-cultural understandings. In other words, the Internet adds a global dimension to humor. This *global* aspect results from the Internet's ability to make visual the *local* by particularizing jokes, humorous events, and experiences. YouTube, which makes available a glimpse at specific cultural and topical humor to millions of people around the world, exemplifies the globalization of the local. For example, rappers Nice Peter and EpicLLOYD, creators of *Epic Rap Battles of History*, each assume different characters spitting rap lines at each other. When *Epic Rap Battles* pits Elvis Presley against Michael Jackson, or Albert Einstein against Stephen Hawking, or Gandalf against Dumbledore, or Santa Claus against Moses, it relies upon specific cultural knowledges and experiences. However, because these rap battles also feature physical humor, one can lack this cultural knowledge and still enjoy the humor. In other words, these raps can evoke laughter from those of us who may not fully get the humor, especially if we enjoy slapstick. This enjoyment explains the popularity and ubiquity of the "Epic Fails," "Scary Snowman," and pranking videos on the web.

The Internet *has* helped to translate humor across cultural lines, nevertheless *specific* social and cultural dimensions greatly influence what we do or do not find funny. For example, Cultural Savvy, a program to help global businesses develop cultural competency, provides "some basic rules to remember" regarding humor: "Each culture has its own style of humor." "Humor is very difficult to export." "Humor requires an in-depth understanding of culture." "Avoid the following: ethnic-type humor, stereotyping, sexist, off-color, cultural, or religious humor" ("Using Humor"). These "rules" clearly indicate the importance of understanding the link between humor and culture. However, as you know we can share laughter with people different from us; we may not always agree on why something is funny, but we all agree that humor is important in our lives and in our world.

Kevin Hart "says he has internalized something Chris Rock once told him: the only thing all people have in common, regardless of race, gender, faith, politics or sexual preference, is that they like to laugh" (Wallace).

HUMOR, LAUGHTER, AND HUMANNESS

As you study humor—read and write about it—you will do more than amass information about a subject because humor, according to philosopher Simon Critchley, tells us about *being* human. Whether tongue-in-cheek or not, Critchley writes that humor makes us human because Aristotle tells us so. His reference to Aristotle reminds us that humor and questions of being (ontological questions) have long fascinated philosophers. Most humor scholars agree with philosopher and humor theorist, John Morreall, author of *Taking Laughter Seriously*, that "our capacity to laugh is anything but a peripheral aspect of human life and to understand our laughter is to go a long way toward understanding our humanity" (x). However, philosophers are not the only scholars who make this claim about the ontological aspects of humor. Identifying their approach as that of theoretical cognitive scientists, Matthew Hurley, cognitive scientist; Daniel Dennett, philosopher; and Reginald Adams, psychologist point out that the jokes we tell and the situations, things, and people at which we choose to laugh reveal to others where we position ourselves in the world (12). In our laughter and through our sense of humor, we may reveal our humanity or perhaps, at times, our inhumanity.

The paradox of humor is that we need the mental dexterity to get and express it, but humor's manifestation and expression almost always involve the physical body, which as some argue, becomes very "animal-like" in certain forms of humor. Take a moment to think about the language we use to describe our laughter: *cackle, howl, shriek, roar, bray, snort, hee-haw, crow*—all very animal-like, indeed! You might wonder if animals laugh, and if they do, whether their laughter means they "get the joke." The abundance of images of laughing animals on the Internet seems to provide ample evidence of both. Do laughing animals make them more human, or do they disprove humor's link to humanness? Neurologist and neuropsychiatrist, Richard Restak tells us that although studies of apes suggest they engage in teasing "accompanied by laughter," apes cannot "make multiple interpretations of a situation" (22). In other words, they may laugh, but they are reacting to the play rather than to a conceptual understanding or appreciation of humor.

Getting humor involves the networks in the brain, networks located in the cerebral cortex "related to speech, general information, and the appreciation of contradiction and illogicality" (Restak 21). For humans, humor very much relies on one or more of these areas. In order to find something funny, we draw on what we know, believe, and expect. We depend on generalized scripts and unrecognized (and unexamined) assumptions on which these scripts rest. Our ability to make sense of an inconsistency between a script and a humorous situation and to *appreciate* the humor in the contradiction and illogicality is a mark of our humanness (22).

Restak also points to the distinction between laughter and humor. We can laugh even in the absence of humor, pointing out we may laugh when we are frightened, sad, or embarrassed.

Many humor scholars note that a difference exists between humor and laughter, yet, as you will discover, it often becomes impossible to address one without addressing the other. Marshall Brain, founder of *HowStuffWorks*, states, in "How Laughter Works," "Laughter is the physiological response to humor." Your first reaction might be that Brain is making an obvious distinction. However, as you explore this topic more fully through the readings, assignments, and activities in *Funny*, you may want to revisit this assumption. Perhaps untangling the physiological—or at least the corporeal—from humor is not quite as straightforward as it seems. Indeed, as noted above, Morreall argues for the centrality of *laughter* in

Sharing a laugh or sharing a joke?

human life. In light of Restak's study, we might conclude that regardless of how animal-like our expression of humor or how human-like animal laughter seems the ability to interpret the joke, humorous event, or experience is a uniquely human characteristic. In addition, we might further conclude that humor's cultural, ontological, and epistemological aspects solidify its link to our humanness. This book encourages you to investigate these arguments and conclusions and to figure out where you stand in relation to the various theories regarding humor's place in our world.

THREE THEORIES OF HUMOR AND HOW HUMOR FUNCTIONS

Many of the readings in *Funny* draw from, rely on, or expand upon well-developed theories of humor. The following theories constitute the foundational explanations of humor—of what we find funny and why we laugh: the incongruity, the superiority, and the relief theories. The incongruity theory of humor aligns with the cognitive aspect of humor and laughter. This theory posits humor as an intellectual response to something that surprises us—to something that differs from the norm or accepted pattern. We laugh at situations, actions, or behaviors we find illogical, unexpected, or inappropriate. However, our ability to "resolve" the incongruity proves crucial for us to appreciate the

Thesis

humor. The superiority theory of humor is, as its name implies, based on the notion that we laugh because we feel superior to other people. Laughter then becomes an expression of this feeling of superiority. This theory is used to ridicule, bully, exclude, as well as to strengthen group solidarity or as a social corrective. In its simplest form, the relief theory of humor ties to the biological function of laughter and expresses a physiological point of view. Humor and laughter release tension or excessive energy. Of course, the incongruity, superiority, and relief theories of humor are more complex than I present them here, and they necessarily overlap in many ways. Each offers slightly different explanatory approaches to the subject. The incongruity theory tells us why we find something funny; the relief theory stresses humor's function. The superiority theory seems to do both and also reveals the personal *and* social dimensions of humor.

Although our sense of humor may be individual and tied to a specific cultural context, humor and laughter are social. Many who study both argue that, in addition to *having* a social aspect, humor and laughter also *serve* a social function. In other words, humor is important not only for the health and well-being of the individual but also for that of a community, society, and culture. Morreall devotes an entire chapter of his book on laughter to "the social value of humor." He sees laughter as contagious; it possesses a "cohesive effect" and is "a friendly social gesture"; "it facilitates social interaction" (114-20). Morreall's view of laughter should resonate with all of us. At some point in our lives, we have "caught laughter," laughed because someone else was laughing. Although the Internet and increased opportunities afforded to us by social media (check out Dave Barry's "Technology" on this subject, page 219 in *Funny*) means that we often are physically alone when we encounter humor, one might argue that we are in a virtual social context. In other words, we have a sense of a communal or shared experience of humor just as we do when we watch TV.

Rod Martin, like Morreall, addresses the social context of humor, noting that "[h]umor can (and frequently does) occur in virtually any social situation" and identifies "the social context of humor [as] one of play" (5). This play, however, can often be very serious, and humor often becomes an effective mode through which to challenge the status quo, confront narrow-mindedness, or enact social protest. The use of humor to address inequality, oppression, and the abuse of power has a long history. While my purpose in *Funny* is not to present this history, I hope that as you encounter the various perspectives on humor and laugh at (or not) the stories and images in this text you will want to learn more about the historical roots of humor. Knowing that humor draws upon a rich tradition enhances our understanding of its potential to change perceptions and practices.

HUMOR'S PERSUASIVE POWER

When we examine the ways individuals unconsciously and consciously employ humor, we find that used skillfully and purposefully it is an effective persuasive strategy or rhetorical tool. This idea—humor's link to rhetoric—is not a new one. Plato, when he conceived of his perfect society, had strong views on laughter, marginalizing those at whom laughter is directed and condemning what he perceived as the inherently derogatory nature of humor. His concern with humor and laughter, however, indicates that Plato saw humor's potential to influence how individuals think and act. Indeed, the Roman orators/rhetoricians Cicero and Quintilian (whose ideas still influence our understanding and practice of rhetoric) acknowledge humor's appropriateness in specific rhetorical situations, and both point out that humor may relieve or diffuse tensions thus benefitting the speaker and his argument (yes, they meant males).

In *On Oratory and Orators*, Cicero provides instructions for invention in oratory, specifically noting that "[a] jocose manner, too, and strokes of wit, give pleasure to an audience, and are often of great advantage to the speaker" (II.LIV 144). Used carefully and artfully, humor strengthens the speaker's position and enhances his ethos (II.LVII 150). Quintilian, like Cicero, instructed orators of his day on the proper and effective techniques of oration, and, like Cicero, he finds value in the strategic use of humor. Specifically, in his textbook on the theory and practice of rhetoric, *Institutes of Oratory*, Quintilian, locates great power in laughter because it "very frequently dissipates both hatred and anger" (VI. III). He is quite clear, however, that the ability to use humor effectively—to the orator's advantage—is rare. Nonetheless, Quintilian spends a considerable amount of time in Book VI providing examples of and explaining humor's rhetorical fitness. In other words, he includes humor as an effective means of swaying an orator's audience and opponents, of gaining an advantage, and of changing perspectives.

Satire may best exemplify the persuasiveness and the promise of humor. Satire, often humorous, critiques human vice and folly in an attempt to improve human institutions or humanity and relies on comedic devices such as parody and exaggeration. Satirists see great power in humor, and in their hands, humor becomes the mirror that reflects our flaws. However, rather than using it as a weapon to destroy humanity, satirists use humor as a tool to expose and dismantle these flaws—to offer social commentary and change perspectives. Television shows like *Saturday Night Live, South Park, The Simpsons, Family Guy, The Daily Show with Jon Stewart, The Colbert Report*, and *Parks and Recreation* offer satirical commentary on a wide range of topics. However, first and foremost, these shows make us laugh.

ETHNIC-RACIAL HUMOR

As today's comedians make us laugh, they also make us think. Much like Shakespeare's fools and clowns who often possess the clearest vision of their fellow human beings and their society, our comedians often force us to see ourselves and others more clearly and to listen more keenly to voices other than our own. Comedians like Richard Pryor, Dave Chappelle, Margaret Cho, Louis CK, and Gabriel Iglesias open a space for us to talk about difficult issues such as racism, sexism, and classism. Although one can use humor to reinforce those "isms," these funny men and women use humor to confront harmful stereotypes and to reveal unexamined assumptions about blacks, Asians, Mexicans, lesbians, gays, and working class Americans. These "isms," stereotypes, and assumptions seem tightly linked to our sense of self and to important social and cultural issues.

Therefore, examining the relationship between humor and race is not always easy. How often have you laughed at a joke that you considered racist? Have you ever stopped someone from telling a racist joke? How does one use humor to challenge racism? Almost universally, ethnic and racial humor works on the model whereby jokes target marginalized groups. In this form of disparaging humor, according to David Gillota, author of *Ethnic Humor in Multiethnic America*, "Very often, the dominant group remains unseen or simply implied" (10). This invisibility extends into the opposing sets of adjectives that drive disparaging jokes (smart/stupid, industrious/lazy), with the positive value (smart, industrious) implicitly aligning with the perceived characteristics of the dominant group (Rappoport 133). Because stereotypes and slurs are staples of ethnic and racial humor, they become important areas to consider. If we look at the history of American ethnic humor, we see, from colonial times until about the 1950s, this humor included "ethnic caricatures in newspapers cartoons . . . in minstrel shows . . . [which] survive[ed] throughout much of the twentieth century" (Gillota 7). By the civil rights movement, ethnic comedians such as African Americans Dick Gregory and Richard Pryor and those of Jewish heritage such as Lenny Bruce, Woody Allen, and Mel Brooks emerged. Although Gillota asserts that "these humorists would rework familiar ethnic stereotypes, often collapsing or subverting them," I urge you to consider how one knows if the humor reinforces or challenges the stereotype (8). Nevertheless, when the difficult becomes funny, the potential for change, or empathy, or understanding does emerge.

BAWDY HUMOR—CHALLENGING TABOOS

However, this notion of "funny" gets stickier when we turn our attention to taste or bawdiness. In his 2013 piece on the backlash caused by Seth MacFarlane's performance as host of that year's Academy Awards, *Chicago Tribune's* chief theater critic, Chris Jones, addresses the subject of offensive humor. Referring specifically to Jon Stewart and *The Onion* (a satirical online newspaper), Jones writes "that even top brand names in comedy are struggling to figure what's actually offensive these days." Like other aspects of humor and laughter that you will read about in *Funny*, questions about humor's bawdiness have a long history. Contemporary comedy and comedic performances of scatological (vulgar, crude, off-color) humor flow from the tradition of the Greek dramatist Aristophanes (c 44-380 B.C.), whose plays abound with implicit and explicit sexual humor tightly wedded to his brilliant political satire. We find further examples of ribald humor in Geoffrey Chaucer's *The Canterbury Tales* (1475), specifically in "The Millar's Tale," a *fabliau*, a story showing high class people in comical or satirical compromising situations involving sex and/or money. The "tradition" of bawdiness continues in the work of William Shakespeare (1564-1616). Almost all of his plays (the tragedies and comedies), contain sexual puns, double entendres, and characters engaged in sexual banter. Shakespeare, like Aristophanes and Chaucer, understood and evoked scatological humor because it makes us laugh, maybe because of or despite its "crudeness." However, many argue humor and laughter remind us that we are human, in a bodily (bawdy) sense.

The current debates regarding off-color or vulgar humor are not new. When the civil rights movement provided a "stage" for ethnic comedians to talk about racial issues, these same comedians, most notably Redd Foxx, Lenny Bruce, and Richard Pryor, also incorporated raunch humor into their performances. However, these comedians' bawdy humor sounded and looked very different from that of Aristophanes, Chaucer, and Shakespeare. Foxx, Bruce, and Pryor each deliberately violated taboos by giving public voice to private lived-experiences of marginalized peoples. Using X-rated language, Foxx spoke what he heard and knew about being a black man in white America. Pryor, too, drew on his own experiences as a black man in America and "defied the boundaries of taste, decency and race to become the comic voice of a generation" (Schudel). Intent on challenging the status quo, everything deemed socially acceptable, and the limits of free

speech, Bruce may be the "poster boy" of scatological humor. This iconoclast of the 1950-60s, brought up on obscenity charges for his night club comedy, defended the comic's right to free speech. Today, humor's bawdiness seems routine in comedy clubs, television programs, films, and other media. However, as comedians, humorists, and satirists use humor to challenge taboos or find new ways to make us laugh, controversies regarding the limits of acceptability and taste will continue. Humor—what it is, how we use it, what it means, and how we interpret it—is messy.

WHAT *FUNNY* WANTS YOU TO DO

Funny embraces this messiness as it asks you to read, write, and think critically about the following questions: When and why is something funny or not? *Who* decides what is funny? Can humor transcend cultures? How do race, class, and gender affect our sense of humor? Does humor promote inclusion or exclusion? What can we learn about ourselves, about others, about our world by examining what we find funny and what other people find funny? Is humor *ever* innocent? Finally, I hope that *Funny* opens up a multitude of other areas for you to explore and that the selections get you thinking and, yes, laughing.

Works Cited

Abbey, Jennifer. "Top Qualities Single Men and Women Seek in the Opposite Sex." *ABCNews. Go.com.* ABC News. 05 Feb. 2013. Web. 08 July 2014.

Brain, Marshall. "How Laughter Works." *HowStuffWorks.* Web. 12 Dec. 2012.

Cicero. *On Oratory and Orators.* Trans. Ralph A. Micken. Carbondale: Southern Illinois UP, 1970. Print.

Critchley, Simon. *On Humor*. New York: Routledge, 2002. Print.

Gillota, David. *Ethnic Humor in Multiethnic America*. New Brunswick: Rutgers University Press, 2013. Print.

Hurley, Matthew, Daniel Dennett, and Reginald Adams Jr. *Inside Jokes: Using Humor to Reverse-Engineer the Mind*. Cambridge: MIT Press, 2011. Print.

Jones, Chris. "When Jokes Go Too Far." *ChicagoTribune.com* The Chicago Tribune. 01 Mar. 2013. Web. 13 Jan. 2014.

Lefcourt, Herbert M. *Humor: The Psychology of Living Buoyantly*. New York: Kluwer Academic/Plenum Publishers, 2001. Print.

Martin, Rod. *The Psychology of Humor: An Integrative Approach*. Burlington, MA: Elsevier, 2007. Print.

Morreall, John. *Taking Laughter Seriously*. Albany: State University of New York, 1983. Print.

Quintilian. *Institutes of Oratory*. Ed. Lee Honeycutt. Trans. John Selby Watson. 2006. Iowa State. Web. 10 Mar. 2014. <http://rhetoric.eserver.org/quintilian/>.

Rappoport, Leon. *Punchlines: The Case for Racial, Ethnic, and Gender Humor*. Westport, CT: Praeger, 2005. Print.

Restak, Richard. "Laughter and the Brain." *The American Scholar* 82 (2011): 18-27. *Academic Search Premier*. Web. 2 Feb. 2014.

Schudel, Matt. "With Humor and Anger on Race Issues, Comic Inspired a Generation." *WashingtonPost.com*. The Washington Post. 11 Dec. 2005. Web. 18 May 2014.

"Using Humor." *Cultural Savvy*, n.d. Web. 07 July 2014.

Wallace, Amy. "Walking Tall with Kevin Hart." *GQ.com*. GQ May 2014. Web. 16 July 2014.

Look at the *Calvin and Hobbes* cartoon by cartoonist Bill Watterson and the political cartoon by Mike Luckovich. Both of these cartoons exemplify the complicated nature of humor and its potential to help to think critically. What are the weighty issues that Watterson's cartoon puts before us? What is Luckovich tackling in his cartoon and what's up with the "Grumpy Cat"? What was your reaction to these cartoons? Whether you "like" the message or not, can you identify how the use of humor helps convey the argument and makes it more persuasive?

Using the Internet, find a meme or view one of the Nice Peter and EpicLLOYD rap battles, or a clip from *The Colbert Report*, *The Daily Show with Jon Stewart*, or one of the other shows mentioned. Write a reflection on your experience with this material by addressing the following questions: Did you find the material funny? Why or why not? Did the material rely on specific cultural references? If so, what were these references? Did you understand them? If not, did you make an effort to find their meaning? If so, what did you do? Can you *describe* the humor? Did you laugh? Did you share the humor with anyone else?

Write a detailed narrative about a time that you laughed "until you cried." Be sure to provide the context for the funny event or incident. Feel free to use dialog. When you finish your narrative, begin a new page and address the following questions:
1. What about this incident and your telling of it might appeal to others beside you and the people (if any) involved in the narrative?
2. What do you think makes this incident funny?
3. At the time of the incident or experience, what function did the humor serve?
4. How does the humor work in your narration of the incident or experience?

In addition to a meme generally possessing a cultural component, it is an idea which replicates and evolves as it is transmitted from one individual to another—or as it goes viral. Internet memes are often short videos, images, pictures, and hashtags. Many, but not all, memes also are humorous.

_____

_____

THREE POPULAR MEMES

CONDESCENDING WONKA

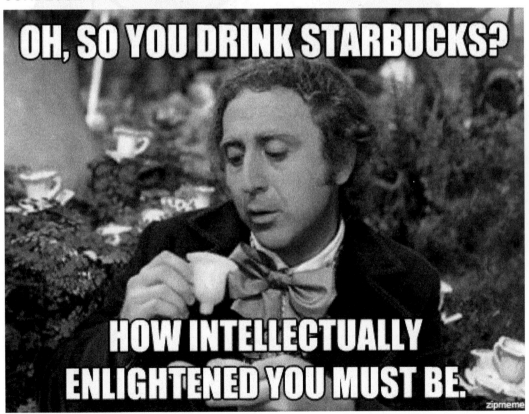

OVERLY ATTACHED GIRLFRIEND

BAD LUCK BRIAN

Identify the idea or ideas that each of the memes attempts to transmit. Do you see a cultural or social aspect to these memes? If you do, explain that aspect; if you do not, explain how the idea or humor transcends a specific cultural or social context. If you have not done so, read the introduction to *Funny* (specifically the section on the theories of humor). Drawing on one or more of these theories, identify and explain the humor in these memes.

Working with a group of your peers, create a meme. If you are not familiar with memes, a quick Internet search will bring up some of the most popular such as "Ancient Aliens," "Philosoraptor," "Kermit the Frog," "Grumpy Cat," or "Confused Black Girl." In addition to finding some images, you will find meme generators and tips for creating memes—the "unofficial" rules. Then write a process report explaining how you created the meme. In your report detail what decisions you had to make regarding the subject, the message, the images, and text. Finally, explain what you had to think about regarding the audience for the meme. Be prepared to share your meme and explain your process with the class.

Henri Bergson, a famous French philosopher in the late 19th and early 20th century, examined the levels of consciousness and the relation of the mind to the body and developed a theory of time which he applied to living beings. In 1927, Bergson won the Nobel Prize for Literature in part for the literary influence of his book, Laughter: An Essay on the Meaning of the Comic. This book, according to Bergson's entry on Nobelprize.org, "provided a theory of comedy and established its place in a survey of aesthetics and the philosophy of art."

THE COMIC IN GENERAL—THE COMIC ELEMENT IN FORMS AND MOVEMENTS— EXPANSIVE FORCE OF THE COMIC

BY HENRI BERGSON

What does laughter mean? What is the basal element in the laughable? What common ground can we find between the grimace of a merryandrew, a play upon words, an equivocal situation in a burlesque and a scene of high comedy? What method of distillation will yield us invariably the same essence from which so many different products borrow either their obtrusive odour or their delicate perfume? The greatest of thinkers, from Aristotle downwards, have tackled this little problem, which has a knack of baffling every effort, of slipping away and escaping only to bob up again, a pert challenge flung at philosophic speculation. Our excuse for attacking the problem in our turn must lie in the fact that we shall not aim at imprisoning the comic spirit within a definition. We regard it, above all, as a living thing. However trivial it may be, we shall treat it with the respect due to life. We shall confine ourselves to watching it grow and expand. Passing by imperceptible gradations from one form to another, it will be seen to achieve the strangest metamorphoses. We shall disdain nothing we have seen. Maybe we may gain from this prolonged contact, for the matter of that, something more flexible than an abstract definition,—a practical, intimate acquaintance, such as springs from a long companionship. And maybe we may also find that, unintentionally, we have made an acquaintance that is useful. For the comic spirit has a logic of its own, even in its wildest eccentricities. It has a method in its madness. It dreams, I admit, but it conjures up, in its dreams, visions that are at once accepted and

From *Laughter: An Essay on the Meaning of the Comic* (1911).

☺ 17 ☺

understood by the whole of a social group. Can it then fail to throw light for us on the way that human imagination works, and more particularly social, collective, and popular imagination? Begotten of real life and akin to art, should it not also have something of its own to tell us about art and life?

At the outset we shall put forward three observations which we look upon as fundamental. They have less bearing on the actually comic than on the field within which it must be sought.

I

The first point to which attention should be called is that the comic does not exist outside the pale of what is strictly HUMAN. A landscape may be beautiful, charming and sublime, or insignificant and ugly; it will never be laughable. You may laugh at an animal, but only because you have detected in it some human attitude or expression. You may laugh at a hat, but what you are making fun of, in this case, is not the piece of felt or straw, but the shape that men have given it,—the human caprice whose mould it has assumed. It is strange that so important a fact, and such a simple one too, has not attracted to a greater degree the attention of philosophers. Several have defined man as "an animal which laughs." They might equally well have defined him as an animal which is laughed at; for if any other animal, or some lifeless object, produces the same effect, it is always because of some resemblance to man, of the stamp he gives it or the use he puts it to.

Here I would point out, as a symptom equally worthy of notice, the ABSENCE OF FEELING which usually accompanies laughter. It seems as though the comic could not produce its disturbing effect unless it fell, so to say, on the surface of a soul that is thoroughly calm and unruffled. Indifference is its natural environment, for laughter has no greater foe than emotion. I do not mean that we could not laugh at a person who inspires us with pity, for instance, or even with affection, but in such a case we must, for the moment, put our affection out of court and impose silence upon our pity. In a society composed of pure intelligences there would probably be no more tears, though perhaps there would still be laughter; whereas highly emotional souls, in tune and unison with life, in whom every event would be sentimentally prolonged and re-echoed, would neither know nor understand laughter. Try, for a moment, to become interested in everything that is being said and done; act, in imagination, with those who act, and feel with those who feel; in a word, give your sympathy its widest expansion: as though at the touch of a fairy wand you will see the flimsiest of objects assume importance, and a gloomy hue spread over everything. Now step aside, look upon life as a disinterested spectator: many a drama will turn into a comedy. It is enough for us to stop our ears to the sound of music, in a room where dancing is going on, for the dancers at once to appear ridiculous. How many human actions would stand a similar test? Should we not see many of them suddenly pass from grave to gay, on isolating them from the accompanying music of sentiment? To produce the whole of its effect, then, the comic demands something like a momentary anesthesia of the heart. Its appeal is to intelligence, pure and simple.

This intelligence, however, must always remain in touch with other intelligences. And here is the third fact to which attention should be drawn. You would hardly appreciate the comic if you felt yourself isolated from others. Laughter appears to stand in need of an echo, Listen to it carefully: it is not an articulate, clear, well-defined sound; it is something which would fain be prolonged by reverberating from one to another, something beginning with a crash, to continue in successive rumblings, like thunder in a mountain. Still, this reverberation cannot go on for ever. It can travel within as wide a circle as you please: the circle remains, none the less, a closed one. Our laughter is always the laughter of a group. It may, perchance, have happened to you, when seated in a railway carriage or at table d'hote, to hear travellers relating to one another stories which must have been comic to them, for they laughed heartily. Had you been one of their company, you would have laughed like them; but, as you were not, you had no desire whatever to do so. A man who was once asked why he did not weep at a sermon, when everybody else was shedding tears, replied: "I don't belong to the parish!" What that man thought of tears would be still more true of laughter. However spontaneous it seems, laughter always implies a kind of secret freemasonry, or even complicity, with other laughers, real or imaginary. How often has it been said that the fuller the theatre, the more uncontrolled the laughter of the audience! On the other hand, how often has the remark been made that many comic effects are incapable of translation from one language to another, because they refer to the customs and ideas of a particular social group! It is through not understanding the importance of this double fact that the comic has been looked upon as a mere curiosity in which the mind finds amusement, and laughter itself as a strange, isolated phenomenon, without any bearing on the rest of human activity. Hence those definitions which tend to make the comic into an abstract relation between ideas: "an intellectual contrast," "a palpable absurdity," etc.,—definitions which, even were they really suitable to every form of the comic, would not in the least explain why the comic makes us laugh. How, indeed, should it come about that this particular logical relation, as soon as it is perceived, contracts, expands and shakes our limbs, whilst all other relations leave the body unaffected? It is not from this point of view that we shall approach the problem. To understand laughter, we must put it back into its natural environment, which is society, and above all must we determine the utility of its function, which is a social one. Such, let us say at once, will be the leading idea of all our investigations. Laughter must answer to certain requirements of life in common. It must have a SOCIAL signification.

Let us clearly mark the point towards which our three preliminary observations are converging. The comic will come into being, it appears, whenever a group of men concentrate their attention on one of their number, imposing silence on their emotions and calling into play nothing but their intelligence. What, now, is the particular point on which their attention will have to be concentrated, and what will here be the function of intelligence?

Bergson asserts that humor, or "the comic does not exist outside the pale of what is strictly human". What reasons does he give for this assertion? He also makes observations regarding the role feelings play in laughter. What does Bergson mean when he says, "laughter has no greater foe than emotion"? In this piece, he offers three fundamental observations necessary for understanding the comic—one about humanness, one about feelings. Identify his third observation and provide at least three of Bergson's key supporting/explanatory points.

Working either in pairs or with two other classmates, read the following two texts in *Funny*: "Early Conceptions of Humor in Religion, Medicine, Philosophy, and Psychology," by Herbert Lefcourt and "The Social Value of Humor" by John Morreall. After reading these pieces, summarize *and* synthesize these writers' ideas. Use your summaries and syntheses to frame a collaboratively written 2–3 page explanation of the relationship between laughter and humanity. Be prepared to share your writing with the class. You may want to create a Google doc in order to facilitate the collaboration.

Herbert Lefcourt, a clinical psychologist and leading researcher in humor, taught at the University of Waterloo, Ontario, Canada. In Humor: The Psychology of Living Buoyantly, *Lefcourt identifies humor as a coping strategy critical for our emotional well-being, particularly during stressful experiences. He also shows the relationship between humor and feelings of connection and community. The following excerpt, which appears early in Lefcourt's book, grounds Lefcourt's argument regarding the "evolutionary" aspect of humor and human beings.*

EARLY CONCEPTIONS OF HUMOR IN RELIGION, MEDICINE, PHILOSOPHY, AND PSYCHOLOGY

By Herbert M. Lefcourt

A motion picture that won three Oscars at the 1999 Academy Awards raised serious questions for those who view humor as a gift with positive evolutionary significance for our species. *Life Is Beautiful* was so well received that it became the biggest U.S. box office hit of any Italian film ever screened in North America. It is the story of a Jewish-Italian man who tries to protect his young son from the horrors of a Nazi concentration camp by pretending that the camp's routines are actually an elaborate game staged for the boy's entertainment. The father who attempts to create this comic vision is played by Roberto Benigni, who was also the film's co-writer and director.

Among his various honors, Benigni was invited to the Vatican to present the film to the Pope. It was one of the very few films that the Pope has seen in his lifetime. After viewing the film with Benigni the Pope embraced him. The Pope seemed to have been overwhelmed by the ressurrective theme of the film wherein the horrors of the Holocaust were diminished by humor. However, not everyone was so enamored. David Denby, movie critic for *The New Yorker* magazine, felt compelled to write two separate reviews of the film (November 16, 1998; March 15, 1999) because he was so disturbed by the premise that agonies such as concentration camp life could be relieved by clownishness. To Denby, the horrors of the Holocaust and the concentration camps were simply beyond the purview of humor. He felt that Benigni was self-deluding

From *Humor: The Psychology of Living Buoyantly* (New York: Kluwar Academic/Plenum Publishers, 2001): 31-40.

in believing that the enormity of such horror could ever be alleviated by so slight a weapon as humor. It was not that humor or laughter never occurred in concentration camps; there have been enough anecdotes from camp survivors to attest to those occurrences. However, to suggest that the horrific oppression of concentration camp life could be so completely altered by humor and clowning was deemed inappropriate and inconceivable by Denby. Showing that humor could undo such horror was said to trivialize it, diminishing the magnitude of the catastrophic and dehumanizing camp existence to the dimensions proposed by Holocaust deniers.

Keith-Spiegel (1972) has described how different thinkers and philosophers vary in their estimations of humor, from those who view it as a "gift handed down from the gods" to those who see it as a "scourge delivered up from the devils" (p. 25).

In a delightful article entitled "A Laugh a Day: Can Mirth Keep Disease at Bay?" Jeffrey Goldstein (1982) presents selected opinions about humor and laughter from early writings in medicine, philosophy, and religion. Among religious writers, Goldstein contends, laughter has usually been held in poor regard. Quoting Robert Barclay in his *Apology for the True Christian Divinity*, Goldstein notes that comedy, along with games, sport, and play, has been said to be inappropriate for Christians because these activities "disagree" with "Christian silence, gravity, and sobriety" (p. 23). Disdain for laughter among the "religiously correct" was likewise manifested in the beliefs of the Pilgrims in America (p. 23). In fact, Goldstein contends, laughter in public has been socially acceptable only for approximately a hundred years.

Before accepting an assumed relationship between religiosity and a lack of humor, however, we should differentiate among religions. As noted by Berger (1997), it is largely the "Abrahamic religions," the monotheistic Judaism, Christianity, and Islam, that "are comparatively underprivileged in the department of mirth" (p. 268). The lack of mirth in Christianity is said to have prompted Nietzsche to have made his renowned quip that he "would find Christianity more believable if only the Christians looked more redeemed."

In contrast to the Abrahamic religions, laughter and humor is common among Zen monks, Taoist sages, and Sufi practitioners, and if one may draw inferences from the multitude of laughing Buddhas on display in the shops of most Chinatowns, laughter would seem to be quite acceptable among Buddhists as well. As noted by Horne (1996), however, "seriousness" is the usual demeanor of Christianity, and Berger (1997) speaks of "Christian theology as a depressingly lachrymose affair" with only occasional exceptions, such as the humor of Martin Luther, which was often used by his critics to discredit him.

Discussions about humor can be found in the writings of Plato *(Philebus)*, Aristotle *(Poetics)*, Hobbes *(Leviathan)*, and Rousseau *(Lettre à M. d'Alembert)*. These works most often focused on the derisive qualities of laughter, asserting that it is most often directed at the ugliness and deformities of others and always has a tinge of venom. Consequently, laughter was said to reflect the more undesirable, aggressive qualities of humans that result in the victimization of others. Aristotle suggested that "comedy aims at representing man as worse, tragedy as better than in actual life" and "the ludicrous is merely a subdivision of the ugly" (Piddington, 1963, p. 153). Bergson (1911) argued that humor and laughter represent powerful social correctives that are used to humiliate and correct persons who do not conform to social expectations. Perhaps the most pejorative comments about laughter were offered by Hobbes, who noted that "the passion of laughter is nothing else but some sudden glory arising from some sudden conception of some eminence in ourselves, by comparison with the infirmity of others or with our own formerly" (Piddington, 1963, p. 160). In Hobbes's consideration, humor resulted from a sense of superiority accompanying the disparagement of other persons or our own past ways of acting or thinking. Zillman (1983) pointed out that where Plato and Aristotle suggested that it is the powerful and unblemished who laugh at the infirm and ugly, Hobbes viewed laughter as characterizing the imperfect and blemished, who laugh at others who are even more unfortunate than themselves to enhance their own self-respect. From this point of view, laughter would seem to be a compensatory act.

These philosophical considerations are often clustered into a grouping defined as *the superiority theory of humor.* Other philosophers, however, were more attentive to the mechanics of humor than to its social ramifications. Many of these *conflict* or *incongruity theories of humor* bear similarity to Koestler's concept of bisociation (Koestler, 1964). Among the earliest writings in this vein is an essay by Beattie (1776, cited by Berlyne, 1969, p. 800) who noted, "Laughter arises from the view of two or more inconsistent, unsuitable, or incongruous parts or circumstances, considered as united in one complex object or assemblage." Schopenhauer (1819) expressed this view most clearly when he described laughter as arising from a sudden perception of an incongruity between an object and an abstract concept under which the object has been subsumed. He ascribed wit to the intentional relating of two radically different objects to the same concept. Spencer (1860) likewise spoke of "descending incongruity" as the essential condition resulting in laughter.

The changeover from a negative to a positive view of humor and laughter is evident in the writings of Freud. His first and larger exploration of humor, *Jokes and Their*

Relation to the Unconscious (1905) dealt prominently with aggressive and tendentious humor. Humor and laughter were perceived as veiled expressions of unconscious wishes, often of a sexual or aggressive nature. Freud's later paper (1928), while brief and less noticed for a good length of time, dealt with what he formally called "humor," a definite gift of forgiveness and reassurance internalized from parental responses to childhood misdemeanors. This form of humor was seen as a more intrapersonal occurrence whereby persons lighten their self-judgments, muting their fears and anxieties with the kinds of reassurances that parents might have offered them when they were children experiencing failures and discomforts.

This transition from perceiving humor and laughter as negative attributes to regarding them as having virtue and therapeutic value may reflect changes in the relationships between people in different ages. Right up until the end of the 19th century, for example, it was routine for the fashionable to visit mental institutions to enjoy a good laugh at the expense of pitifully disheveled inmates who were often shackled to their cages. The film *The Elephant Man* offered a good reminder of how people would visit carnivals to view and laugh at deformed and diseased persons.

Among physicians, however, humor—or at least laughter—seems to have been held in positive regard for some time. The first association drawn between health and humor is a biblical maxim attributed to Solomon that states, "The joyous heart is a good remedy, but a crushed spirit dries up the bones" (Proverbs 17:22). Goldstein (1982) noted that the idea that laughter could be therapeutic occurs frequently in medical writings throughout the centuries. Citing the contributions of physicians and philosophers from the 13th through the 19th centuries, Goldstein presented a series of priceless testimonials to humor's value for health. Gottlieb Hufeland, a 19th-century professor, is quoted as follows:

> Laughter is one of the most important helps to digestion with which we are acquainted; the custom in vogue among our ancestors, of exciting it by jesters and buffoons, was founded on true medical principles. Cheerful and joyous companions are invaluable at meals. Obtain such, if possible, for the nourishment received amid mirth and jollity is productive of light and healthy blood (p. 22).

In the 13th century, Henri de Mandeville, a surgeon, suggested that laughter could be used as an aid in the recovery from surgery: "The surgeon must forbid anger, hatred, and sadness in the patient, and remind him that the body grows fat from joy and thin from sadness" (Koestler, 1964).

Another testimonial noted by Goldstein was from Richard Mulcaster, a 16th-century physician who believed that laughter could be thought of as a physical exercise promoting health. He wrote that laughter could help those who have cold hands and cold chests and are troubled by melancholia, "since it moveth much aire in the breast, and sendeth the warmer spirites outward" (p. 22).

In his *Treatise on Laughter*, Laurent Joubert (1579), another physician, discussed how laughter could alter the direction of illnesses, though he also warned how "inordinate laughter" could have untoward effects that might exacerbate some medical conditions. Describing how the presence of pet monkeys caused mirth and recovery from illness, Joubert went on to say:

> In these illnesses the pleasant acts of the monkeys (an animal laughable in itself) excited and raised up the nature that was burdened, broken, and as if suffocated by sickness. The pleasure acquired from laughter can do this very easily. For such joy moves the languishing and crushed heart, spreads the pleasure throughout the body, and makes it come to the aid of Nature, which, seizing upon these means and proper instruments, finds itself once again healthy, and strengthened by such help, combats the sickness with great vigor until it vanquishes the illness. For it is, properly speaking, Nature that cures illness. The doctor, the medicine, and the aid of the assistants are but the helps which encourage Nature. . . . The dignity and excellence of laughter is, therefore, very great inasmuch as it reinforces the spirit so much that it can suddenly change the state of a patient, and from being deathbound render him curable (p. 128).

It would seem then that where many philosophers, theologians, and those concerned with morality and religion in earlier centuries excoriated humor and laughter—which was said to derive from malicious delight at the failings and misfortunes of others—physicians were more observant of the benefits of laughter and humor for restoring health. Joubert wrote about how laughter helped to create healthy-looking complexions and vitality in facial features due to the excessive blood flow that accompanies it. In turn, this was used as evidence that laughter was aligned with recuperative forces that contributed to a patient's wellness.

Given the relatively brief history of psychology as an empirical science separate from philosophy, what we will call early psychological contributions to the literature on humor are really quite recent. Beginning in the 20th century, social psychologists and sociologists concerned with our species' social nature spoke of "instincts" such as "primitive passive sympathy" (McDougall, 1908). This instinct would result in our sharing emotions with others, crying when others cry, feeling angry when others express anger. This tendency was said to make us highly vulnerable to emotional arousal during our social interactions. Along with suggestion and imitation, emotional arousal—derived from primitive passive sympathy—was seen as a source of irrational behavior. Social theorists like Le Bon (1895) regarded these forces as helping to produce a "group mind," which submerged rationality in the rush to group-directed, emotionally charged behavior.

It was McDougall (1903, 1922) who first suggested that laughter could play a role in reducing the impact of these social forces that undermined rational behavior. Laughter was described as a device for avoiding excessive sympathy, saving us not only from depression and grief but from all other forms of vicarious sympathy, a position not unlike that of recent writings about humor serving to alleviate distress (emotional arousal):

> The possession of this peculiar disposition (laughter) shields us from the depressing influence which the many minor mishaps and shortcomings of our fellows would exert upon us if we did not possess it, and which they do exert upon those unfortunate persons in whom the disposition seem to be abnormally weak or altogether lacking. It not only prevents our minds from dwelling upon these depressing objects, but it actually converts these objects into stimulants that promote our well-being, both bodily and mentally, instead of depressing us through sympathetic pain or distress. And now we see how the acquirement of laughter was worthwhile to the human species; laughter is primarily and fundamentally the antidote to sympathetic pain (p. 299).

Although technically not a psychologist, Sigmund Freud examined the subject matter of concern to psychologists, albeit from limited samples of behavior. His book *Jokes and Their Relationship to the Unconsious* (1905) was a landmark in the literature about humor, later amplified in the writings of others (Koestler, 1964). Working from a "closed energy model," Freud described laughter as a release of defensive tension that had been aroused by circumstances preliminary to the laugh. The tension was said to be created by anything that could provoke primary emotions, anger, and sexuality in situations where their expression would be inappropriate (subject to superego condemnation). When the ego defenses preventing the release of id-derived emotional expressions prove to be unnecessary—as when a joker provides a punch line to his story and relieves listeners of possible emotional responses—the energy exerted to inhibit responses is released in laughter. Though Freud's focus on energy is now regarded as a quaint reminder of the scientific thinking of the 19th century, his writings, like McDougall's, hinted at the beneficial effects of humor as a means of reducing the impact of emotional duress.

Freud's later paper entitled *Humor* (1928) was another pioneering effort that has had a delayed but welcome effect on the literature concerned with humor. Freud suggested that humor represents parental forgiveness that, having been internalized into the superego, enables the individual to gain perspective and absolution from disappointments and failures. Reinterpreting failures as being of lesser importance than initially believed, "mere child's play" becomes a means of coming to terms with them and therefore of averting anxiety and depression. It is this form of humor that eventually comes to be regarded as among the most mature ego defenses (Vaillant, 1977).

In the writings of many early philosophers, especially religious philosophers, humor and laughter were thought of in critical terms, in contrast to the way they were evaluated by early physicians and psychologists. The former emphasized the derisive and hostile characteristics of humor and laughter, whereas the latter addressed their virtues as stress reducers. Among the seminal thinkers of the 19th century, Charles Darwin (1872) suggested that laughter was an innate expression of joy and a form of social communication that fostered survival. This positioning of humor within the cluster of survival enhancing instincts probably influenced Freud, who described humor and laughter as instinctive means of reducing emotional arousal and thus emphasized their positive effects. Conceivably, the different evaluations of humor by early philosophers and later psychologists may reflect their times. Innocuous or nonhostile, self-deprecating forms of humor may actually have become more common in recent years. On the other hand, it is also plausible that writers with greater interest in religious matters may have been more attentive to the "subversive" qualities of humor, as Umberto Eco's novel described. Laughter, with its associated dismissal of seriousness, may have been seen to lead humans astray from the very things they should regard with utmost seriousness. These antithetical viewpoints are mirrored in recent psychological research into the role of mourning. Whereas it has long been thought that humans are helped by fully expressing their grief in mourning, recent investigations have found that laughter, humor, enjoyment, and amusement exhibited during interviews six months after the loss of a spouse were good predictive indicators of how well persons had been able to come to terms with bereavement (Bonanno & Keltner, 1997; Keltner & Bonanno, 1997)....For now, we see that seriousness and humor have been considered in widely contrasting ways. Those with religious proclivities emphasized the need to remain serious and emotionally engaged in tragic events, whereas others viewed humor as a means of escaping from the persisting agonies of life. The latter would argue that tragedies are all too common and that humor allows us to escape their deleterious consequences.

If humor is a "hardwired" characteristic of our species that has evolved because of its usefulness as a defense against becoming emotionally over whelmed, then we would expect it to be universal.

Herbert Lefcourt points out that "laughter and humor is common among Zen monks, Taoist sages, and Sufi practitioners," and he also references the laughing Buddha. Use the Internet and the library to find more information about the place or function of humor in Zen, Dao, or Sufi practices and to explain the laughing Buddha. How does this information relate to some of the other points that Lefcourt makes? Do you see similarities or differences between some of these Eastern perspectives on humor and the Western ones that Lefcourt explains? As you were searching for this information, did you come across anything that surprised you? If so, what? How has your researcher furthered your understanding of the conceptions of humor? Write a 1-2 page summary of your findings that you can share with the class.

Working with two or three of your classmates, revisit Lefcourt's explanation of how the early philosophers (Plato, Aristotle, Hobbes, Rousseau, Bergson) viewed humor. Choose one of the philosophers and look at what he argues about humor. (For example, read the section in Aristotle's *Poetics* where Aristotle discusses comedy.) Together address the following questions: What are the philosopher's specific views on and arguments regarding humor, comedy, or laughter? What insights about the values of this philosopher and his society do these views/arguments provide? What rhetorical appeals and strategies can you identify in the presentation of the philosopher's position? As a group, write a fuller explanation of this philosopher's views that you share with the class.

Robert Provine is a neuroscientist and Professor of Psychology at the University of Maryland, Baltimore County (UMBC). He published Laughter: A Scientific Investigation *in 2000. In* Curious Behavior: Yawning, Laughing, Hiccupping and Beyond *published in 2012, Provine explores, according to the UMBC website "neglected human instincts." He is well-known for advocating "small science" and "sidewalk neuroscience," science performed on a small scale, by individuals with minimal resources. In the following piece, Provine summarizes some of his findings as he addresses the question of laughter for msnbc.com. The piece appeared on the msnbc.com website in 1999.*

_____

A BIG MYSTERY: WHY DO WE LAUGH?

By Robert Provine

Laughter is part of the universal human vocabulary. All members of the human species understand it. Unlike English or French or Swahili, we don't have to learn to speak it. We're born with the capacity to laugh.

One of the remarkable things about laughter is that it occurs unconsciously. You don't decide to do it. While we can consciously inhibit it, we don't consciously produce laughter. That's why it's very hard to laugh on command or to fake laughter. (Don't take my word for it: Ask a friend to laugh on the spot.)

Laughter provides powerful, uncensored insights into our unconscious. It simply bubbles up from within us in certain situations.

Very little is known about the specific brain mechanisms responsible for laughter. But we do know that laughter is triggered by many sensations and thoughts, and that it activates many parts of the body.

When we laugh, we alter our facial expressions and make sounds. During exuberant laughter, the muscles of the arms, legs and trunk are involved. Laughter also requires modification in our pattern of breathing.

From *NBC News* (1999).

We also know that laughter is a message that we send to other people. We know this because we rarely laugh when we are alone (we laugh to ourselves even less than we talk to ourselves).

Laughter is social and contagious. We laugh at the sound of laughter itself. That's why the Tickle Me Elmo doll is such a success—it makes us laugh and smile.

The first laughter appears at about 3.5 to 4 months of age, long before we're able to speak. Laughter, like crying, is a way for a preverbal infant to interact with the mother and other caregivers.

Contrary to folk wisdom, most laughter is not about humor; it is about relationships between people. To find out when and why people laugh, I and several undergraduate research assistants went to local malls and city sidewalks and recorded what happened just before people laughed. Over a 10-year period, we studied over 2,000 cases of naturally occurring laughter.

We found that most laughter does not follow jokes. People laugh after a variety of statements such as "Hey John, where ya been?" "Here comes Mary," "How did you do on the test?" and "Do you have a rubber band?". These certainly aren't jokes.

We don't decide to laugh at these moments. Our brain makes the decision for us. These curious "ha ha ha's" are bits of social glue that bond relationships.

Curiously, laughter seldom interrupts the sentence structure of speech. It punctuates speech. We only laugh during pauses when we would cough or breathe.

AN EVOLUTIONARY PERSPECTIVE

We believe laughter evolved from the panting behavior of our ancient primate ancestors. Today, if we tickle chimps or gorillas, they don't laugh "ha ha ha" but exhibit a panting sound. That's the sound of ape laughter. And it's the root of human laughter.

Apes laugh in conditions in which human laughter is produced, like tickle, rough and tumble play, and chasing games. Other animals produce vocalizations during play, but they are so different that it's difficult to equate them with laughter. Rats, for example, produce high-pitch vocalizations during play and when tickled. But it's very different in sound from human laughter.

When we laugh, we're often communicating playful intent. So laughter has a bonding function within individuals in a group. It's often positive, but it can be negative too. There's a difference between "laughing with" and "laughing at." People who laugh at others may be trying to force them to conform or casting them out of the group.

No one has actually counted how much people of different ages laugh, but young children probably laugh the most. At ages 5 and 6, we tend to see the most exuberant laughs. Adults laugh less than children, probably because they play less. And laughter is associated with play.

We have learned a lot about when and why we laugh, much of it counter-intuitive. Work now underway will tell us more about the brain mechanisms of laughter, how laughter has evolved and why we're so susceptible to tickling—one of the most enigmatic of human behaviors.

Explore

Go to your campus student union, cafeteria, or similar gathering place and conduct your own "small science." Observe a group of students and count how many times each individual laughs. Note and describe how their bodies were involved in the laughter. Who initiated the laughter? If the group was comprised of both male and female, note who laughed the most often—males or females? Based on these observations, respond to the following questions: How do you think laughter functioned in this particular group? How do you think laughter functions in general? Did your observations correspond to Provine's research? Write a 2–3 page paper summarizing your observations and responding to these questions.

Invent

Robert Provine wrote "A Big Mystery: Why Do We Laugh?" for msnbc.com under the subject "technology." What is Provine's primary purpose in this piece? How does he achieve this purpose? In other words, what rhetorical or compositional decisions does he make? How do the conventions of the genre—a short informational piece for an online new source—determine presentation and content?

Collaborate

In "A Big Mystery: Why Do We Laugh?", Robert Provine describes what occurs to our bodies when we laugh. He also addresses the social aspects (and hints at the emotional aspects). In addition, he offers an evolutionary explanation. Working with several of your classmates, list Provine's key points under the various categories. Then together design a visual presentation, including images *and* text, of this information.

This report was published on Health.org in 2009.

HEALTH CARE SAVVY: HEART BENEFITS OF A HEARTY LAUGH

By Health.org

Laughter is contagious. But don't worry about spreading it around. Growing research suggests that regularly getting your giggles going offers several health benefits beyond the emotional ones. Specifically, laughing appears to:

Increase blood flow. Researchers at the University of Maryland Medical Center measured the blood-moving capacity of arteries after volunteers watched humorous or stressful films. After volunteers laughed through scenes from *There's Something About Mary* their arteries expanded, but they constricted after viewing battle scenes from *Saving Private Ryan*. And in a small one-year study of heart-attack patients, those who watched comedies for 30 minutes a day were less likely to suffer a second heart attack than those who did not watch funny videos.

Lower blood sugar. People with type 2 diabetes maintain better blood sugar-control after watching comic performances, research suggests. A Japanese study of 10 people with the condition suggests that might stem from beneficial changes in immune regulation that prevent damaging inflammation from undermining blood-sugar control.

Regulate the immune system. In another small study, laughter significantly reduced levels of inflammation-triggering cytokines in people with rheumatoid arthritis. Other research suggests that after viewing humorous films, people with asthma become more resistant to flareups, those with allergies suffer fewer symptoms, and children with allergic skin rashes sleep more easily. A good laugh might also stimulate production of disease-fighting T cells and natural killer cells.

From *Health.org* (2009).

Burn calories. Laughing boosts energy expenditure by 10 to 20 percent, according to Vanderbilt University researchers. They calculated that 15 minutes of hearty laughter could burn up to 40 calories, enough to shed more than 4 pounds a year if done daily.

Ease pain. Laughter contracts and relaxes muscles in the abdomen, face, and shoulders, which might ease muscle tension and spasms that contribute to pain. And the temporary distraction helps too.

Recommendation: While 4-year-olds laugh about every 4 minutes, adults do it about once an hour. So spend time each day having fun. Trade jokes, watch comedies, horse around with your kids or grandkids, or share a laugh while in line at the grocery store. It will brighten your day—and maybe provide a much-appreciated dose of mirthful medicine.

James Gorman, a science reporter for The New York Times, *writes about evolutionary biology, brain science, conservation, and other subjects. In this article published in 2011, Gorman looks to science to explain why laughing may be good for us.*

SCIENTISTS HINT AT WHY LAUGHTER FEELS SO GOOD

BY JAMES GORMAN

Laughter is regularly promoted as a source of health and well being, but it has been hard to pin down exactly why laughing until it hurts feels so good.

The answer, reports Robin Dunbar, an evolutionary psychologist at Oxford, is not the intellectual pleasure of cerebral humor, but the physical act of laughing. The simple muscular exertions involved in producing the familiar ha, ha, ha, he said, trigger an increase in endorphins, the brain chemicals known for their feel-good effect.

His results build on a long history of scientific attempts to understand a deceptively simple and universal behavior. "Laughter is very weird stuff, actually," Dr. Dunbar said. "That's why we got interested in it." And the findings fit well with a growing sense that laughter contributes to group bonding and may have been important in the evolution of highly social humans.

Social laughter, Dr. Dunbar suggests, relaxed and contagious, is "grooming at a distance," an activity that fosters closeness in a group the way one-on-one grooming, patting and delousing promote and maintain bonds between individual primates of all sorts.

In five sets of studies in the laboratory and one field study at comedy performances, Dr. Dunbar and colleagues tested resistance to pain both before and after bouts of social laughter. The pain came from a freezing wine sleeve slipped over a forearm, an ever tightening blood pressure cuff or an excruciating ski exercise.

From *The New York Times* (2011).

The findings, published in the *Proceedings of the Royal Society B: Biological Sciences*, eliminated the possibility that the pain resistance measured was the result of a general sense of well being rather than actual laughter. And, Dr. Dunbar said, they also provided a partial answer to the ageless conundrum of whether we laugh because we feel giddy or feel giddy because we laugh.

"The causal sequence is laughter triggers endorphin activation," he said. What triggers laughter is a question that leads into a different labyrinth.

Robert R. Provine, a neuroscientist at the University of Maryland, Baltimore County, and the author of *Laughter: A Scientific Investigation*, said he thought the study was "a significant contribution" to a field of study that dates back 2,000 years or so.

It has not always focused on the benefits of laughter. Both Plato and Aristotle, Dr. Provine said, were concerned with the power of laughter to undermine authority. And he noted that the ancients were very aware that laughter could accompany raping and pillaging as well as a comic tale told by the hearth.

Dr. Dunbar, however, was concerned with relaxed, contagious social laughter, not the tyrant's cackle or the "polite titter" of awkward conversation. He said a classic example would be the dinner at which everyone else speaks a different language and someone makes an apparently hilarious but incomprehensible comment. "Everybody falls about laughing, and you look a little puzzled for about three seconds, but really you just can't help falling about laughing yourself."

To test the relationship of laughter of this sort to pain resistance, Dr. Dunbar did a series of six experiments. In five, participants watched excerpts of comedy videos, neutral videos or videos meant to promote good feeling but not laughter.

Among the comedy videos were excerpts from *The Simpsons*, *Friends* and *South Park*, as well as from performances by standup comedians like Eddie Izzard. The neutral videos included *Barking Mad*, a documentary on pet training, and a golfing program. The positive but unfunny videos included excerpts from shows about nature, like the "Jungles" episode of *Planet Earth*.

In the lab experiments, the participants were tested before and after seeing different combinations of videos. They suffered the frozen wine sleeve or the blood pressure cuff in different experiments and were asked to say when the pain reached a point they could not stand. They wore recorders during the videos so that the time they spent laughing could be established. In the one real-world experiment, similar tests were conducted at performances of an improvisational comedy group, the Oxford Imps.

The results, when analyzed, showed that laughing increased pain resistance, whereas simple good feeling in a group setting did not. Pain resistance is used as an indicator of endorphin levels because their presence in the brain is difficult to test; the molecules would not appear in blood samples because they are among the brain chemicals that are prevented from entering circulating blood by the so-called blood brain barrier.

Dr. Dunbar thinks laughter may have been favored by evolution because it helped bring human groups together, the way other activities like dancing and singing do. Those activities also produce endorphins, he said, and physical activity is important in them as well. "Laughter is an early mechanism to bond social groups," he said. "Primates use it."

Indeed, apes are known to laugh, although in a different way than humans. They pant. "Panting is the sound of rough-and-tumble play," Dr. Provine said. It becomes a "ritualization" of the sound of play. And in the course of the evolution of human beings, he suggests, "Pant, pant becomes ha, ha."

Gretchen Reynolds writes a weekly column about fitness for The New York Times Magazine *and covers fitness for* Women's Health. *This blog appeared in* The New York Times Magazine *in 2012, and like James Gorman, in "Scientists Hint at Why Laughter Feels So Good," Reynolds draws on recent scientific studies to tout the health and social benefits of laughter. As you read Reynolds blog, pay close attention to how she uses Robin Dunbar's findings.*

LAUGHTER AS A FORM OF EXERCISE

BY GRETCHEN REYNOLDS

Is laughter a kind of exercise? That offbeat question is at the heart of a new study of laughing and pain that emphasizes how unexpectedly entwined our bodies and emotions can be.

For the study, which was published this year in Proceedings of the Royal Society B, researchers at Oxford University recruited a large group of undergraduate men and women.

Then they set out to make their volunteers laugh.

Most of us probably think of laughter, if we think of it at all, as a response to something funny—as, in effect, an emotion. But laughter is fundamentally a physical action. "Laughter involves the repeated, forceful exhalation of breath from the lungs," says Robin Dunbar, a professor of evolutionary psychology at Oxford, who led the study. "The muscles of the diaphragm have to work very hard." We've all heard the phrase "laugh until it hurts," he points out. That pain isn't metaphoric; prolonged laughing can be painful and exhausting.

Rather like a difficult workout.

But does laughter elicit a physiological response similar to that of exercise and, if so, what might that reveal about the nature of exertion?

From *The New York Times* (2012).

To find out, Dr. Dunbar and his colleagues had their volunteers watch, both alone and as part of a group, a series of short videos that were either comic or dryly factual documentaries.

But first the volunteers submitted to a test of their pain threshold, as determined by how long they could tolerate a tightening blood pressure cuff or a frozen cooling sleeve.

The decision to introduce pain into this otherwise fun-loving study stems from one of the more well-established effects of strenuous exercise: that it causes the body to release endorphins, or natural opiates. Endorphins are known "to play a crucial role in the management of pain," the study authors write, and, like other opiates, to induce a feeling of euphoric calm and well-being (they are believed to play a role in "runner's high").

It's difficult to study endorphin production directly, however, since much of the action takes place within the working brain and requires a lumbar puncture to monitor, Dr. Dunbar says. That is not a procedure volunteers willingly undergo, particularly in a study about laughing. Instead, he and his colleagues turned to pain thresholds, an indirect but generally accepted marker of endorphin production. If someone's pain threshold rises, he or she is presumed to be awash in the natural analgesics.

And in Dr. Dunbar's experiments, pain thresholds did go up after people watched the funny videos, but not after they viewed the factual documentaries.

The only difference between the two experiences was that in one, people laughed, a physical reaction that the scientists quantified with audio monitors. They could hear their volunteers belly-laughing. Their abdominal muscles were contracting. Their endorphin levels were increasing in response, and both their pain thresholds and their general sense of amiable enjoyment were on the rise.

In other words, it was the physical act of laughing, the contracting of muscles and resulting biochemical reactions, that prompted, at least in part, the pleasure of watching the comedy. Or, as Dr. Dunbar and his colleagues write, "the sense of heightened affect in this context probably derives from the way laughter triggers endorphin uptake."

The physical act of laughing contributed to the emotional response of finding something to be funny.

Why the interplay of endorphins and laughing should be of interest to those of us who exercise may not be immediately obvious. But as Dr. Dunbar points out, what happens during one type of physical exertion probably happens in others. Laughter is an intensely infectious activity. In this study, people laughed more readily and lustily when they watched the comic videos as a group than when they watched them individually, and their pain thresholds, concomitantly, rose higher after group viewing.

Something similar may happen when people exercise together, Dr. Dunbar says. In an experiment from 2009, he and his colleagues studied a group of elite Oxford rowers, asking them to work out either on isolated rowing machines, separated from one another in a gym, or on a machine that simulated full, synchronized crew rowing. In that case, the rowers were exerting themselves in synchrony, as a united group.

After they exercised together, the rower's pain threshold—and presumably their endorphin levels—were significantly higher than they had been at the start, but also higher than when they rowed alone.

"We don't know why synchrony has this effect, but it seems very strong," Dr. Dunbar says.

So if you typically run or bike alone, perhaps consider finding a partner. Your endorphin response might rise and, at least theoretically, render that unpleasant final hill a bit less daunting. Or if you prefer exercising alone, perhaps occasionally entertain yourself with a good joke.

But don't expect forced laughter to lend you an edge, Dr. Dunbar says. "Polite titters do not involve the repeated, uninhibited series of exhalations" that are needed to "drive the endorphin effect," he says. With laughter, as with exercise, it seems, there really is no gain without some element of pain.

 Although both James Gorman and Gretchen Reynolds draw on the same source, Robin Dunbar's study, for their respective articles, each article has a slightly different focus. Identify where and explain how each writer uses the same information to convey a slightly different message. Of course, a place to begin would be with identifying each writer's purpose and to mark specific passages where Gorman and Reynolds refer to, paraphrase, or quote Dunbar.

 Working with several of your classmates design a visual image (brochure, PowerPoint, Prezi, poster) explaining the health benefits of laughter. Make sure that you include documentation for your claims.

 Using the information in "Scientists Hint at Why Laughter Feels So Good," "Laughter as a Form of Exercise," "Health Care Savvy: Heart Benefits of a Hearty Laugh," and at least one other reading in *Funny*, draft a proposal to the Dean of Student Affairs making a case for an on-campus comedy club. (See "Humor and Physical Health" and "Humor and Mental Health" by Rod Martin; "The Social Value of Humor" by John Morreall.)

Rod A. Martin, a clinical psychologist, teaches at the University of Western Ontario, Canada. The following excerpts are from his book The Psychology of Humor: An Integrative Approach.

HUMOR AND PHYSICAL HEALTH

BY ROD A. MARTIN

The idea that humor and laughter are good for one's health has become very popular in recent years, among the general public as well as many health care practitioners. This is actually not a new idea; the health benefits of laughter have been touted for centuries. The medicinal value of mirth and cheerfulness, as well as the health-impairing effects of negative emotions, were affirmed thousands of years ago in a biblical proverb which states that "a merry heart does good like a medicine, but a broken spirit dries the bones" (Proverbs 17:22).

Since the time of Aristotle, a number of physicians and philosophers have suggested that laughter has important health benefits, such as improving blood circulation, aiding digestion, restoring energy, counteracting depression, and enhancing the functioning of various organs of the body (for reviews, see Goldstein, 1982; Moody, 1978). This idea has become increasingly popular in recent years, as modern medical discoveries like endorphins, cytokines, natural killer cells, and inununoglobulins have been added to the list of bodily substances that are thought to be beneficially affected by humor and laughter.

[A] burgeoning "humor and health movement" has developed, made up of nurses, physicians, social workers, psychotherapists, educators, clowns, and comedians, who enthusiastically promote the therapeutic benefits of humor through conferences, seminars, workshops, books, videotapes, and Internet websites. The Association for

From *The Psychology of Humor: An Integrative Approach* (MA: Elsevier Academic Press, 2007): 269-07, 309-35.

Applied and Therapeutic Humor (AATH) is a professional society of individuals whose members are interested in the application of humor and laughter in medicne, social work, psychotherapy, education, and so on (available at www.aath.org).

In addition, the "laughter club movement," which was started in India in 1995 by a physician named Madan Kataria, has witnessed remarkable growth in the past decade, forming chapters throughout the world. Believing that even non-humorous laughter is beneficial for physical, mental, interpersonal, and spiritual health, adherents of this movement meet regularly to engage in group laughter as a form of yogic exercise. According to Kataria (2002), the mission of the movement is nothing less than to bring about "world peace through laughter!" The humor and health movement also received a boost in 1998 with the release of the movie *Patch Adams*, starring Robin Williams, which depicted the true story of an unconventional physician who augmented his medical interventions by making his patients laugh in response to his comic interactions with them (described also in P. Adams and Mylander, 1998). Laughter rooms, comedy carts, and "therapeutic clowns" have now become familiar sights in many hospitals.

The remarkable range of bodily functions that are said to be helped by laughter and humor, according to contemporary claims, reminds one of the advertised benefits of patent medicines a century ago. Laughter is said to provide exercise for the muscles and heart, produce muscle relaxation, improve blood circulation, reduce the production of stress-related hormones such as catecholamines and cortisol, enhance a wide range of immune system variables, reduce pain by stimulating the production of endorphins, reduce blood pressure, enhance respiration, regulate blood sugar levels, and remove carbon dioxide and water vapor from the lungs (W. F. Fry, 1994; McGhee, 1999). As such, laughter has been said to provide some degree of protection against cancer, heart attacks, stroke, asthma, diabetes, pneumonia, bronchitis, hypertension, migraine headaches, arthritis pain, ulcers, and all sorts of infectious diseases ranging from the common cold to AIDS (W. F. Fry, 1994; McGhee, 1999). With such a range of effects, it would seem that laughter threatens to put the major pharmaceutical companies out of business!

Many of the claimed health benefits of laughter are unproven and appear quite fanciful. For example, although it is often claimed that laughter provides the same health benefits as jogging and other forms of physical exercise, there is no published research evaluating this claim. It seems likely that one would need to laugh for quite a long time in order to consume a significant number of calories; people are likely better off taking up a more vigorous form of exercise if they wish to lose weight or enhance their cardiovascular fitness.

Part of the attraction of humor and laughter as a form of alternative medicine is that it is inherently enjoyable and, unlike many other health-promoting activities, it does not require giving up pleasurable habits like smoking and overeating. The fact that it is free, in contrast to the high costs of many traditional and nontraditional treatments, makes it even more attractive. Given the popularity of these views, one runs the risk of being labeled as a killjoy if one questions whether humor and laughter actually produce the medical benefits that are claimed. However, a scientific approach requires that we examine the evidence.

[T]here is good reason to believe that laughter can improve one's mood and that a healthy sense of humor can be beneficial for coping with stress and enriching one's relationships with others, enhancing one's quality of life. What is the evidence, however, that humor and laughter can also have a beneficial impact on aspects of physical health, such as strengthening the immune system, reducing pain, or prolonging the duration of one's life? [T]he existing evidence is rather weaker and more inconsistent than the media reports would lead us to believe.

Of all the health benefits claimed for humor and laughter, the most consistent research support has been found for the hypothesized analgesic effects. After watching humorous films in the laboratory, individuals tend to be able to tolerate increased levels of pain, and there is some limited clinical evidence that humor can reduce postsurgical pain. The research suggests that the observed pain-reducing effects are likely due to amusement-related positive emotion, rather than to laughter per se, although similar effects are also found with negative emotions. The popular idea that these effects are mediated by the production of endorphins or other opiates in the brain has not yet been investigated, although this appears to be a plausible explanation. More extensive research is needed to explore these mechanisms and to determine whether these effects are strong enough to be useful for applications of humor in the treatment of pain resulting from clinical conditions.

With regard to possible effects of humor and laughter on immunity, the research to date is not as consistent or conclusive. Some short-term effects of exposure to comedy on some components of immunity have been observed in the laboratory, and recent findings of reduced allergic reactions are intriguing. However, these studies tend to be quite small, with many methodological limitations, and some of the findings have been inconsistent across studies. More systematic and rigorous research is needed to replicate these findings and explore possible mechanisms before firm conclusions can be drawn. Research in the general field psychoneuroimmunology of indicates that emotional states can influence immunity through the many communication channels linking the brain and the immune system. There is therefore reason to expect interactions between the emotion of mirth and immunity as well. However, these complex interactions are still not well understood, and there does not appear to be a simple one-to-one relation between specific emotions and particular changes in immunity (Booth and Pennebaker, 2000).

Although the research offers some interesting suggestions of possible effects of humor on immunity, there is little evidence that people who have a better sense of humor and laugh more frequently have better immunity, enjoy better health overall, or live longer lives. There is even some research suggesting that more humorous and cheerful people may actually die at an earlier age than their more serious counterparts. This may be due to high-humor individuals having less concern about health issues, a more risky lifestyle, or a reduced tendency to take health problems seriously and seek appropriate medical treatment when needed.

Nonetheless, even though more humorous and cheerful people may not live longer, they may enjoy a better quality of life and greater overall life satisfaction. It also remains possible that different types of humor may affect different aspects of health in different ways. Although a cheerful sense of humor might contribute to earlier mortality by causing people to take less care of themselves overall, it remains possible that mirth could produce biochemical changes having some health benefits, or that the use of certain styles of humor could facilitate coping with stress or enhance intimate relationships, indirectly producing some positive health effects.

Those who advocate humor and laughter as a pathway to better health seem to have moved too quickly to promote their views on the basis of rather flimsy research evidence. Besides the need for more basic research in this area, the effectiveness of humor-based interventions needs to be carefully evaluated before they are widely implemented. For some proponents, this health fad may be seen as an opportunity for making money through promotional books and workshops, but many others appear to be motivated by genuine concern about helping others. In either case, a strong commitment to belief in health benefits of humor and laughter can make it difficult for advocates to evaluate the research objectively.

One could perhaps argue in defense of proponents of the "humor and health" movement that, although humor may not produce all the health benefits that have been claimed, at least it is not likely to be harmful and it can enhance people's enjoyment if not the duration of their lives. There is certainly some merit to this line of argument. There is undoubtedly nothing wrong with encouraging people to enjoy humor and to laugh more often, especially if they are suffering from a serious illness that would otherwise reduce their enjoyment of life. However, there is a risk that unfounded claims of health benefits of humor and laughter may raise false hopes in sick individuals.

There is also a danger that an emphasis on the health benefits of humor and laughter could lead to an unjustified perception that people have more control over their health than they actually do, fostering a subtle tendency to blame people for their illnesses. Consequently, those who become ill may begin to feel guilty because they supposedly did not laugh enough. In addition, exaggerated claims about unfounded health benefits of humor and laughter can contribute to perceptions that this is nothing more than a fringe movement and a passing fad, which could dissuade researchers and funding agencies from conducting and funding well-designed large-scale experiments in this field, thereby delaying progress in identifying those health effects that may be genuine.

Theories about possible health benefits of humor need to be based on plausible biological mechanisms. From an evolutionary perspective, it seems unlikely that the primary function of humor and laughter is to improve people's physical health. [C]omparative research suggests that the positive emotion associated with humor is related to social play, and that laughter is an expressive behavior communicating playful emotions and intentions to others. . . . Thus, the origins of humor and laughter seem to have more to do with social interaction and the social nature of human existence than with physical health. Nonetheless, it remains possible that these emotions and behaviors may have some physiological and psychological concomitants that could indirectly affect aspects of health.

"HUMOR AND MENTAL HEALTH"

In recent decades, a sense of humor has come to be viewed not only as a very socially desirable personality trait but also as an important component of mental health. Besides boosting positive emotions and counteracting negative moods like depression and anxiety, humor is thought to be a valuable mechanism for coping with stressful life events and an important social skill for initiating, maintaining, and enhancing satisfying interpersonal relationships (Galloway and Cropley, 1999; Kuiper and Olinger, 1998; Lefcourt, 2001). A good deal of research in the psychology of humor in the past two decades has focused on the relation between humor and various aspects of mental health.

When people engage in humor and laughter, they tend to feel more cheerful and energetic, and less depressed, anxious, irritable, and tense. In the short term, at least, humor seems to boost positive moods and counteract negative emotions. Thus, one way a sense of humor may be beneficial to mental health is by contributing to one's ability to regulate or manage emotions, which is an essential aspect of metal health (Gross and Muñoz, 1995).

The effects of humor on mood have been demonstrated in a number of laboratory experiments. . . . The . . . experiments provided fairly consistent evidence of short-term effects of humor on positive and negative moods and feelings of well-being in the laboratory. Based on these findings, one would expect that exposing people to humorous stimuli repeatedly over a number of weeks or months should result in overall improvements in their prevailing moods and general outlook on life. However, when researchers have investigated longer-term psychological effects of repeated exposure to humorous stimuli over fairly extended time periods, the results have generally been rather disappointing.

A second general way humor may potentially be beneficial to mental (as well as physical) health has to do with its use in coping with stressful life experiences. . . . Many authors have noted that humor, because it inherently involves incongruity and multiple interpretations, provides a way for individuals to shift perspective on a stressful situation, reappraising it from a new and less-threatening point of view. As a consequence of this humorous reappraisal, the situation becomes less stressful and more manageable, and the individual is less likely to experience a stress response (Dixon, 1980). Walter O'Connell (1976) described humorous people as being "skilled in rapid perceptual-cognitive switches in frames of reference" (p. 327), an ability that presumably enables them to reappraise a problem situation, distance themselves from its immediate threat, and thereby reduce the often paralyzing feelings of anxiety and helplessness. Similarly, Rollo May (1953) stated that humor has the function of "preserving the self. . . . It is the healthy way of feeling a 'distance' between one's self and the problem, a way of standing off and looking at one's problem with perspective."

A number of experiments have been conducted to investigate the effectiveness of a humor manipulation in mitigating the emotional or psychophysiological effects of mildly stressful laboratory stressors. . . . [A]lthough the results have not always replicated, these experimental laboratory studies provide some support for the hypothesized stress-buffering effects of humor. When participants actively create humor during mildly stressful experiences, or when they are exposed to comedy before or after such events, they tend to report more positive and less negative moods and show less stress-related physiological arousal as compared to participants in control groups. These studies extend the findings of the [previous] laboratory experiments . . . indicating that the general effects of humor on moods also occur in mildly stressful conditions.

[H]umor is a complex process involving cognitive, emotional, and interpersonal aspects. All of these facets of humor have implications for mental health and emotional well-being. When people joke with one another about their problems or about a potentially threatening life situation, they are able to change their perceptions of the situation, their emotional state, and the nature of their relationships with each other. However, the research reviewed in this chapter suggests that the link between humor and psychological health is more complex than it might first seem.

Overall, then, it would appear that humor is inherently neither psychologically healthy nor unhealthy. Just because someone is very funny and able to make others laugh does not necessarily mean that he or she is particularly well-adjusted psychologically. As suggested by earlier psychologists such as Maslow (1954) and Allport (1961), the role of humor in mental health seems to have as much to do with the kinds of humor an individual does not display as the kinds of humor he or she does express.

Another way of putting this is that a healthy sense of humor is an important component of overall mental health. People who are psychologically well-adjusted, with satisfying personal relationships, tend to use humor in ways that enhance their own well-being and closeness to others. For example, they may engage in friendly joking to communicate an optimistic outlook on a stressful situation, to encourage others during times of distress, or to express underlying feelings of acceptance and affection in the midst of an argument. However, less well-adjusted individuals who are aggressive and hostile, or those with low self-esteem and a vulnerability to negative emotionality, tend to use humor to communicate their aggression and cynicism, to manipulate, demean, or control others, to ingratiate themselves, or to hide their true feelings from others. Indeed, since no one is completely psychologically healthy or completely unhealthy, most people likely use humor to some degree in all of these ways at different times and in different contexts.

Rod Martin gives a nod to what he describes as a "burgeoning 'humor and health movement'". Using the Internet and the library databases, investigate this movement in order to find out just how "burgeoning" this movement is. In your research locate the vision, mission, philosophy statements or guiding principles of the various organizations that you find. You may also want to locate those documents for the Association for Applied Therapeutics (AATH) and the laughter club movement, both of which Martin includes in this chapter. Based on your exploration, what can you conclude about the importance of humor to our overall health and well-being?

a. Look carefully at each paragraph of Martin's conclusion to "Humor and Physical Health." Restate (summarize), in two or three sentences, each paragraph's key points. Using these sentences, explain Martin's position on the relationship between humor and physical health.

b. In this excerpt from Martin's chapter on "Humor and Mental Health," you read information about the following areas: humor and emotions, stress, and coping. Summarize the key points of in each area. What do you conclude about the relationship between humor and mental health? Does your conclusion agree with Martin's?

Write a 3–4 page reflection paper on the place of humor in your life. As you write, think about what makes you laugh, who makes you laugh, whether you make others laugh and why you do so. Once you can answer some of those questions, you may want to think about how you feel, physically and mentally, when you laugh. You may also want to consider how you use humor and how those around you use it. There are many ways to write a reflection paper; however, you should have a controlling idea, and you should show critical engagement with some of the ideas you have encountered in Rod Martin's work as well as some of the other readings in this book.

John Morreall, a professor of religious studies at William and Mary College in Virginia, has served on the editorial board of Humor: International Journal of Humor Research *and on the board of the* International Journal for Humor and Health. *In addition, as speaker/seminar leader, he has worked with clients such as AT&T, IBM, and the IRS explaining the benefits of integrating humor into the workplace as well into our everyday lives.*

THE SOCIAL VALUE OF HUMOR

By John Morreall

[H]umor is primarily a social phenomenon, as are other forms of human enjoyment. We rarely laugh when alone, even at things that would evoke our laughter if we were with others. And if we are in a group and find that we are the only one laughing at something, we will usually cover our mouth and stifle our laughter, at least until others join in. This social aspect of laughter shows, too, in its contagiousness. Group laughter tends to work like atomic fission. Your laughter makes me laugh harder, and mine in turn reinforces your laughter. Indeed, sometimes another person's laughing is enough to get us started, even though we don't know what is making him laugh. Comedians and theater owners have long been aware that it is much easier to get a full house laughing than just half a house, especially if the smaller crowd is spread out so that they don't reinforce one another's laughter. It is because of the contagious nature of laughter, too, that television comedies often use "laugh tracks."

Perhaps the most extreme manifestation of the contagious laughter is the "laughter epidemic" in which large numbers of people are made to laugh convulsively not by any organic cause but just by the laughter of the others. The most famous of these epidemics occurred in Africa in the mid-1960s. It started among girls at a Catholic high school, who "gave" it to their mothers and sisters when they went home. Their laughter, often mixed with heavy sobbing, lasted from a few hours to more than two weeks, and usually prevented them from eating. Many "victims" collapsed from exhaustion. Over a thousand women and girls were affected, and the epidemic lasted two months.[1]

From *The Social Value of Humor* (New York: State University of New York, 1983): 113-20.

Laughter is not only contagious, but in spreading from person to person, it has a cohesive effect. Laughing together unites people. Those who hold the superiority theory *of* laughter often point to the fact that groups unite in laughter against outsiders as evidence for their theory. But ridicule is not the only kind of group laughter that has a binding effect. To laugh with another person for whatever reason, even if only at a piece of absurdity, is to get closer to that person. Indeed, humor can even be directed at the laughers themselves, and still have this unifying effect. Getting stuck in an elevator between floors with people, or running into people at the bank door on a bank holiday, often makes us laugh at our common predicament, and this laughter brings us together.

When two people are quarreling, one of the first things they stop doing together is laughing; they refuse to laugh at each other's attempts at humor, and refuse to laugh together at something incongruous happening to them. As soon as they begin to laugh once more, we know that the end of the quarrel is at hand.

The cohesive effect of humor is connected with its ability to distance us from the practical aspects of the situation we're in, and with the shared enjoyment which it involves. To joke with others is to put aside practical considerations for the moment, and doing this tends to make everyone relax. Sharing humor is in this respect like sharing an enjoyable meal. It is precisely because the quarrelers do not want to put aside practical considerations and do not want to relax together, that they will not respond to each other's attempts at humor. . . .

Sharing humor with others, then, is a friendly social gesture. It shows our acceptance of them and our desire to please them. When we are anxious about meeting someone because we're not sure how that person will react to us, the first laugh we share (if it occurs) will be important, for it will mark the other person's acceptance of us. We often start off conversations with new acquaintances with a small joke, of course, for just this reason—to set up the mood of acceptance and make the other person relax. And public speakers have for centuries begun speeches with a joke for the same reason.

Humor also facilitates social interaction in a number of situations where it is added to a basically serious piece of communication to eliminate the offensiveness which that communication might otherwise have. When we have a complaint to make to a friend, for example, we often do so with a jocular gripe. By making our complaint amusing, we show the person that the problem is not of overwhelming importance and that we have maintained our perspective on it—"It's not the end of the world," as we sometimes say. And our humor not only shows that we have some distance from the problem, but it also tends to allow our friend some distance. He isn't put on the spot and forced to defend himself in the way that people often are when their actions are criticized in a serious tone. By using the jocular gripe we don't set up a confrontation; rather we invite the person to step back and laugh with us. The tension often associated with serious criticism is thus reduced and the person is more likely to consider the reasonableness of the complaint. Indeed, most people seem able to take almost any criticism from a friend if it is expressed in a humorous way.

Humor serves to create distance and smooth out social interaction not just in making complaints, of course, but in asking potentially offensive questions, admitting to blunders, accepting praise graciously, and in many other interchanges.

Even when humor is used (or abused) for some end other than simply amusing another person, we should note, humor for that person can still be an end in itself. If we present humor to someone to make him like us, for example, *he* does not enjoy the humor as to achieving some further goal, even though *we* have an ulterior motive. He simply enjoys it. Humor is like other aesthetic objects in this respect. If I give you a piece of sculpture so that you'll owe me a favor, that doesn't destroy the self-contained-ness of your aesthetic enjoyment of that sculpture.

We enjoy humor the most, perhaps, when we feel that it is offered with no ulterior motive—not even the altruistic one of getting us to relax. We want the other person simply to amuse us, with no strings attached. This is the kind of humor found among close friends. Indeed the frequency of nonmanipulative humor in a group's interaction is a good indicator of the intimacy of the group. We can usually determine who someone's best friends are by determining whom he enjoys humor with the most—people who talked without an humorous interchange by all odds just couldn't be close friends.

In many ways the sharing of humor in a group is like the sharing of a meal, or any other pleasurable experience. But humor, because it requires no specific setting or equipment, is especially versatile as a form of enjoyable interchange. And unlike, say, listening to a concert together, humor is not just passive but calls for imagination and creativity from its participants. Humor is versatile, too, in that it mixes so well with other kinds of conversation. Friends often share a good deal of their daily experience, and so in a conversation there may be little new information that they are able to give one another. But making a funny comment doesn't require any new information; it requires only a new way of looking at things which everyone may already know about. People who have a common store of experience may be unable to inform each other, but they can always amuse each other, by playing with the reality which they have in common. In many conversations, indeed, imaginative humor is valued more than information.

In humorous conversation we may play not just with reality outside the conversation, but also with the very moves of conversation itself. We can get a humorous effect ... by playfully violating the conventions governing serious conversation. Instead of saying what we believe, and uttering sentences of warning and criticism sincerely, for example, we may engage in kidding—mock claims, mock warning, and mock criticism. Kidding is funny and enjoyable because we are taking forms of speech intended for serious communication and discarding the serious purpose. Like mock physical fighting, mock criticism can be enjoyed by both parties because they know it is only play. Indeed, it can even be an expression of affection, as in the "roast," the banquet where someone's friends take turns at giving speeches full of wisecracks about him.

Human beings seem to have a basic need for playing, not just with the conventions of conversation, but with all conventions.[2] As a species we need customs to structure and regulate our relationships, of course, but we seem to have just as strong a need to occasionally let our hair down and act silly with one another. For thousands of years we have even institutionalized silly action with festivals where the ordinary rules are temporarily suspended. At least as far back as the ancient Egyptians, the courts of pharaohs and kings have had their jesters, whose job it was to introduce playful silliness into the ruler's otherwise serious day. In most cases, court jesters were even allowed to make fun of the king. Among the American Indians of the Southwest, tribal clowns formed a priestly class, and in their ritual clowning were allowed to say or do almost anything, including the breaking of sexual taboos.

In Western cultures, of course, institutionalized silliness has had a long history. The Greeks and Romans had festivals tied to the seasons, which were a time for breaking loose and acting foolishly. All kinds of sexual activity were allowed, in part because these festivals were based on fertility rites. Clowning and fertility go together, some have suggested, in that both overcome the individual's suffering and death.[3] In medieval Christian Europe we find a "Feast of Fools"; modeled on liturgical feats, it included such things as replacing the usual vespers for the day with a mixture of all the vespers throughout the year. Wilder abuses also took place, and the Feast of Fools was eventually suppressed by the Council of Basel in 1435. Nonetheless, much of it survived and traces can be found even today in Mardi Gras celebrations.

The intellectual ferment of the fifteenth and sixteenth centuries produced a heightened appreciation of the value of humor and silliness, especially as an antidote to blind allegiance or orthodoxy. In sixteenth-century Poland a "fool society" called the Babinian Republic was established. When nonmembers did something sufficiently foolish, they were invited to join, by assuming an office appropriate to what they had done. One could be made an archbishop, for example, for speaking publicly on issues about which he was ignorant. The society soon grew to include almost every important church and government official in the country. When the King of Poland asked if the Babinian Republic also had a king, he was told that as long as he was alive the society would not dream of electing another.[4]

A better known example of the "fool movement" of this period was Erasmus's *In Praise of Folly*, a book which so nicely captures the social value of humor and silliness, that we might cite its central argument as a fitting conclusion to this chapter. The work is a long speech made by the goddess Folly on her own behalf. She argues that it is foolishness and not the calculations of reason that makes possible everything we treasure most in life. It is folly, especially, that allows us to live together and even love one another. To have a friend or spouse we have to have a sense of humor and foolishly overlook that person's faults; a rational assessment of what a friendship or marriage was going to involve would keep us aloof from the rest of our species. Even to have a good opinion of ourselves, without which no one else would love us, we need a foolish, unrealistic self-image.

The completely rational and realistic person, Dame Folly suggests, would love neither himself nor anyone else; indeed he would probably despair and kill himself.

> In sum, no society, no union in life, could be either pleasant or lasting without me [Folly]. A people does not for long tolerate its prince, or a master tolerate his servant, a handmaiden her mistress, a teacher his student, a friend his friend, a wife her husband, a landlord his tenant, a partner his partner, or a boarder his fellow-boarder, except as they mutually or by turns are mistaken, on occasion flatter, on occasion wisely wink, and otherwise soothe themselves with the sweetness of folly.[5]

1. A. H. Rankin and R. J. Philip, "Epidemic of Laughing in Bukoba District of Tanganyika," Central *African Journal of Medicine,* 9 (1963), quoted in *Newsweek,* 26 August 1963, pp. 74-75.

2. Cf. J. Huizinga, Homo Ludens: *A Study of the Play-Element* in *Culture* (London: Routledge & Kegan Paul, 1949).

3. William Willeford, *The Fool and His Scepter: A Study in Clowns and Jesters and Their Audience* (Evanston: Northwestern University Press, 1969), pp. 85-87.

4. Ibid., p. 226.

5. Erasmus, *The Praise of Folly,* trans. Hoyt Hopewell Hudson (Princeton: Princeton University Press, 1941), p. 28.

In the beginning of "The Social Value of Humor," what metaphor does John Morreall use to explain how humor functions? Can you identify and explain the other metaphors that he uses to define humor and how it functions in society? How would you describe or explain humor?

Morreall mentions several instances where humor, silliness, or absurdity is ritualized and/or celebrated. Using the Internet and your library databases, research one of Morreall's specific references or find another example of a ritual or tradition where humor plays a significant part. Describe the humor in the ritual or tradition. What social value does the humor hold, if any?

Working with a partner, scan "The Social Value of Humor" looking for and marking all the "humor is" or "laughter is" statements. After you have isolated what humor/laughter is, repeat this process looking for and marking all the statements indicating what humor/laughter does. (For example, "humor facilitates . . .") Finally, one of you read aloud the "humor/laughter is" sentences and then the other read aloud the "humor/laughter does" sentences. Based on this reading, answer this question: What is the social value of humor?

Describe a time when you consciously used humor and/or laughter to your advantage or when you felt excluded because of others' use of humor. Once you have described this incidence, put your narrative in conversation with Morreall's ideas. In other words, use your personal experience to support, extend, or challenge Morreall's arguments.

Robin Tapley teaches at Thompson Rivers University, British Columbia, Canada. In "The Value of Humor," an academic essay which appeared in The Journal of Value Inquiry, *Tapley spends considerable time explaining other scholars' views and arguments regarding humor's place in society. Understanding these arguments is crucial to understanding Tapley's key point. As you read, try to identify how Tapley situates her own claims in relation to the debate between humor theorists John R. Moreall and Jean Harvey.*

THE VALUE OF HUMOR

By Robin Tapley

Humor is a human character trait and a ubiquitous human practice. But is it a good practice, and how do we go about evaluating it? Does humor further us in some way, or facilitate our endeavors, or better us ethically? An evaluation of the proclaimed goods of humor is the focus of "Humor as social act: Ethical issues" by Jean Harvey.[1] John Morreall gives voice to the goods of humor, and Harvey argues that no such goods exist. In part this is a familiar refrain. Much of the focus in the literature on the ethics of humor is on the power of humor to harm. Humor reinforces negative sexist and racist stereotypes. Humor masks negative messages. Humor perpetrates social harm. Most writers on the ethics of humor try to ascertain when it might be appropriate to participate in humor by laughing. But Harvey goes too far when she suggests that contrary to Morreall's reasonable claims, humor is of little or no value at all. Harvey claims that humor is a dangerous social weapon. Harvey argues that humor is essentially a social act that occurs in groups of people of mixed social status. What happens is that the joking reinforces the power differential in favor of individuals with a high social status. Additionally only people who already have power can enjoy a sense of humor as a positive character trait.

HARVEY'S ARGUMENTS

Harvey's argument rests primarily on two passages from a book by John Morreall called "Taking Laughter Seriously." One passage is as follows:

From *The Journal of Value Inquiry* 40 (2006): 421-31.

The nonpractical stance in humor, along with its openness to novelty in experience, keeps us from anxiety. . . . With a sense of humor we are especially well equipped to face new situations, and even failure, with interest, since humor is based on novelty and incongruity, on having one's expectations violated. The distance in humor, too, gives us a measure of objectivity in looking at ourselves. . . . Hence we are less egocentric and more realistic in our view of the world. We are more humble in moments of success, less defeated in times of trouble, and in general, more accepting of things the way they are.[2]

The second passage is this:

When the person with a sense of humor laughs in the face of his own failure, he is showing that his perspective transcends the particular situation he's in, and that he does not have an egocentric, overly precious view of his own endeavours. This is not to say that he lacks self-esteem—quite the contrary. It is because he feels good about himself at a fundamental level that this or that setback is not threatening to him. The person without self-esteem, on the other hand, who is unsure of his own worth, tends to invest his whole sense of himself in each of his projects. Whether he fails or succeeds, he is not likely to see things in an objective way; because his ego rides on each of the goals he sets for himself, any failure will constitute personal defeat and any success personal triumph. He simply cannot afford to laugh at himself, whatever happens. So having a sense of humor about oneself is psychologically healthy.[3]

Harvey sets out to examine "the value and uses of humor."[4] What she finds is that what we might have thought formed the solid foundation of the desirability of humor is a morally corrupt crumbling hull. Harvey uses John Morreall's work to give voice to the virtues of humor. Morreall's claim is that, among other things humor gives a person a certain perspective on his self, his accomplishments, failures, and life. This perspective allows for a balanced outlook which in turn allows for a healthy, but not overblown ego, a happy outlook, and a general sense of well being. Morreall does not say that a sense of humor alone does this, but that having a certain lightness of attitude and willingness to see the humor in a situation can greatly relieve us of stress and anxiety that might otherwise leave us facing day to day routines with a sombre and cheerless disposition.

Harvey has at least two criticisms of Morreall's recounting of the value of humor. The first is that since humor is a social act usually involving three parties, Morreall's individual-based approach is inappropriate. Morreall talks about having a sense of humor instead of acts of humor or humorous events, or joking as an activity. For Harvey this means that Morreall is missing the whole point of humor, the whole function and significance of humor. Humor is fundamentally social. Laughing is not something we do alone. It is not that people do not laugh when they are the only actual person in the room. For example someone could be remembering a funny thing that happened or a joke told. In which case, there is a virtual, though not actual, social situation occurring. Another example might be laughing at a television show, in which case we are part of a virtual social situation. Granting that laughter and amusement are social, taking a purely individual approach to humor is, according to Harvey, flawed.

Moreover, it is morally flawed as it would have us ignore the moral dangers of humor. Harvey does not directly charge Morreall with this form of irresponsibility but it is implicit in the article. Because Morreall is individual-based in his approach he irresponsibly ignores the inherent moral implications of the social nature of humor. When we have a social situation in which parties are of mixed social status, it is often the case that humor is at the expense of people of lower social status. When this is the case, the humor is most often morally objectionable because of the power difference between the teller and the butt of the joke, if the content of the joke is harmful in some way. The harm of the joke can be magnified by members of the laughing audience who are not mere bystanders but who become secondary agents endorsing the joke by laughing. The parties involved then, are the agent, or teller, the victim, and the audience, or secondary agents. According to Harvey, humor is not very desirable because it is not really the perspective granting device envisioned by Morreall. Instead, humor is more a social weapon used with abandon to cut down social inferiors. Harvey claims that:

> [I]t is not a random matter who tends to initiate humor or who can typically rely on secondary agent endorsement. . . . In mixed groups where some people are highly vulnerable in various ways and others are extremely secure, it is not an accident that humor tends to be initiated by the secure. It is also not an accident that the readiness of others to become secondary agents increases in proportion to the security and power of the joke's initiator. When Caligula tells a joke, people laugh.[5]

Harvey paints a nasty picture for humor focussed on the social evils of humor, with no thought to how, or even if, humor might be employed in socially neutral or positive ways.

Harvey's second criticism is that Morreall's account applies only to privileged individuals in society. Anyone experiencing poverty or oppression, for example, may be justifiably sombre and cheerless but according to Harvey's take on Morreall this lack of a sense of humor is somehow a failing. At one point Morreall claims that being able to laugh at our failures and being humble in the face of our successes is psychologically healthy. Harvey takes offense to this and takes Morreall to task over the callousness of this statement when millions of people have no power whatsoever over their failures or their successes. In the case of oppression or poverty the power differential is so great that the only value humor can really have, according to Harvey is as a weapon against the oppressor.[6] The victims of tyranny might mimic or make jokes about the tyrant in order to relieve stress or to bond together in their fight or struggle. Here powerless individuals use humor against unjustly powerful individuals, and according to Harvey, this is morally acceptable.

Harvey goes on at length about put-down humor, but in the main her argument is really about the use of power. Her ethic of humor is straightforward. Humor is a weapon. It is a weapon of power, used to maintain or gain power. If we have a social advantage over someone and we make a put-down joke about the person, we are according to Harvey, trying to either attack her power-status to lessen her, or justify some lesser status, or perhaps delight in some reduced status.[7] If the butt of our joke is standing right there, she is in the position of having to laugh along or otherwise take it, or be a poor sport. She is doubly wounded. We have abused our power over her and have wronged her. If however the butt of our jokes is a dictatorial boss, our jokes are acceptable. By cutting her down we are not then abusing our power over her since we do not have any, and consequently we do nothing wrong. The key element here is that she is dictatorial, and her power over us must be unjust. If she were a good boss, we would not be morally able to make jokes according to Harvey. How we go about deciding when someone has "morally justifiable constructed power" is a bit of a mystery.[8]

REBUTTAL: HUMOR AND INDIVIDUALS

It should be obvious that Harvey's real concern is with power and people who abuse what power they might have to gain more at the expense of people who are power deprived. In this case, humor is just the vehicle for wielding power. Other common vehicles of power are money, jobs, and sex. It is not always the case that humor by itself is as destructive or damaging as Harvey suggests. People with power use humor as a means to exert power over others.

By claiming, as Harvey does in her first objection to the desirability of humor, that humor is solely a social act, Harvey misses as much of the phenomenon of humor as we would miss of ethics if we were to claim that all there were to it were act based theories. There is a strong and almost ubiquitous social aspect to humor. We can also talk about humor as a character trait, or an aspect of personality. We frequently say things like "George has a great sense of humor," or "Jess cannot take a joke," or "Sally is so funny." We require the much maligned individual approach to make sense of these sorts of things. Since the individual approach and the social approach are not mutually exclusive, it is curious that Harvey would take such issue with one of them. Possibly her reasons have to do with her ethics of humor, but leaving speculation aside for a moment, she gives no reason except for her claim that since humor is social, a social perspective ought to be taken in analysis. But, we cannot have a social act of humor without individual agents. This is a weak reason, and gives us only the following easily defeated argument: Harvey suggests that viewing humor from the perspective of individual agents is wrongheaded and thereby discussing any value of humor to the agents is also wrongheaded. However since we need the agents to create the social acts of humor, it is not wrongheaded, and the value of humor to the agents is relevant. Therefore, what Morreall says about perspective and self-esteem stands. Furthermore, according to other scholars such as Robert C. Roberts, an ability to view events with an objective distance, to enjoy incongruity, to be amused by poetic justice, to take pleasure in a certain sort of irony, to have a certain sort of wit, are all virtues of a sort.[9] This is a sense of humor, and it is of value to the individual.

In addition to the mental goods of an individual, there are also numerous physical goods that come from a sense of humor and from laughing. Laughing reduces stress which is good for the heart, depression, and many other illnesses. But Harvey objects that Morreall takes an individual-based approach to humor and that this is wrongheaded and morally irresponsible. There are real and significant goods to the individual who has a sense of humor, not the least of which is a freedom of mind. Part of Harvey's objection is that the goods of a sense of humor are not available to most of the world's population who still struggle under poverty and oppression. The people who would benefit most from freedom of the mind and who would need it the most are people who are struggling under oppression and poverty. There are people of good humor everywhere, under any condition. There are people whose struggling and strife is made that much easier by their sense of humor. There are people who face oppression and poverty owning nothing but their character and spirit. What Morreall says about a sense of humor applies equally to such people.

Harvey objects to the individual approach in the first place, claiming that since humor is social, we require a social analysis. While it goes unacknowledged by Harvey, Morreall agrees that humor is a social act of great import. He gives humor a social function similar to that of sharing food or a meal. Humor and laughing bind people, put people at ease and signify acceptance and friendliness, caring, or sharing. He says:

> To joke with others is to put aside practical considerations for the moment, and doing this tends to make everyone relax. Sharing humor is in this respect like sharing an enjoyable meal. It is precisely because the quarrellers do not want to put aside practical considerations and do not want to relax together, that they will not respond to each other's attempts at humor (if, indeed, any are made). Similarly, people who are quarrelling often refuse to eat together.[10]

It is clear that unless it is used to alienate, humor is seen by Morreall as a social good. Laughing together is generally a good thing. While Harvey does not see social humor as innocuous, she takes more seriously the cases of alienation, and believes them to be common.

REBUTTAL: HUMOR AND THE PRIVILEGED

The second objection made by Harvey to humor being a good is that humor is the luxury of privileged individuals. She cites Morreall as crediting humor as a way to cut fat cats down to size in a good natured way, and bolster defeated people, cajoling them to try again. Harvey reminds us of the millions of people still struggling around the world under poverty and oppression. She says:

> Even more disturbing is Morreall's implied characterization of the contrasting type of person, the person who does not approach failure with a sense of humor. This person now lacks self-esteem, is not objective, has an ego problem, and is in fact psychologically unhealthy. These seem to be presented as serious personal defects.[11]

When practical matters are close at hand, or when tragedy, or strife, or even mundane tasks require our close attention there is no humor. If survival requires most of our time, then there may not be much humor. But, it is fundamental to human nature that there be some humor at some time. It is correct to say:

> Lurking behind all these examples is the question of the relation between moral understanding and a sense of humor. The relation can be best seen in Jewish humor, which I would call the serious form of humor. It is a humor that has been distilled over centuries of pain and anguish. In a recent article A. Wood states that Jewish humor attempts "to root out the meaning of experiences, to point a certain control over them [sic] and exercise some independence from them, to penetrate the heart of suffering so as to rise above it, to save

some sanity to find just a little compensation."[12] Jewish thought has been nourished by misfortune, but the Jews have frequently met it with laughter. But the laughter was more than being cheerful or mere frivolity. It was more than a diversion. It drew the sting out of their tragedy and grief.[13]

Even in adversity there is humor. Perhaps it does not occur at the moment the adversity is suffered, but there is humor. It seems that we cannot do without it. The humor may not be the same as the fat-cat humor, but it is humor nonetheless and it has a value.

Morreall counts humor as a sort of freedom of the mind. People who are oppressed by poverty, tyranny, or captivity may have such freedom of mind as their only liberty. Humor may be their only refuge. Morreall quotes Viktor Frankl as follows:

> To the extent that we can achieve this distance from the practical side of any situation, we are free from being dominated by that situation. In some cases, such as during wartime, humor can become almost a prerequisite of survival. Viktor Frankl, who survived Auschwitz and Dachau and later came to incorporate humor into his psychotherapeutic techniques, said of the concentration camps: "unexpectedly most of us were overcome by a grim sense of humor. We knew we had nothing to lose except our ridiculously naked lives. . . . Humor was another of the soul's weapons in the fight for self preservation. . . . Humor more than anything else in the human make-up can afford an aloofness and ability to rise above any situation, if only for a few seconds."[14]

Even people in a concentration camp needed humor. Harvey is incorrect to assume that humor is only for people in power and is only used by people with power against people who have none. She is also incorrect to assume that Morreall thinks that people who are oppressed would be sombre and have flawed characters.

ETHICS OF HUMOR

No one would deny that humor could be used badly, with negative intentions. Humor can be manipulative, hurtful, or degrading. As well, people in a position of power have leverage when it comes to using social weapons, humor included. While an abuse of power is a good starting place for any ethic, unfortunately Harvey's ethic never gets off the ground. While admittedly an ethic of humor was never her main objective, she clearly believes that the problem with put-down humor is moral:

The underlying moral objection is to the aggrandizement or relishing of power for its own sake, to the savouring of an attack on the less powerful. The objection [to put down humor] does not depend on the effects of the action, but has to do with the lack of an appropriate attitude toward unequal power.[15]

She does not seem to allow for joking among peers, or for non-power driven joking between non-peers. Power always wins out over what might have been a well-intended jest. Harvey claims: "A significant difference in power brings with it the inherent danger of abusing the greater power with impunity, perhaps even without conscious awareness."[16] She adds: "Not all subjects of jokes are victims. Joking between peers, even mutual teasing, may involve no genuine victim. No serious prudential constraints prevent their "fighting back."[17] However, she also says: "But intimacy of affection is no guarantee of genuine peer status. In many families, for example, children and teens are prudentially constrained in their response to put-down jokes from parents."[18] Indeed throughout her whole article she uses the family to demonstrate power differentials. There is no innocent joke. Among peers there may be hidden restraints to fighting back, thereby creating a power difference. Where power differences are obvious we may be unconsciously using our power even when we do not mean to.

Harvey uses the term "put-down humor" in the title of several of her sections as though she is only talking about one kind or type of humor. Someone might mistakenly think that what she says does not apply to other kinds of humor such as teasing or knock-knock jokes. For Harvey, however, there is no other kind of humor. In Harvey's ethics of humor, a fair-play joke would require that two parties of equal status engage in humor where neither party's humor is an attempt to lessen the other party's power, justify lesser power for the other party, or delight in the other party's reduced status. However, in Harvey's view a fair-play joke can never happen because no two people are really of equal status, and even if they were, their humor would not maintain the status. Our ethic of humor has to take into account that true peers do not exist. Power differentials must be taken into consideration in any reasonable ethics of humor. Power differentials must be dealt with in any workable ethic. But every joke is not a play for power.

According to Harvey, there can be no fair-play joke because there is no true peer relationship and a power play will always be made. While the equality of peers might be merely perceived equality instead of true equality, there is a problem with the condition that a power play will always be made. The condition that there is no true peer relationship is mainly structural or formal, either it is the case or it is not. But the condition that a power play will always be made has to do with the joker's motivation. According to Harvey there is only one motivation and that is the attainment or sustainment of power. This seems narrow, even on the view Hobbes advances. Unless we build a contorted and deformed picture of human motivation, it is hard to account for why people do things with only one drive. To assume, as Harvey seems to, that we crack a joke only to get or maintain power is to cling to a phantom of a one-dimensional person who just does not exist. People are capable of being motivated by altruism, justice, meanness, pain, and sometimes just fun. We function and joke, from more than just one motive.

If we follow Harvey, because there can be no fair-play joke, joking is inherently morally flawed. It is flawed for the same reasons there can be no fair-play joke. In joking there is no such thing as equality, and there is always a power struggle. Joking then is inherently morally suspect. It is highly unlikely that social goods can come of something that is inherently morally bad. What Harvey seems to have shown is that joking is morally corrupt, and as a social act, it corrupts society. Joking is a bad thing that does bad things to the societies in which it is practiced. People in power use it to batter people without power.

But there can be fair-play joking, and joking is not inherently morally flawed. Joking, like many other social practices and constructs can be used or practised for good or bad. Harvey only becomes locked into the inherently flawed view because she becomes locked into the no fair-play view of joking. If we reject her idea that there is no fair-play joking then we do not have to accept her idea that joking is inherently morally flawed. People can tell jokes for many purposes. One of which might be to hurt the feelings of people. But jokes can also be used for many other positive purposes, not the least of which is simply to entertain. Like other powerful motivators, humor can be used to manipulate people, or it can be innocently enjoyed. While Harvey is not wrong to include humor in this group of social puppet strings, she is wrong to think it the puppet master.

Notes

1. Jean Harvey, "Humor as Social Act: Ethical Issues," *Journal of Value Inquiry,*
2. Vol 29, No. 1 (1995).
3. John Morreall, *Taking Laughter Seriously,* (Albany: State University of New York Press, 1983) p. 128.
4. Ibid. p. 106.
5. op. cit., p. 19.
6. Ibid. pp. 20–21.
7. Ibid. p. 24.

8. Ibid. p. 25.

9. Ibid. p. 27.

10. See: Robert C. Roberts "Humor and the Virtues," *Inquiry: An Interdisciplinary Journal of Philosophy and The Social Sciences* 31, June 1988.

11. Ibid. p. 115–116.

12. op. cit., p. 23.

13. D. Ieuan. Lloyd, "What's In a Laugh? Humour and Its Educational Significance" *Journal of Philosophy of Education,* Vol 19, No. 1 (1985) p. 78.

14. Ibid. p. 78.

15. op. cit., p. 104.

16. op. cit., p. 28.

17. Ibid. p. 26.

18. Ibid.

In "The Value of Humor," Robin Tapley "takes on" Jean Harvey's arguments regarding the social aspects of humor. What flaws does Tapley find in Harvey's theories? What is Tapley's stance regarding the value of humor? What reasons does Tapley offer for her position, and what evidence does she present to support her reasons and claims? Share your answers with several of your classmates and discuss the effectiveness of Tapley's piece. Do you find her reasons, arguments, and evidence persuasive?

Read John Morreall's "The Social Value of Humor" (p. 59) and one of the other essays in *Funny*. Write a 4-5 page essay, supported by evidence, examples, and reasoned argument, expressing your position on the value of humor and its place in our society.

Nicholas Kuiper teaches in the Department of Psychology at the University of Western Ontario, Canada. He specializes in the personality and social psychological aspects of humor. Dana Klein is a practicing psychologist in London, Ontario, Canada. Klein and Kuiper published this research in the journal Humor. *Their research utilizes existing models that recognize the importance of adaptive and maladaptive humor styles. In the excerpt that follows, the authors explain the various humor styles and their influence in middle childhood, and they offer suggestions for the direction that the research in this field should take. As you read this psychological study, think about what it adds to your understanding of the social aspects of humor.*

HUMOR STYLES, PEER RELATIONSHIPS, AND BULLYING IN MIDDLE CHILDHOOD

BY DANA KLEIN AND NICHOLAS KUIPER

Sense of humor begins to develop during the preschool years, but it is not until middle childhood (ages 6–12) that the ability to use humor effectively in social situations is displayed. By the age of 11 or 12, most children have acquired sufficient cognitive and social skills to appreciate and use humor as an effective form of social interaction and communication (see Bergen, 1998 and McGhee, 1974 for detailed reviews). Middle childhood is a crucial time, as it is during this period that the child must learn to interact effectively within larger peer groups. Successful social development during this period can lead to beneficial social relationships, including greater peer acceptance (Zigler and Finn-Stevenson, 1987). Conversely, poor social development can lead to lower social status, increased peer rejection, neglect, and even peer victimization (Craig and Pepler, 2000). As these detrimental effects can become long-term and persist through adolescence and adulthood (Ladd, 1999), it is important to understand more fully how the expression of humor during middle childhood may impact on social interactions and relationships.

From *Humor* 9.4 (2006): 383-04.

A CONTEMPORARY MODEL OF HUMOR STYLES

Although some theorizing and research has been conducted regarding the development of humor during childhood (see Bergen, 1998; McGhee, 1974), there is a relatively limited consideration of the underlying individual difference models that may apply. Thus, to set the stage for our examination, we first provide a brief overview of a contemporary model of humor, based upon research with adults, that has recently been advanced by Martin et al. (2003). In developing their individual differences approach to humor, Martin and his colleagues reviewed past literature on the relationship between humor and well-being, in order to identify various styles of humor that have been described as being either adaptive or maladaptive. The resulting four styles of humor are self- enhancing, affiliative, self-defeating, and aggressive humor. Both the self-enhancing and affiliative humor styles generally tap the positive or adaptive aspects of sense of humor, whereas the self-defeating and aggressive humor styles generally tap the negative or maladaptive aspects of sense of humor.

As described by Martin et al. (2003), those high on self-enhancing humor have a humorous outlook on life and can maintain a humorous perspective, even when faced with potentially stressful events and situations. These individuals also use humor as a beneficial coping strategy to minimize negative emotions, while still maintaining a realistic perspective on life. Self-enhancing humor thus serves to buffer and protect the self, but not at the expense of others. Affiliative humor is the second adaptive style, and focuses on the use of humor to enhance interpersonal and social relationships. Humor is employed here to raise group moral, identity, and cohesiveness by reducing conflicts and increasing others' feelings of wellbeing. This non-hostile use of humor also involves joking and banter to reduce interpersonal tensions, and facilitate relationships with others.

In contrast to the two adaptive styles, which are tolerant and accepting of both self and others, the two maladaptive styles are detrimental and potentially injurious to either the self (i.e., self-defeating humor) or others (i.e., aggressive humor). Those high on self-defeating humor, for example, use excessive self-disparaging and ingratiating humor in inappropriate attempts to gain the approval of others, and thus enhance their interpersonal relationships. Humor is expressed in a self-detrimental style that is at high personal cost. . . . The final maladaptive style identified in the Martin et al. (2003) model is aggressive humor. Here, individuals may use a variety of negative humor techniques, including teasing, ridicule, sarcasm, and disparagement to denigrate and put down others. Aggressive humor is displayed with little regard for its potential negative impact on others, ultimately alienating these individuals and seriously impairing social and interpersonal relationships.

HUMOR STYLES IN MIDDLE CHILDHOOD

We propose that Martin et al.'s (2003) humor styles model is also quite relevant to the humor displayed by children, especially during the latter phase of middle childhood. As children proceed through this period, their cognitive and social development matures to the point that they can readily understand and express many different forms of humor (see Bergen, 1998; McGhee, 1974 for extensive reviews). Thus, congruent with the humor styles model, some children in the latter part of middle childhood (i.e., ages 10–12) may often use affiliative humor to help maintain group cohesiveness, or gain support of a peer group. In addition, self-enhancing humor may be used more often by certain children, in order to help maintain or even enhance their self-esteem. Similarly, we suggest that the expression of the two maladaptive humor styles may also be quite evident in middle childhood. As one illustration, aggressive humor may often be used against peer victimized children, as one means of maintaining their lowered status within the peer group. Thus, if a bully makes fun of a peer rejected child, this could serve to decrease the rejected child's self-esteem and value within the group. Furthermore, this use of aggressive humor could also serve to enhance the bully's morale and entertain the group, thereby maintaining group solidarity. Finally, some children in middle childhood may also display a strong self-defeating humor style....

Our examples suggest that different children may use different humor styles to achieve their desired goals. Thus, while some children may be more proficient in using adaptive humor styles, others may tend to favor maladaptive humor styles. For example, a more prosocial child may favor affiliative styles of sense of humor, whereas a bully may be more proficient at using an aggressive humor style. Additionally, the style of humor the child uses could then impact on their social relationships, as different styles of humor may be more favored by the peer group as a whole. To illustrate, affiliative humor may be more conducive to the development of friendships, whereas aggressive humor may be related to rejection by one's peers.

HUMOR STYLES, PEER RELATIONSHIPS, AND BULLYING IN MIDDLE CHILDHOOD

In accord with other researchers (Bergen, 1998; Gest et al. 2001; McGhee, 1974; Warnars-Kleverlaan et al. 1996), we view humor as one of the important social competencies that develops during middle childhood. Accordingly, this portion of the paper discusses the four humor styles in the context of two social issues of particular relevance during this period, namely, peer relationships and bullying. Here, we will indicate how each humor style may relate to either peer acceptance versus victimization, or direct versus indirect bullying. As one illustration, recall that affiliative humor is an adaptive style used to enhance interpersonal and social relationships, but at no one's expense. Accordingly we will propose that this humor style is quite characteristic of successful social development in middle childhood, and is linked to greater peer acceptance. Rather ironically, we will also propose that this humor style may sometimes characterize the indirect bully, who displays superior social skills and adept management of the peer group. A similar pattern will then be described for the self-enhancing humor style, with this characteristic also being quite evident in both peer acceptance and indirect bullying. In contrast to these two humor styles, we will describe how aggressive humor may be one of the strong contributors to peer victimization, and is a humor style that is used by both direct and indirect bullies. Finally, we will propose that self-defeating humor may pertain primarily to increased peer victimization, but may not be a strong aspect of either direct or indirect bullying.

AFFILIATIVE HUMOR

Affiliative humor refers to humor that enhances one's relationship with others. This style of humor can be described as adaptive, pleasant, and enjoyable to most individuals (Martin et al., 2003; Kuiper et al., 2004). Because affiliative humor is generally a pleasant and desirable style of humor, children utilizing affiliative humor may have an advantageous position within the peer group. As such, this humor style may pertain to both peer acceptance and indirect bullying.

4.1.1 *Peer acceptance.* Affiliative humor may be used by more popular children to help achieve and maintain peer group identity and cohesiveness. Peer accepted, popular children may be more proficient at using affiliative humor for several reasons. First, since peer accepted children are generally the most prosocial and well-adjusted within the group (Ladd, 1999), it is more likely that these children will gravitate towards the use of an adaptive humor style, such as affiliative humor (Gest et al., 2001), rather than use a negative and aggressive humor style. . . . Peer accepted children may also use affiliative humor to help maintain social support, facilitate harmony, and increase in-group pride. . . . Furthermore, since peer accepted children have a greater understanding of social norms and rules (Ladd, 1999), these children would have a better concept of what constitutes socially acceptable humor within their peer group. In turn, this may result in a greater ability to understand and express affiliative humor within their social network. Finally, prior research has shown that children's use of humor increases when social interactions are viewed as being more comfortable and safe (Bergen, 1998). Since peer accepted children are much more likely to feel socially safe and comfortable (when compared with rejected or victimized children), they may express affiliative humor much more often within their social settings.

4.1.2 *Indirect bullying.* Whereas peer accepted children may use affiliative humor in a prosocial manner, for example, to facilitate group harmony and cohesiveness, an indirect bully may use affiliative humor to harass, victimize and even exclude children from the group. As described earlier, indirect aggression may require sophisticated social skills, since the bully must understand the rules and norms that govern the network of peers, in order to manipulate the peer group and gain their support (O'Connell et al., 1999). Thus, a bully who uses indirect forms of aggression would likely possess superior social skills (Sutton et al., 1999), which, in turn, would foster the greater use of differing styles of humor, including affiliative humor, to manipulate the group.

Indirect bullies with superior social skills may be better able to use affiliative humor within the peer group to accomplish two goals. First, the indirect bully may use affiliative humor as one means to increase in-group cohesion and morale. By doing so, this bully may gain additional support and respect from the in-group members. The use of affiliative humor in this fashion may also help accomplish the indirect bully's second goal, namely, that of exclusion. That is, by increasing in-group cohesion, this bully may be better able to exclude other select members of the peer group. For example, an indirect bully may make an inside joke that only the members of the in-group would understand. When a rejected child fails to get this joke, this would then serve to distance the rejected child from the group. In this case, the indirect bully would cause the victimized child distress by increasing the social discrepancy between that child and members of the in-group.

SELF-ENHANCING HUMOR

4.2.1 *Peer acceptance.* Given that the use of humor increases within comfortable, safe situations (Bergen, 1998), a child accepted by the peer group may have more opportunity to practice humor, thus developing superior skills. Peer accepted children may also use different styles of humor more often, to successfully achieve their goals within their social network. Thus, peer accepted children may not only be proficient at using affiliative humor, but may also effectively use a different adaptive style, namely, self-enhancing humor, depending on the demands of the particular social situation.

Whereas affiliative humor is often used to enhance one's relationships within a group, self-enhancing humor is often used to promote and maintain personal psychological well-being (Martin et al., 2003). Thus, peer accepted children may use self-enhancing humor to appear confident and self-assured. This may help them to appear as leaders to the other members of the group, thus serving to solidify their desirable position within the peer network. This use of self-enhancing humor could also impact on their self-esteem in a positive manner, thus serving to increase their subjective feelings of self-worth. In turn, higher self-esteem may lead to greater social adjustment, and could thus contribute to even more prosocial behavior. Overall, the greater use of self-enhancing humor by peer accepted children could serve to increase their self-esteem, increase others' opinions of them, increase overall prosocial behaviors, and help to maintain their position within the peer group.

4.2.2 *Indirect bullying.* In the same way that peer accepted children might use self-enhancing humor, socially skilled bullies might also use self-enhancing humor to promote the self and subsequently influence the manner in which their peers view them. Indirect bullies could use self-enhancing humor to increase their own self-esteem and to feel important within the social group. Additionally, indirect bullies may use positive humor styles to increase the impression that they are confident, worthy leaders that deserve the respect of the group. An indirect bully could make jokes that emphasize her dominant position within the group, and impart the impression that she is a strong member of the peer network. Thus, by appearing confident and self-assured, this indirect bully may gain respect from peers. Overall, socially skilled indirect bullies may use self-enhancing humor to increase their own self-esteem, and ultimately to gain the respect of others, improve their social status, and present an impression of confidence and leadership ability to their peers.

AGGRESSIVE HUMOR

In our approach we view the aggressive humor style as being a strong contributor to peer victimization, and one that is used by both direct and indirect bullies. Accordingly, the differential use of this humor style to foster peer victimization within each form of bullying is elaborated below.

4.3.1 *Indirect bullying.* Aggressive humor may be used by indirect bullies to exclude rejected children from the group, by lowering their value in the eyes of the other children. For example, a socially skilled bully may be able to joke about the victim in a manner that diminishes the victim's status, but at the same time increases the bully's support within the peer group. This could be done by ensuring the level of aggression displayed in the humor does not exceed the socially acceptable bounds defined by the group. Similarly, an indirect bully may also spread rumors and make aggressive jokes behind the victim's back, to both damage the victim's reputation and entertain the crowd, thereby gaining social support. Again, by accurately gauging the limits of acceptable aggression to include in these jokes, the socially skilled bully could succeed in diminishing and degrading the victim, while simultaneously maintaining their own prominent position and respect within the larger peer network.

4.3.2 *Direct bullying.* Whereas the socially skilled bullies may use aggressive humor as a form of indirect aggression, direct bullies may use aggressive humor as a form of overt aggression. These direct bullies may use aggressive styles of humor to overtly make fun of their victims, rather than covertly harass their victims and manipulate the peer group. Crick and Dodge's (1994) social deficit model of bullying best describes these direct, overt forms of aggression. In their model, bullies who use more primitive forms of direct aggression also display deficits in their abilities to interact in a more prosocial, effective manner. The research supporting this model indicates that these bullies often lack social skills pertaining to leadership or communication.

In light of these various social skills deficits, and a limited ability to understand and manipulate the peer group, direct bullies may also lack the ability to effectively use a wider variety of humor styles with their peers. In particular, we suggest that although socially skilled bullies may be able to effectively use self-enhancing, affiliative, and aggressive humor styles, the direct bully may lack the ability to effectively use the two more positive humor styles. As a result, direct bullies may rely primarily on aggressive humor as a way of attacking their victims. For example, the socially deficient bully may approach another child and make fun of the child's clothing. However, this form of aggressive humor may be considered less sophisticated and socially skilled because it is more easily detected by others (e.g., teachers, parents), and it does not as easily allow the bully to manipulate the peer group to gain social support. Moreover, overtly aggressive humor may be seen as a social deficit by other members of the peer group, particularly when this humor routinely exceeds the socially accepted bounds defined by the group. Thus, as Ladd (1999) points out, peer rejection can be related to behavioral excess, as well as deficits. In particular, excessive aggressive humor may become one of the reasons why a particular child is not accepted by the peer group. Overall, then, socially deficient direct bullies may be less proficient at using a broader range of humor styles, thus coming to rely predominately on overt, aggressive humor to achieve their social goals. Ultimately, however, the over reliance on an aggressive humor style may seriously damage and jeopardize the direct bully's social reputation and status within the group.

SELF-DEFEATING HUMOR

In much the same way as a direct bully may not fully understand how to use a wide variety of humor styles to interact effectively within the peer group, this may also be true for the victimized child. Recall that the development of humor flourishes more readily in comfortable and safe social situations (Bergen, 1998). As such, children that interact frequently and freely with their peers may be better able to use humor, and various humor styles, depending on the demands of their social circumstances. In particular, peer accepted children may be able to better use differing styles of positive humor to effectively achieve both their social and personal goals within the peer group. In contrast, peer victimized children are provided with much less opportunity to interact freely with their peers (Craig and Pepler, 2000), and therefore may be at a marked disadvantage with regard to both the development and practice of humor competence. As such, we suggest that peer victimized children may not be able to use either of the adaptive humor styles as effectively within the peer group. If peer victimized children are unable to effectively use affiliative humor to develop and maintain friendships and peer acceptance, this could then contribute to their continued rejection from the larger peer network. These children may not be able to joke with their peers, and may not be able to fully understand the jokes that the other children make. Additionally, these children may not know how to effectively use self-enhancing humor to bolster their self-esteem, and gain the respect of the other children. In summary, the effective use of adaptive humor styles may be a social competency that these peer victimized children lack, placing them at a disadvantage when attempting to interact with their peers.

Peer victimization and self-defeating humor. Since peer victimized children may not be proficient at using affiliative or self-enhancing humor styles, they may gravitate towards the excessive use of a self-defeating humor style. Many of these victimized children have been bullied by their fellow classmates, and have come to identify with their lower status (Bukowski and Hoza, 1989; O'Connell et al., 1999). In particular, victimized children may believe that the jokes that the bully makes at their expense are actual indicators of their own self-worth. Thus, peer victimized children may also begin to make negative, self-directed jokes, reflecting their low self-esteem. As one illustration, a victimized child may also begin to joke about their own personal appearance in a negative manner, as they are very self-conscious about this aspect of self.

Compounding further the difficulties faced by peer victimized children, it may be that the aggressive jokes made by both direct and indirect bullies are their prime exemplars of social interaction humor. In particular, victimized children may learn about humor primarily through the negative, maladaptive aggressive humor displayed by bullies. Thus, the self-defeating jokes that these victimized children make, may actually reflect the aggressive jokes the bullies make about them, as they have very limited opportunities to develop and practice the more positive, adaptive humor skills. For instance, if a bully makes fun of a victim's clothing, the victim may learn that this type of joke is funny to others, and then convert this to negative self-defeating humor, in a vain attempt to make others laugh.

The self-defeating humor style used by victimized children may also help explain the behaviors of the "class clown." According to Fabrizi and Pollio (1987), these children tend to be of low social status, and make jokes at their own expense, in an attempt to make their peers laugh. Although these children can be seen as quite amusing, their humor style reflects underlying neediness and low self-esteem. Overall, then, victimized children and children of low social status may use self-defeating humor because it reflects their feelings of low self worth, and they want to try and gain the acceptance of their peers through any means possible.

FURTHER THEORETICAL CONSIDERATIONS AND RESEARCH DIRECTIONS

Central to our approach is the proposal that humor can have a strong impact on the various types of social relationships evident during middle childhood. Congruent with this notion, the limited amount of research conducted thus far does indeed show that humor is one of the important social competencies that can contribute to the child's status within the social group (Bergen, 1998; Gest et al., 2001; McGhee, 1974; Warnars-Kleverlaan et al., 1996). Although this existing research is certainly promising, it has been based primarily on the implicit assumption that humor should be viewed as a unitary positive personal attribute that serves to facilitate well-being and social relationships. Thus, little, if any, theorizing or research has considered the impact of both negative and positive facets of humor on social interactions and bullying during middle childhood.

In considering this issue, we would propose that the relationship is most likely reciprocal in nature. Young children who are socially skilled may develop a more positive sense of humor. In turn, these children may be more likely to develop friends and become accepted into the peer group. As a consequence of this acceptance, they will have more opportunity to interact with other children, thus enabling them to practice and improve their humor skills. This interaction with peers may lead to the development of superior social skills, and consequently, a more well-developed adaptive sense of humor. As it seems likely that humor styles do have an impact on one's social status, future research should carefully examine the nature of this relationship to clarify causality. In particular, the potential role of humor in social development should no longer be neglected, as different humor styles may strongly impact a child's degree of acceptance into the peer group, ultimately bearing on overall social, psychological and emotional adjustment.

Bergen, Doris

1998 Development of the sense of humor. In Ruch, Willibald (ed.), *The Sense of Humor: Explorations of a Personality Characteristic*. Berlin/New York: Mouton de Gruyter, 329–360.

Bippus, Amy

2005 Humor usage during recalled conflicts: The effects of form and sex on recipient evaluations. In Shohov, Serge P. (ed.), *Advances in Psychology Research*, vol. 34. Hauppauge, NY: Nova Science, 115–116.

Bukowski, William M., and Betsy Hoza

1989 Popularity and friendship: Issues in theory, measurement, and outcome. In Berndt, T. J., and Gary W. Ladd (eds.), *Peer Relations in Child Development.* New York: Wiley, 15–45.

Craig, Wendy, and Debra J. Pepler

2000 Observations of bullying and victimization in the school yard. In Craig, Wendy (ed.), *Childhood Social Development: The Essential Readings.* Malden, MA: Blackwell, 116–136.

Crick, Nicki R., Juan F. Casas, and Monique Mosher

1997 Relational and overt aggression in preschool. *Developmental Psychology* 33 (4): 579–588.

Crick, Nicki R., and Kenneth A. Dodge

1994 A review and reformulation of social-information-processing mechanisms in children's social adjustment. *Psychological Bulletin* 115, 74–101.

DeKoning, Elizabeth, and R. L. Weiss

2002 The relational humor inventory: Functions of humor in close relationships.

The American Journal of Family Therapy 30, 1–18.

Dubow, Eric F.

1988 Aggressive behavior and peer social status of elementary school children. *Aggressive Behavior* 14, 315–324.

Fabrizi, Michael S., and Howard R. Pollio

1987 A naturalistic style of humorous activity in a third, seventh, and eleventh grade classroom. *Merrill-Palmer Quarterly* 33, 107–128.

Frewan, Paul, Jaylene Brinker, Rod A. Martin, and David Dozois

(in press) Humor styles and personality-vulnerability to depression. *Humor: International Journal of Humor Research.*

Furman, Wyndol, and Philip Robbins

1985 What's the point? Issues in the selection of treatment objectives. In Schneider B. H., K. H. Rubin, and J. E. Ledingham (eds.), *Children's Peer Relationships: Issues in Assessment and Intervention.* New York: Springer, 41–54.

Gest, Scott D., Sandra A. Graham-Bermann, and Willard W. Hartup

2001 Peer experience: Common and unique features of number of friendships, social network centrality, and sociometric status. *Social Development* 10 (1), 23–40.

Kazarian, Shahe S., and Rod A. Martin

2004 Humor styles, personality, and well-being among Lebanese university students. *European Journal of Personality* 18 (3), 209–219.

Kirsh, Gillian, and Nicholas A. Kuiper

2003 Humor use in adolescent relationships and associations with psychological well-being. Paper presented at the Annual Conference of the Canadian Psychological Association, Hamilton.

Kuiper, Nicholas A., Melissa Grimshaw, Catherine Leite, and Gillian Kirsh

2004 Humor is not always the best medicine: Specific components of sense of humor and psychological well-being. *Humor: International Journal of Humor Research* 17 (1/2), 135–168.

Ladd, Gary W.

1999 Peer relationships and social competence during early and middle childhood. *Annual Reviews: Psychology* 50, 333–359.

Martin, Rod A., Patricia Puhlik-Doris, Gwen Larsen, Jeanette Gray, and Kelly Weir

2003 Individual differences in the uses of humor and their relation to psychological well-being: Development of the Humor Styles Questionnaire. *Journal of Research in Personality* 37, 48–75.

McGhee, Paul E.

1974 Cognitive mastery and children's humor. *Psychological Bulletin* 81, 721–730.

O'Connell, Paul, Debra J. Pepler, and Wendy Craig

1999 Peer involvement in bullying: Insights and challenges for intervention. *Journal of Adolescence* 22, 437–452.

Olweus, Dan

1991 Bully/victim problems among schoolchildren: Basic facts and effects of a school-based intervention program. In Pepler, Debra J., and K. H. Rubin (eds.), *The Development and Treatment of Childhood Aggression*. Hillsdale, NJ: Lawrence Erlbaum, 411–448.

Rubin, Zick

1980 *Children's Friendships*. Cambridge, MA: Harvard University Press.

Saroglou, Vassilis, and Christel Scariot

2002 Humor Styles Questionnaire: Personality and educational correlates in Belgian high school and college students. *European Journal of Personality* 16, 43–54.

Sutton, Jon, Peter K. Smith, and John Swettenham

1999 Bullying and 'theory of mind': A critique of the 'social skills deficit' view of anti-social behavior. *Social Development* 8, 117–127.

Warnars-Kleverlaan, Nel, Louis Oppenheimer, and Larry Sherman

1996 To be or not to be humorous: Does it make a difference? *Humor: International Journal of Humor Research* 9 (2), 117–141.

Zigler, Edward F., and Matia Finn-Stevenson

1987 *Children: Developmental and Social Issues*. Toronto: D. C. Heath and Company.

In their study on humor, peer relationships, and bullying, Dana Klein and Nicholas Kuiper use the term "humor competence." Explain humor competency. What examples do they provide of this competency? Why is it an important aspect of their study?

Using the Internet and the library databases, find news stories about middle-school bullying. How many incidents involve some form of humor such as pranks or teasing? How many involve one "teaser" or bully, and how many involve a group of bullies or teasers? How many incidents involve some form of social media? Klein and Kuiper published their study in 2006. What do your findings suggest about humor and bullying in middle childhood today? What might Klein and Kuiper have to take into consideration today that they did not in 2006?

Working with several of your classmates, create a Public Service Announcement (PSA) "about the positive and negative facets of humor on social interactions and bullying during middle childhood" (Klein and Kuiper). Be prepared to share your PSA with the class.

Filmmaker, photographer, and broadcaster Toby Amies has written comedy for MTV, and ar
and newspapers. In the following article for bbc.com Magazine, Amies elevates the prank
practical joke.

THE ART OF THE PERFECT PRANK

As April Fools jokers hatch their plans, what's the secret to a perfect prank,
asks broadcaster Toby Amies. And how far do the very best tricksters go in
preparing their practical jokes?

This article is not a hoax. I promise you. It's a serious work about the practical joke.

How far would you go to pull off a prank? The dole queue? In 1987, a young British broadcaster called Chris Morris let off helium into the BBC Bristol studio, causing the newsreader's stories to reach a higher and higher pitch. Chris lost his job. And started his career in satire.

Would you risk prison? Pranks are often protests, against unfairness or authority or reality. And protest is increasingly risky in the 21st Century.

As the film director Billy Wilder said: "If you are going to tell people the truth, be funny or they will kill you."

Whether personal or public, the prank has a point to make, but if you're planning on tricking someone, it's best to ensure everyone gets the joke.

Russian Art Collective Voina might have gone furthest in making fun of the unfair. Two of their members went to prison.

From *BBC News* (2011).

Although Voina's manifesto is political, their activities make more immediate (non) sense, from launching live cats at workers in McDonald's to their most notorious "action"—daubing graffiti on a raised bridge opposite the headquarters of the federal security service in St Petersburg, with an enormous, crude phallus that erected every time the bridge did.

Perhaps inevitably, two Voina members were arrested—not for the abstract insult of the penis but for overturning police cars. Voina's name means "war" and they see themselves as part of another Russian revolution, one that refuses to take the very serious seriously at all, even if it means loss of liberty.

The pranksters have been bailed out of prison by the world's most internationally famous "anonymous" street artist, Banksy.

With its roots in the mythological trickster who mediated between Heaven and Earth—known by many names in many cultures, like Loki, Anansie, Prometheus, Coyote, Eshu or Brer Rabbit—a good prank allows boundaries to be crossed, including the ones between art and crime, or amateur and professional.

When unemployed Mancunian Karl Power became, for a brief moment the 12th man in Manchester United's team against Munich in 2001 by walking on to the pitch at the right moment in the right kit, he turned every fan's fantasy into reality.

But it was the result of two years of careful strategy, he said. "We planned it like a military campaign and brought three United kits with us—red, white and blue." The choice of three kits meant Karl the imposter could blend in with the reality of a Champions League match unnoticed till it was too late.

Legendary American media hoaxer Joey Skaggs has devoted his whole life to the prank. For more than 30 years, Joey's been making up ridiculous lies that get disseminated so far by the mass media we are forced to wonder if the same media might not be fact-checking every other story so closely.

"I am an artist. To me the media is a medium and I create plausible but non-existent realities and I stage for the news media to make social, political, satirical commentary."

Joey simplifies the process as "the hook, line and sinker."

The hook has the bait, a ready-written story, so sexy that a journalist wants it to be true so much they don't bother to check.

The line is a record of the process. Joey uses clippings services and devices like Google alerts help him chart the reach of the hoax. "I watched how the news media would change the intent, content, meaning of the message to suit their own agendas."

Joey has duped the media into covering an embarrassing number of weird but wonderful stories, from his canine brothel, The Cathouse for Dogs, to his celebrity sperm bank, and probably several other stories that are works in progress that have yet to be revealed.

The sinker is the reveal, the moment when the lights go on and we all realise how easy it is to be fooled.

It's hard work to overturn reality. Joey creates shell companies, puts out official press releases, hires actors, installs dedicated phone lines, whatever it takes to make the false seem real. It's a wonder he hasn't been headhunted by the financial services industry. The prank on his scale is an art form and consequently a mix of inspiration, craft and industry, imagination and talent is needed.

FALSE REALITY

Even so, pranking has proved extremely popular as a form of television, the hidden camera pioneered in Allen Funt's Candid Camera in the US allowed the delicious dramatic irony of watching a carefully planned plot unfold from several angles.

Television turned the prank into an expensive business with millions at risk. The budgets of TV and film allowed for exactly the kind of careful dramatic plotting that a good prank needs, fortunes were spent in creating versions of reality that were are at once, ridiculous to the viewer and plausible to the victim.

Nigel Crowle, an associate producer for Noel Edmonds and Jeremy Beadle, describes it as creating "layer upon layer of absurd situations build it up, to a climax, which really if you analysed it make absolutely no sense whatsoever."

You almost need to bully your target into accepting a false reality, by not giving them the opportunity to consider the alternatives. Of course this is how advertising works.

Pranksters are the special forces of comedy, getting out into the field to tell truth through laughter and using the public space as a theatre.

Charlie Todd's Improv Everywhere most famously froze time in New York's Grand Central Station in a performance that has received millions of views on YouTube. He has used social media as effectively as revolutionaries in the Middle East for feel-good pranks.

If nothing else, the advent of social media has helped the prank become the perfect art for our times. It's anti-authoritarian, hard to commodity or monetise, full of social comment, anti-violent and revolutionary. The opposite of the kind of art a billionaire would buy.

But as I write this, I wonder if I've been unfair to authority and the status quo: the bosses, the parents, the teachers, the politicians, the forces of darkness who would stop us laughing and joking.

On reflection perhaps not, because you might say they've been playing the most terrible joke on us 364 days a year.

Several kinds of pranks emerge throughout Amies's piece. How would you classify the various pranks that he describes? Do you see commonalities among them? List them. What differences do you see? List them. What conclusions do you draw from these commonalities and differences?

Working with several of your peers do the following: first, list the criteria for the "perfect prank," according to Amies; second, view several clips or full episodes of a recent TV prank show such as *Impractical Jokers* or *Da Ali G Show*; third, choose the clip that best meets Amies's criteria; fourth, prepare a short in-class presentation in which you show the clip and explain how it fits Amies's criteria.

Using the library databases and/or the Internet research one or more of the trickster figures that Amies names in his piece, identify the trickster's defining characteristics and cultural functions. Now that you have a better understanding of the trickster and how this figure uses "pranks," do you think that Amies's point that the roots of a good prank rest in the mythology of the trickster is effective and relevant. Why or why not?

Amies writes that the prank is "anti-authoritarian, hard to commodity or monetise, full of social comment, anti-violent and revolutionary." Write a 3-4 page paper, extending, complicating, or challenging this statement. As you develop your ideas, you may find it helpful to think about the trickster figure (see "Explore") and the various kinds of pranks Amies details (see "Invent"). You also might consider viewing current YouTube videos of Charlie Todd's *Improv Everywhere*, checking out the TV prank show *Impractical Jokers*, as well as other self-proclaimed pranksters who use pranks to create absurdity to challenge the status quo.

Peter Funt, one time producer and host of Candid Camera, *is a speaker, columnist, and President of the Laughter Therapy Foundation. He writes op-ed pieces for* The New York Times *among other publications.*

THE JOKE'S ON WHOM?

By Peter Funt

I've pranked several thousand people, although I never favored that term. Much of my career was spent doing hidden-camera stunts on "Candid Camera," following a path charted for decades by my father, Allen Funt. We always worried about what might go wrong, particularly involving the physical and emotional health of unsuspecting subjects. Our gags were relatively tame, and we sought to find greater social meaning in each sequence. Our track record was pretty good. Still, we had our share of critics.

Tens of millions heard, or heard about, the telephone gag conducted last week by two Australian radio hosts, who called a hospital in London pretending to be Queen Elizabeth II and Prince Charles. Despite their admittedly awful attempts at British accents, they were transferred to a nurse caring for the Duchess of Cambridge, Kate Middleton, who was hospitalized with severe morning sickness.

The joke seemed harmless, until a few days later when news came that the nurse who took the call, Jacintha Saldanha, was dead, a possible suicide.

This tragic turn will undoubtedly prompt debate about practical joking in the digital age, when everything is magnified by the potential for viral distribution.

The practical joking itself—usually on video—has intensified in both volume and crudeness. This is in part a result of desensitizing among viewers, for whom the barrage of clips becomes so overwhelming that it's easy to lose track of the inherent risks involved.

From *The New York Times* (2012).

People in flash videos are sometimes thought of almost as avatars or digital creations, rather than actual human beings, whose feelings and health are always potentially in jeopardy.

The facts are still not fully clear in the case of the nurse's death, but it seems that once again the medium is more to blame than the message. A phone prank confined to those directly involved in the call is not likely to cause much stress. Even a radio broadcast heard only in Australia would not seem too damaging for a "victim" in Britain. But a viral prank that flashes around the globe on radio, TV, the Internet and newspapers can make even a silly joke seem to carry the weight of the world.

The very morning that the news came from London, NBC's *Today* show was replaying for the umpteenth time a clip from Brazil in which people in an elevator were frightened by the unexpected appearance of a ghostly figure—actually a prankster who entered through a secret door. The video, which has established a record for views worldwide, has no shred of comedic content beyond the screams, tears and shocked expressions of those caught unaware. If ever a prank posed health risks for its victims, this would seem to be it. But the NBC hosts hooted with laughter.

In my view, the Australian D.J.'s did nothing wrong other than attempt a sophomoric gag that had an awful, but unpredictable, consequence. Yet everything is magnified and made permanent in the digital environment.

Pranksters must always be accountable for their actions, but in the digital age the burden of responsibility also lies with those who use the echo chamber to amplify things to the point of distortion and stress. Unless we're careful, the joke is on us.

Identify Peter Funt's argument and the support he offers for his argument. What stated and unstated assumptions about humor can you find in Funt's op-ed piece? How does the title of his piece relate to various points that he makes? What do you think Funt's views tell us about the "nature" of humor?

Funt claims that "practical joking itself—usually on video—has intensified in both volume and crudeness." Because this is an op-ed piece, he does not have to provide "evidence" to support this claim. Put Funt's assertion to the test by conducting some informal research on the Internet. First, find information about *Candid Camera* and what constituted the shows hidden-camera stunts. Second, view some current pranking videos, and third, using your own criteria, respond to Funt's claim. You must provide evidence to support or challenge Funt's claim.

Ari Shapiro, an award-winning journalist, is an NPR international journalist. He has also served as a White House and Justice Correspondence for NPR. In his blog Shapiro reminds us that humor is "serious business" in the political arena. Although he does not reference academic and scientific studies, you might see some connections to other studies that you have read in Funny.

NOT JUST FOR LAUGHS: WHY HUMOR CAN BE A POWERFUL CAMPAIGN TOOL

BY ARI SHAPIRO

At the end of the month, President Obama will deliver a string of punch lines at the White House Correspondents' Dinner. It's an annual tradition, a chance for the man at the top of the pyramid to poke fun at his political opponents and himself.

Humor is an essential tool in any politician's kit—all the more so in an age of instant, constant media. It can disarm an opponent, woo a skeptical voter or pierce an argument. This year, both Obama and presumptive GOP nominee Mitt Romney are using it to try to win the upper hand in the presidential race.

President Obama has a chance to make fun of his opponents—and himself—when he addresses the annual White House Correspondents' Association gala later this month. Last year he joked about Donald Trump and the "birther" issue.

So far in this campaign, Obama and Romney have been the butt of a lot more jokes than they've made themselves. Anyone in the White House is a nightly source of material for comedians of all kinds. Romney, meanwhile, has been mocked for saying the trees in Michigan are the right height, and for telling Mississippi voters that he learned to say "y'all."

Romney has been trying to reverse his reputation as a humorless aristocrat. When he stiffly told CNN last December, "I live for laughter," the line had the opposite effect, reinforcing his buttoned-up image.

From *NPR News* (2012).

And when he cited his comedic preferences in that same interview, "Laurel and Hardy, the Three Stooges, even the Keystone Kops," the examples were not exactly the laugh track of 2012.

Yet occasionally, a genuinely funny side of Romney slips out. At the end of a particularly bad day campaigning in Michigan, the candidate seemed a bit slap-happy when he took the stage at Western Michigan University in Kalamazoo. He talked about driving through the town of Brighton, where his parents are buried.

"My dad is a very frugal man, and he checked all over for where the best deal was on a gravesite," Romney told the audience. Sounding incredulous at his family's quirks, he wrapped up the story with this advice: "If you're looking for the best deal on a gravesite, check Brighton. They've got a good spot. And you're near the former governor and former first lady!"

It was a human moment that endeared Romney to his audience. That is the most valuable use of humor in politics, says former White House speechwriter Landon Parvin. "If you can make fun of yourself, it says that I'm just like you."

Parvin has written speeches for the last three Republican presidents, and he is known for his comedy. He says the connective power of humor could be especially important this year. Each candidate is trying to portray the other as an out-of-touch elitist who doesn't understand the American people. A joke shared with an audience can serve as anti-venom. It's a way of telling voters, "We get each other."

Parvin thinks both men are missing opportunities to forge these kinds of connections. "Neither of the candidates that I see are using genial, good-natured humor," he says. "What I've seen on the campaign so far is the insult and the cut."

The cut can serve a purpose too, says former Obama speechwriter Jon Lovett, who's now writing a sitcom for NBC.

"If you can make someone laugh about something that your opponent or your opposition thinks, that means you've done a really good job of highlighting what's wrong with their argument or their position," says Lovett.

He points to an immigration speech that President Obama delivered on the Texas border last May. The president argued that every time he met Republican demands, the Republicans moved the goalposts.

"They said we needed to triple the border patrol," Obama said. "Well now they're gonna say we need to quadruple the border patrol. Or they'll want a higher fence. Maybe they'll need a moat. Maybe they want alligators in the moat!"

Most of that speech was a rehash of arguments the president had made before. But thanks to the joke about alligators, the speech was all over the news.

"So not only is it about having that connection with an audience; it's also about figuring out ways to bust through a culture of politics and media that makes conveying substantive arguments so difficult," says Lovett.

That media culture makes humor in politics more valuable now than it has ever been, says communications professor John Meyer of the University of Southern Mississippi.

"I think the more we have had media involved in our presidential campaigns, the more humor has become a force for presidents to use both in becoming elected and in becoming an effective president," says Meyer.

Still, there are examples of presidential humor stretching back more than 150 years. In a debate, Abraham Lincoln was once accused of being two-faced. The famously homely man replied, "If I had two-faces, would I be wearing this one?"

In "Not Just for Laughs: Why Humor Can Be a Powerful Campaign Tool," Ari Shapiro uses at least two metaphors to make his points. Identify these metaphors and explain what they suggest about how humor is used in the realm of politics. What other aspects of humor are especially important in politics in general and in political campaigns specifically?

Find at least three videos of debates among or between candidates running for a political office. As you watch the videos, note the use of humor by each of the candidates and answer the following questions (you will have to watch the video more than once!): When did the candidate use humor? How? What kind of humor (satire, irony, self-effacing, shared, aggressive)? How did the audience react to that humor? Write a brief report on your findings, noting if they correspond to Shapiro's observations. If they did not, explain why. You may want to think about issues raised by Christie Nicholson in "The Humor Gap" and/or "Males versus Females, Gays versus Straights, and Varieties of Gender Humor" by Leon Rappoport.

This selection, featured on NPR's news radio program All Things Considered, *comes from award-winning journalist, Allison Keyes.*

POLITICAL HUMOR'S HYSTERICAL HISTORY

BY ALLISON KEYES

If you have a computer or a television, you can hardly have missed the viral videos spoofing the presidential candidates and their running mates. Videos have a bit of fun with everything from Republican vice presidential nominee Sarah Palin's background to *Saturday Night Live*'s weekly jabs at, well, everyone—like this sendup of John McCain and Barack Obama's first debate. Or the spoof of last week's vice presidential debate.

There's a whole flurry of funny stuff floating around out there, including elaborate flights of fancy by talented amateurs with a lot of time on their hands. Try the Obama Bollywood video with images of the Democrat seeming to lip-sync to a love song.

And then, of course, there are the glitzy, Hollywood-level productions by networks like NBC and Comedy Central. It's all very cutting-edge, but it's hardly new.

"We can go all the way back to ancient Egypt to find examples of political humor," says Jody Baumgartner, assistant professor of political science at East Carolina University. He says editorial cartoons have a long history.

"They were actually around since Colonial times, but didn't become really popular 'til the penny press in the mid- to later 19th century."

Older political satire was sharp, like Mark Twain's quip, "Fleas can be taught nearly anything that a congressman can." Whether or not today's humor is any more vicious, it is often more salacious, like this primary season video from *Mad TV*, which simulates

---

From *NPR News* (2008).

an intimate relationship between Democratic presidential nominee Barack Obama and his former rival Sen. Hillary Clinton.

"It's gotten a lot tougher and bloodier through the years," says Gerald Gardner, a historian of presidential humor and former speechwriter for Robert F. Kennedy. In the mid-20th century, Gardner says, the leading practitioners of political humor were people like newspaper columnist Art Buchwald and TV comedian Johnny Carson.

"Political humor was kind of a benign art form at that time, perhaps because Buchwald knew he would lose newspapers, and Carson knew he would lose affiliates."

Gardner says that is likely the same reason that political cartoons in newspapers and magazines are fairly tame. Online and on TV, however, there are fewer censors or monitors at work. But when humor gets as explicit as the *Mad TV* video, aren't we undermining respect for national leaders? Isn't there some sort of line that just shouldn't be crossed?

"What's the line? I have no idea anymore—I don't know it 'til I've crossed it," says Lizz Winstead, a comedian, writer and co-creator of *The Daily Show*. She scoffs at the idea that politicians should be put on some sort of pedestal, and thinks it's the satirist's job to keep politicians in check with humor. One should always be skeptical of people who have amassed power, Winstead says.

"The fundamental problem with a politician is that they've assessed the world and looked in the mirror and said, 'You know what's wrong with society? I'm not in charge!' So right off the bat, you should not trust them," she says.

Gardner notes that both candidates and even sitting presidents incorporate humor into their speeches to polish their images or to make themselves look like regular folks. But he agrees it can go too far.

"You can make a case for the fact that humor—at least in politics—is most effective when it is drawing a little blood. Mind you, it shouldn't be a battle-ax, it should be a rapier."

He also says "thank heaven" for the comic relief that's injected into campaigns, especially marathons like this one. Otherwise, he says, it would be almost unendurable.

Explore

"Political Humor's Hysterical History" was aired during the 2008 Presidential Campaign between Barack Obama and John McCain, which generated a lot of political humor, especially when McCain chose Sarah Palin as his running mate. However, as Jody Baumgartner notes in this piece, political humor is not new. Using the Internet and the library, find examples of political cartoons from at least three different eras. Identify and describe the similarities and differences in humor in these examples. Explain what these examples suggest about the values of the societies they represent and how humor functioned in each of those societies.

Invent

Gerald Gardner, the historian quoted in "Political Humor's Hysterical History," points to the "fairly tame" nature of political cartoons and magazines compared to the political humor on TV and online. Do you find evidence of this difference? What does Lizz Winstead add to this discussion?

Compose

Read Robin Tapley's article "The Value of Humor." and John Morreall's "The Social Value of Humor." Considering their theories about the ethics and social value of humor, write a 500-word "blog" response to several of the points in "Political Humor's Hysterical History." In addition, in one or two paragraphs describe your writing process—the decisions you made in order to convey your points. To which points in the original NPR story did you choose to respond? Why? If you decided to quote "experts," whom did you choose and why? What choices did you make about the tone of your blog?

Collaborate

Working with several of your classmates, choose one of the five political cartoons to analyze. Consider these cartoons as presenting a visual argument through the use of humor. As a group analyze the cartoon's content, cartoonist's use of humor and rhetorical strategies. Discuss the effectiveness of the cartoon. Be prepared to share your conclusions and the reasons for those conclusions with the class.

Alison MacAdam is a Senior Editor at All Things Considered. *This transcript from* National Public Radio's *news show* All Things Considered *provides insights into the complex and multifaceted nature of political cartoons.*

FOR CARTOONISTS WHO COVER OBAMA: FOUR MORE EARS

BY ALISON MACADAM

ROBERT SIEGEL, HOST:

From NPR News, this is ALL THINGS CONSIDERED. I'm Robert Siegel.

AUDIE CORNISH, HOST:

And I'm Audie Cornish.

Four years ago, a group of people known for being irreverent created some unusually reverent drawings. Editorial cartoonists, the jokes and critiques on hold as they mark the inauguration of the first African-American president. Now, four years later, those same cartoonists are figuring out how to depict Barack Obama's second inauguration. And we asked two of them to join us. Matt Wuerker is editorial cartoonist for Politico, and he's the 2012 recipient of the Pulitzer Prize. Matt, welcome.

MATT WUERKER: Hi.

CORNISH: And Scott Stantis comes to us from the president's adopted hometown, Chicago, where he is editorial cartoonist for the *Chicago Tribune*. Hi there, Scott.

SCOTT STANTIS: Hey. Thanks for having me.

CORNISH: So to start, I'm going to ask you both to describe your drawings from four years ago. And, Scott, starting with you, you described yourself as a conservative, not

---

From *NPR News* (2013).

exactly an Obama supporter, but you did draw a cartoon—I have the image here—that is honoring the moment. Describe it to me.

STANTIS: Well, I think there are times in our history where we can just take half a step back from our partisanship and revel in the history and the wonder of something. And this was a cartoon—I had actually drawn for *USA Today*. And it's Uncle Sam looking at a big screen TV, and there is President Obama being sworn in, and Uncle Sam is simply saying wow.

CORNISH: And he has his hat off, and the drawing is still pretty, you know, it's still kind of a caricature image of President Obama.

STANTIS: Yeah. That.

CORNISH: The ears are very prominent.

(LAUGHTER)

STANTIS: That's as close as I can come to reverence. I'm sorry. It comes with the territory.

CORNISH: And, Matt, for you, you drew something that is sort of, in a way, depicting the inaugural scene outside the Capitol.

WUERKER: Yes. It's the swearing-in, and it was, again, sort of, you know, it was a very epic moment. I think it's interesting how quickly we moved on from it. But I depicted the swearing-in, and Obama is standing there on the platform and is a cutaway, and you can see inside the platform. And he's literally standing on the shoulders of MLK, the civil rights workers, Abraham Lincoln, abolitionists and all of the people who sort of led to that historic moment.

CORNISH: Though as you kind of look back on your art from that period, what most strikes you about the evolution of the Obama image because his image was such a big part of the pop culture feeling around him? I mean, Matt, what's different this time around?

WUERKER: Oh, boy, it's so entirely different. I mean, four years ago, I think the country was sort of stunned. We are coming out, frankly, from eight years of Bush-Cheney. You know, we forget. The economy was cratering. It was a moment where I think that everybody was really suddenly embracing this moment of idealism. And I think four years later, so much of that is gone for different reasons. And there's just this drumbeat of hysteria, and I think that politically it boxes Obama in, in a way.

CORNISH: But at the same time, if you look at this—and I don't know. Scott, if you want to jump in here, you know. . .

STANTIS: Sure.

CORNISH: . . . the Obama campaign courted this. You know, there was Obama kind of iconography.

WUERKER: Oh, yeah.

CORNISH: There's lots of images and the art of Obama and the pop stars and . . .

STANTIS: He has a logo.

CORNISH: Right. Exactly.

(LAUGHTER)

STANTIS: He has a logo, a registered trademark. What I find interesting, as a cartoonist, is the evolution or lack thereof of his images over the last four years. I mean, you look at four years of, well, Jimmy Carter would be one example, where he, you know, was diminished to about—he was standing like three and a half feet tall. You had Bill Clinton who just became this big, doughy, sort of, you know, sensualist kind of character. You had, you know Richard Nixon, of course. And you had George W. Bush devolved into, like, a demonic Keebler elf.

(LAUGHTER)

STANTIS: This caricature has not—what's interesting to me looking at my work, looking at Matt's work and looking at work of other cartoonists over the last four years, the caricature—and, Matt, tell me if you disagree with me—I don't think the caricature has changed dramatically from four years ago, has it?

WUERKER: I think it's changed a little bit. I think that one of the changes that happened in the beginning I think the first years of the administration, a lot of cartoonists were very careful about dealing with the caricature of an African-American.

STANTIS: Absolutely.

WUERKER: And it was a minefield that people were tiptoeing across in a lot of ways. And a couple of people stepped on some mines and some—one of our boneheaded brethren drew him as a monkey for Rupert Murdoch or something. And people began to have to sort of, you know, you had to deal with the legacy of some really virulent racist imagery in American cartoons going back centuries. But we got over it. And the cartoon gods work in mysterious ways, just as we're having to grapple with drawing the first black president. The cartoon gods gave us the first orange house speaker so. . .

(LAUGHTER)

WUERKER: And so . . .

CORNISH: I'm sure John Boehner would quibble with that description.

WUERKER: Well—but it was suddenly, you know, it was like, OK, we're drawing people of color here, so this is fun and . . .

(LAUGHTER)

WUERKER: . . . everyone has been having a good time, and I think actually there's this evolution in the Obama caricature that I think is all perfectly healthy and gets back to the significance of the second inaugural in some ways. And what was extraordinary four years ago is ordinary, and I think that the caricature has actually sort of evolved. And Obama is now just another goofy guy that we get to have fun with and, you know, play with his big smile and make his ears bigger and all that kind of stuff.

CORNISH: Yeah. I have to say the ears on Scott's alone in each of his drawings . . .

(LAUGHTER)

CORNISH: . . . the ears are a little bit bigger. I'm looking at one where in your art, Scott, it's Obama smoking like four, five cigarettes at once, and he's holding a box of cigarettes that says unfiltered spending, and he thinks to himself I can't seem to quit. But his ears . . .

(LAUGHTER)

CORNISH: . . . take up I think fully 40 percent of his head in this picture.

(LAUGHTER)

STANTIS: Well, you know, here's the thing. Here's—let me give you a quick. . . .

STANTIS: . . . a quick lesson on caricature is what human beings find attractive in each other and this crosses ethnic lines, preference—sexual preference lines, all lines is that we like symmetry. And the fact of the matter is this president is actually a pretty good-looking fellow, except for those big jug handles on either side of his head. And so I can talk to grade schools. I could talk to colleges or rotary clubs. I draw just an outline of his head and if you put those ears on, instantaneously, people know who he is. So, of course, yeah, we're going to jump all over that.

WUERKER: I think that cartoonists have gotten lazy, too, because I mean, in all fairness or in our defense a little bit, I mean, we did the same thing to George W. Bush. I mean, by the end of his administration, he was just Dumbo.

(LAUGHTER)

WUERKER: I mean, his ears were just immense.

CORNISH: Now, going into the inauguration then, can you guys give us a preview of what you're thinking of drawing? I know actually on the way in here, Matt, you were doing some sketching in the studio.

WUERKER: I'm still flummoxed. I don't quite know what to do. I'm playing with an idea of everybody on the inaugural standing extremely well-armed with assault rifles and whatnot, and it's something about the way the NRA would like to see the inauguration. But my wife actually had a good idea. I should probably do something ripping off of—remember Aretha's hat at the last inauguration?

CORNISH: Yes, yeah.

(LAUGHTER)

WUERKER: I think that there's something about inaugural bonnets out there that would be really fun to do, but I've got to figure that out this afternoon.

CORNISH: And, Scott, for you?

STANTIS: Oh, my gosh, it's not 20 minutes before deadline, so I really don't have anything solid.

(LAUGHTER)

STANTIS: But I would go, you know, some of the stuff—I love drawing critters. I mean—so—and just innocuous, almost non sequitur, so I would have like a rhinoceros or a hippopotamus, and, you know, it could be—I think he is still facing—frankly, still facing the same issues he did four years ago. Unemployment is still unacceptably high even though it's going down slightly. We've got debt. We've got war. We've got Guantanamo. We've got civil liberties. We've got all those things, and they were, you know, I'd love having them in the stands, and they're saying, yeah, we're here four years ago.

WUERKER: That's good. I'm going to steal that.

(LAUGHTER)

WUERKER: Dang it.

(LAUGHTER)

CORNISH: Well, Scott Stantis, thank you so much for speaking with me.

STANTIS: Well, thanks for having me.

CORNISH: And, Matt Wuerker, thank you for coming in to talk to us.

WUERKER: Thanks, Audie.

CORNISH: Editorial cartoonists Matt Wuerker of Politico and Scott Stantis of the *Chicago Tribune*. You can see drawings by both of them at npr.org, including their cartoons from the inauguration four years ago.

What did editorial cartoonists Matt Wuerker and Scott Stantis each seek to convey in his cartoon of Barack Obama's first inauguration? Without the explanation provided by each cartoonist, how well do you think the visual image conveys the intended message? What specifically enhances or hinders the message? Do you think that each cartoon successfully stepped back from partisanship, to paraphrase Stantis? If not, why not, and if so, how so?

According to Wuerker and Stantis what proved challenging to editorial/political cartoonists who depicted Obama during his presidency? This discussion raises larger issues regarding the relationship among humor, caricature, and stereotypes. What do Wuerker's and Stantis's explanations imply about these relationships?

Once you have addressed these questions, discuss them with a classmate.

Choose a past president (or Uncle Sam or Lady Liberty) and using the Internet and the library find political cartoons showing the evolution of his or her caricature. Find information that may account for this change and then create a PowerPoint, Prezi, or some other visual presentation showing and explaining this evolution.

Working with a partner choose a politician, political, or social issue and create a political cartoon to share with the class. Write a short 2-3 page paper describing the process of creating this cartoon. In this collaboration, you and your fellow cartoonist should explain how you chose your subject, decided on the images, on the inclusion of text, on whether to include written text, on what text, on the tone, and so on.

Luke Harding, award-winning foreign correspondent reports for The Guardian. *Kim Willsher, also recognized for her work in journalism is a foreign correspondent for* The Guardian. *This story is one of many that appeared across the globe after the Danish newspaper,* Jyllands-Posten, *printed twelve editorial cartoons of Muhammad, the Islamic prophet.*

ANGER AS PAPERS REPRINT CARTOONS OF MUHAMMAD

By Luke Harding and Kim Willsher

Newspapers in France, Germany, Spain and Italy yesterday reprinted caricatures of the prophet Muhammad, escalating a row over freedom of expression which has caused protest across the Middle East.

France Soir and Germany's *Die Welt* published cartoons which first appeared in a Danish newspaper, although the French paper later apologised and apparently sacked its managing editor. The cartoons include one showing a bearded Muhammad with a bomb fizzing out of his turban.

The caricatures, printed last September in Denmark's *Jyllands-Posten* newspaper and reprinted by a Norwegian magazine, have provoked uproar across the Middle East.

Italy's *La Stampa* printed a smaller version on an inside page yesterday, while two Spanish papers, Barcelona's *El Periódico* and Madrid's *El Mundo*, carried images of the cartoon as it appeared in the Danish press. The pictures also appeared in Dutch and Swiss newspapers.

There have been protests in several countries yesterday, as well as a boycott of Danish goods. Saudi Arabia has withdrawn its ambassador to Copenhagen, Syria recalled its chief diplomat, while Libya has closed its embassy. On Monday, gunmen from al-Aqsa Martyrs Brigade briefly occupied the EU's office in the Gaza Strip, demanding that Denmark and Norway apologise. There was a bomb hoax at the Danish embassy in the Syrian capital, Damascus, yesterday.

From *The Guardian* (2006).

The front page of the daily *France Soir* carried the defiant headline: "Yes, we have the right to caricature God," and a cartoon of Buddhist, Jewish, Muslim and Christian gods floating on a cloud. Inside, the paper ran the drawings.

But last night it was reported that the paper's managing editor had been sacked and an apology issued. According to Agence France Presse, *France Soir's* owner, Raymond Lakah, said that he removed Jacques Lefranc "as a powerful sign of respect for the intimate beliefs and convictions of every individual."

The paper's initial decision drew condemnation from the French foreign ministry, which acknowledged the importance of freedom of expression but said France condemned "all that hurts individuals in their beliefs or their religious convictions." The rare governmental rebuke revealed domestic sensitivity; France is home to western Europe's largest Muslim community with an estimated 5 million people. Germany has about 3 million.

The centre-right *Die Welt* also ran the caricature on the front page, reporting that Muslim groups had forced the Danish newspaper to issue an apology. It described the protests as hypocritical, pointing out Syrian TV had depicted Jewish rabbis as cannibals. Yesterday Roger Koppel, editor-in-chief of *Die Welt*, said he had no regrets. He told the *Guardian*: "It's at the very core of our culture that the most sacred things can be subjected to criticism, laughter and satire. If we stop using our journalistic right of freedom of expression within legal boundaries then we start to have a kind of appeasement mentality. This is a remarkable issue. It's very important we did it. Without this there would be no *Life of Brian*."

Muslim groups in both countries were furious. "It's odious and we totally disapprove of it," said Dalil Boubakeur, president of the French Muslim Council. "It's a real provocation towards the millions of Muslims in France." The council planned legal action against *France Soir*, he said, and he intended to complain to Denmark's ambassador.

The "blasphemous" cartoons were reminiscent of the caricatures of Jews published by the Nazi propaganda sheet Der Sturmer, Michael Muhammad Pfaff, of the German Muslim League, told the Guardian."Press freedom shouldn't be used to insult people. We Germans need to know our history."

Denmark's prime minister, Anders Fogh Rasmussen, on Monday begged Arab countries not to boycott Danish products. Lego and Bang & Olufsen have been boycotted, and a Danish milk firm in Riyadh has had to close. The Arab League condemned the cartoons, demanding those responsible "be punished."

On the net, Iraqi groups threatened attacks against the 500 Danish soldiers in southern Iraq. Muslim hackers have tried to shut the Danish newspaper's website and a hoax bomb threat yesterday forced its building to be evacuated.

EXTRACT FROM YESTERDAY'S *FRANCE SOIR*

It is necessary to crush once again the infamous thing, as Voltaire liked to say. This religious intolerance that accepts no mockery, no satire, no ridicule. We citizens of secular and democratic societies are summoned to condemn a dozen caricatures judged offensive to Islam. Summoned by who? By the Muslim Brotherhood, by Syria, the Islamic Jihad, the interior ministers of Arab countries, the Islamic Conferences— all paragons of tolerance, humanism and democracy.

So, we must apologise to them because the freedom of expression they refuse, day after day, to each of their citizens, faithful or militant, is exercised in a society that is not subject to their iron rule. It's the world upside down. No, we will never apologise for being free to speak, to think and to believe.

Because these self-proclaimed doctors of law have made this a point of principle, we have to be firm. They can claim whatever they like but we have the right to caricature Muhammad, Jesus, Buddha, Yahve and all forms of theism. It's called freedom of expression in a secular country . . .

For centuries the Catholic church was little better than this fanaticism. But the French Revolution solved that, rendering to God that which came from him and to Caesar what was due to him.

The history of political cartoons is linked with questions of free speech, rights of the press, issues of tolerance and intolerance as this 2006 news story about political cartoons depicting the prophet Muhammad makes clear. Using the library's resources and the Internet, find more details about this incident and its aftermath. Choose one of the items that you find (a letter to the editor, an editorial, an op-ed piece, a blog, a news story) to bring to class. Before you bring it to class, make sure that you fully understand the writer's views and how he or she conveyed them. Annotating the piece—marking it up by highlighting, adding comments, and sticky notes helps!

Luke Harding and Kim Willsher include the terms of each side of debate in their coverage of the controversy over the initial appearance and the reprints of the cartoons of Muhammad. Working with a group of your classmates, identify those terms. What is at stake for all involved? Read (or revisit) "For Cartoonists Who Cover Obama: Four More Ears and "Political Humor's Hysterical History." What do these two pieces contribute to the conversation/debate about the ethics of political/humor cartoons?

Iain Ellis writes regularly for the online journal Pop Matters *and teaches in the English Department at the University of Kansas. In the following column, which Ellis wrote October 2012 for* Pop Matters, *he poses multiple questions about the pervasiveness and efficacy of political humor and humorists. Keep these questions in mind as you read "Political Humor and Its Diss-Content" as well as the other articles and essays in* Funny *on this subject.*

POLITICAL HUMOR AND ITS DISS-CONTENT

BY IAIN ELLIS

More than ever, today's political humor infects, inflects, and injects into our national state of affairs. This is not just via our daily doses of Jon Stewart, Stephen Colbert, and the late night talk show hosts, either. A cursory glance through your Facebook, Twitter, and e-mail posts today will no doubt reveal that your friends and associates also fancy themselves as skilled and authoritative political wits. Nowadays, it seems, everyone is a political comedian—or at least they think they are. This ubiquity of political humor certainly brings a lot of joy and laughter into our often humdrum lives—as well as into the dour landscape of day-to-day politics—but is America's laugh fest a good thing for the nation at large?

Furthermore, do political humor's incessant and incisive barbs ever unduly influence the behavior and decisions of our elected representatives? Do these constant waves of wit distract us from the serious concerns of our time? Has this humor's lure and appeal encouraged our hard news sources to go "soft," as ratings are sought in the shallower waters of entertainment? And has its all-pervasive repertoire of diss and discontent skits transformed us into bitter, cynical, and detached citizens with little-to-no faith in either our leaders or the institutions they operate within?

Alternatively, one might rhetorically question: do political humorists instead *serve* the republic, offering insight into, and critiques of, corruption, hypocrisy, and extremism, all the while engaging citizens in ways neither the traditional news media nor academia can (or will) do? At its best, political humor not only attracts and delights, but teaches,

From *Pop Matters* (2012).

too, such that options for an alternative polity and real change are either offered or inferred. Aristophanes, Jonathan Swift, and Mark Twain are among the many outspoken humorists whose stinging satire and broad appeal were instrumental in informing, enlightening, and inspiring their respective publics into curtailing the worst excesses of their governments. This tradition sees political humor not as breeding detachment, but as encouraging vigilance and participation. One might note the censorship (and thus paucity) of critical political humor to be found in the public media of totalitarian regimes like Nazi Germany or modern day North Korea; presumably their leaders would not have silenced such expression if they felt it had little or no effect.

Much recent argumentation around the effects and/or effectiveness of political humor has been sparked by the popularity of *The Daily Show with Jon Stewart*. Spearheading a recent wave of news/humor hybrids (alongside *Real Time with Bill Maher*, *The Colbert Report*, and *The Onion*), *The Daily Show* not only entertains, but also serves as a primary source of news and information for a large—particularly young and young adult—contingent of the American populace (See Jody C. Baumgartner & Jonathan S. Morris (eds). *Laughing Matters: Humor and American Politics in the Media Age*. New York: Routledge, 2008. p. xvi). On the face of it, this would appear to be a disturbing cultural phenomenon, but recent research also informs us that the audience that watches *The Daily Show* is actually amongst the most informed and intelligent in the nation (See Brandon Rottinghaus et al. *Laughing Matters*. p. 279-295).

So what does one make of political humor and its omnipresence? Thus far, critics have largely lined up around these two schools of thought: those that consider *The Daily Show* and its ilk to be damaging and dangerous, responsible for breeding a cynical, disinterested electorate; and a contrary camp that finds such humor to be engaging, fostering critical thinking through its satirical provocations and parodies while official information outlets merely maintain the status quo.

The naysayers tend to bring a certain pessimism and nostalgia to their complaints, arguing that political humor is both the producer and product of a larger cultural demise. For them, political humor is meaner than ever, responsible for reducing our leaders to little more than absurd caricatures. Stereotypes overwhelm, they say, with politicians cast as liars, hypocrites, fools, or narcissists. Under this barrage of negative characterizations it's little wonder, they argue, that citizens are skeptical and lack trust in their representatives. And while types and exaggerations may be the very stuff of satire, too much too often tends to subsume and supplant any objective reality. Moreover, it's only getting worse in a climate where nothing and no-one is off-limits, claim these critics.

Defenders of political humorists—at least of the Jon Stewart kind—contend just the opposite. Yes, we are contemptuous of our leaders and our news media, but so we should be. It is they, not the comedians, who have been derelict in their duties. But for the vigilance of the latter, they claim, we would be largely ignorant of political malfeasance and of the contributory negligence of our slanted, sensationalizing, and profit-obsessed news corporations. Rather than the hybrid news-comedies diminishing the value of the news, arguably they offer a more open-minded and informed alternative, one which takes pride in digging for truths (i.e., muckraking) and in providing additional perspectives and points-of-view.

The comedic angles Stewart, Colbert, and Maher bring to our national affairs offer a different model from that provided by the mainstream news services. Because the latter only consider socio-political concerns through the prism of the two-party system, they are loath to entertain any viewpoints or opinions that (might) exist beyond the parameters of the propaganda machines provided by each side. As Stewart often points out, *Fox News*, *MSNBC*, and *CNN* do not offer variant voices on issues or the news, only counter-weight shouters hired to create political drama and higher ratings. Articulating this argument, Stewart's on-air evisceration of the hosts of *Crossfire* in 2004 has since become legendary in the annals of critical humor.

Using satirical argument and art, critical humorists deconstruct the "fair and balanced" myths of the news systems, in the process chastising the party spokespeople they predictably trot out and pander to for access. By observing and documenting this media-politico conspiracy of convenience from behind the scenes, Stewart et al. perform the age-old functions of satire: to expose, ridicule, and—implicitly—call for action and change. Ironically, this demystification of the news and its processes actually makes the comedians more reliable than journalists as truth-tellers, for, as outsider operatives, the news-humorists are neither beholden to their subjects nor to the machinery that has reduced our political dialogue to Republican versus Democrat talking points.

When we think of political humor our minds naturally gravitate to the kind of hybrid news-comedy shows being discussed here; or perhaps to variety shows like *Saturday Night Live*; or to the late night talk shows of Jay Leno, David Letterman, and Conan O'Brien, each of which doles out such humor in large and regular doses. However, from within the political realm, too, humor output flourishes today as never before. During election season it has become almost compulsory for presidential candidates to do the rounds of the late night talk shows, and they are not just expected to show up and answer questions, but to be funny, too.

Further, humor ripples expand outwards beyond the candidates, as well, as their families and associates also get in on the act, as do their speechwriters, media representatives, and base supporters. Nowadays, presidents are as reliant upon their teams of comedy writers and strategists as is any talk show host. As long as "likeability" continues to be cited as a significant criteria of importance for voters, candidates can ill afford to appear dull, out-of-touch, or elitist; thus, displays of (particularly self-deprecating) humor can contribute much to (re)defining impressions and perceptions. Gerald Ford, Al Gore, and John Kerry can all testify lamentably to what happens when the media and the opposition—rather than the candidate and campaign staff—carve out, craft, and control the image of a presidential contender.

Peter M. Robinson perceives the three primary purveyors of humor—media, politicians, and public—as being in a perpetual "three-way dance" featuring multiple moves and interchangeable partners. What kind of dance he envisages is not made clear, though it sometimes appears more like slamming than waltzing. For Robinson, the comedy crossfire we witness between these three forces is a positive political phenomenon for it "empowers its participants to reexamine, renegotiate, and often redefine the roles of all concerned" (*The Dance of the Comedians: The People, The President, and the Performance of Political Standup Comedy in America*. Boston: University of Massachusetts Press, 2010. p. 4). Sometimes politicians will attempt to counter incoming humor attacks, as Gore did in the 2000 election when he attempted to inject some levity into his public appearances in a concerted effort to redress the perception—particularly perpetuated by *Saturday Night Live*—that he was stiff and humorless. As is so often the case when a caricature rings true, though, Gore's comedy bits invariably fell embarrassingly flat.

A more effective dance move is for the politician to use self-parody, playing directly *to* his/her stereotype trait. While this means conceding to the general character attack, strategically it enables the earning of new, additional images of the candidate as being down-to-earth, one of the people, and able to laugh at him/her self. Both George W. Bush and Sarah Palin distracted observers from their various negatives by taking this comedic route. Palin's self-effacing performance on *Saturday Night Live* in the wake of a week of various media debacles has become a notable precedent regarding the power of comedic damage control and image rehabilitation, such that today most politicians see more upside in chatting with comedians like Jay Leno than with harder-hitting journalists like Soledad O'Brien (or, in Palin's case, Katie Couric).

On the talk shows, candidates can be guaranteed a welcoming environment where they will be encouraged to parade their wit and charm, where they will be fielding soft-ball questions, and where they will be accredited with communicating in plain-speak directly to the average Joe and Joanne. For today's politicians, this wide world of soft wit (half wit?) provides an appealing win-win situation; conversely, press conferences and hard news interviews have become increasingly rare public events on the campaign trail.

The communication network of political comedy is a complex one of constant transactional missives, each contributing to an emerging consensus narrative about a candidate. Nevertheless, as Bush's two-term presidency showed us, a constant barrage of critical and/or insulting comedy from media and public does not guarantee political capital for any side. Much obviously depends upon the reception and appreciation (or lack thereof) of America's splintered publics, as well as the spontaneous dexterity of the moves and maneuvers made by the politician (and his camp) within the overall dance. In the end, to emerge from the dance marathon as a politician that can laugh, provide laughs, and be accepting of being laughed at plays positively to that perennial election-time question: which candidate would you rather have a beer with?

While presidents and politicians have sharpened their wits as a necessary requisite of our modern media age, the separation between (the roles of) comedians and politicians has grown increasingly blurry. Yet, while America's history is littered with comedians running as funny-but-fake candidates (Will Rogers, Gracie Allen, Pat Paulsen, and others), could anyone have predicted 20 years ago that a cast member of *SNL* would one day *seriously* stand for, run in, and win a US Senatorial race? Such is the case with current Minnesota Senator Al Franken.

Which of the many questions that Iain Ellis asks at the beginning of "Political Humor and Its Diss-Content" do you find the most significant? Why? Which ones does he answer and what is *the* answer? When Ellis shifts his discussion to Peter Robinson's theory about "the primary purveyors of humor—media, politicians, and public—as being in a perpetual 'three-way dance,'" he makes several points about our beliefs about people who possess a sense of humor. What key assumptions about the value of humor emerge here? Why do politicians, according to Ellis, now rely on "the power of comedic damage control and image rehabilitation" through self-parody?

Watch an episode of *Real Time of Bill Maher, The Colbert Report,* or *The Daily Show* or explore *The Onion* choosing an article to read in-depth. Write a 4–5 page rhetorical analysis of the TV show or article. In this paper, identify the political issue or social problem at the heart of the political humor and analyze its rhetorical appeal and effectiveness as satire. Consider Ellis's observation that the "age-old function of satire [is] . . . to expose, ridicule, and—implicitly—call for action and change."

With several of your classmates, "cover" a political candidate or current issue. Designate one team to take a mainstream news approach and the other that of a political humorist/satirist. Choose the medium through which to convey your coverage to the class—text-based (online news source such as the *Huffington Post, The New York Times, The Onion*) or performance-based (skit, video). In addition, in two or three paragraphs describe the decisions that each team made about how to cover and then present the information. In this explanation, you might want to identify the primary purpose of the piece and intended audience.

Jonathan Swift (1667–1745) was an Irish author, clergyman, and satirist. He published his essay "A Modest Proposal," which many consider epitomizes the genre of satire, in 1729. Understandably, many readers reacted violently to his suggestions; however, astute readers recognize Swift's razor wit and satirical bit. Although the language may present some challenges, I urge you to read attentively, attuned to Swift's message with an eye to the elements of satire that he employs.

A MODEST PROPOSAL

By Jonathan Swift

For preventing the children of poor people in Ireland, from being a burden on their parents or country, and for making them beneficial to the publick.

It is a melancholy object to those, who walk through this great town, or travel in the country, when they see the streets, the roads and cabbin-doors crowded with beggars of the female sex, followed by three, four, or six children, all in rags, and importuning every passenger for an alms. These mothers instead of being able to work for their honest livelihood, are forced to employ all their time in stroling to beg sustenance for their helpless infants who, as they grow up, either turn thieves for want of work, or leave their dear native country, to fight for the Pretender in Spain, or sell themselves to the Barbadoes.

I think it is agreed by all parties, that this prodigious number of children in the arms, or on the backs, or at the heels of their mothers, and frequently of their fathers, is in the present deplorable state of the kingdom, a very great additional grievance; and therefore whoever could find out a fair, cheap and easy method of making these children sound and useful members of the common-wealth, would deserve so well of the publick, as to have his statue set up for a preserver of the nation.

But my intention is very far from being confined to provide only for the children of professed beggars: it is of a much greater extent, and shall take in the whole number of

From *A Modest Proposal* (1729).

infants at a certain age, who are born of parents in effect as little able to support them, as those who demand our charity in the streets.

As to my own part, having turned my thoughts for many years, upon this important subject, and maturely weighed the several schemes of our projectors, I have always found them grossly mistaken in their computation. It is true, a child just dropt from its dam, may be supported by her milk, for a solar year, with little other nourishment: at most not above the value of two shillings, which the mother may certainly get, or the value in scraps, by her lawful occupation of begging; and it is exactly at one year old that I propose to provide for them in such a manner, as, instead of being a charge upon their parents, or the parish, or wanting food and raiment for the rest of their lives, they shall, on the contrary, contribute to the feeding, and partly to the cloathing of many thousands.

There is likewise another great advantage in my scheme, that it will prevent those voluntary abortions, and that horrid practice of women murdering their bastard children, alas! too frequent among us, sacrificing the poor innocent babes, I doubt, more to avoid the expence than the shame, which would move tears and pity in the most savage and inhuman breast.

The number of souls in this kingdom being usually reckoned one million and a half, of these I calculate there may be about two hundred thousand couple whose wives are breeders; from which number I subtract thirty thousand couple, who are able to maintain their own children, (although I apprehend there cannot be so many, under the present distresses of the kingdom) but this being granted, there will remain an hundred and seventy thousand breeders. I again subtract fifty thousand, for those women who miscarry, or whose children die by accident or disease within the year. There only remain a hundred and twenty thousand children of poor parents annually born. The question therefore is, How this number shall be reared, and provided for, which, as I have already said, under the present situation of affairs, is utterly impossible by all the methods hitherto proposed. For we can neither employ them in handicraft or agriculture; we neither build houses, (I mean in the country) nor cultivate land: they can very seldom pick up a livelihood by stealing till they arrive at six years old; except where they are of towardly parts, although I confess they learn the rudiments much earlier; during which time they can however be properly looked upon only as probationers: As I have been informed by a principal gentleman in the county of Cavan, who protested to me, that he never knew above one or two instances under the age of six, even in a part of the kingdom so renowned for the quickest proficiency in that art.

I am assured by our merchants, that a boy or a girl before twelve years old, is no saleable commodity, and even when they come to this age, they will not yield above three pounds, or three pounds and half a crown at most, on the exchange; which cannot turn to account either to the parents or kingdom, the charge of nutriments and rags having been at least four times that value.

I shall now therefore humbly propose my own thoughts, which I hope will not be liable to the least objection.

I have been assured by a very knowing American of my acquaintance in London, that a young healthy child well nursed, is, at a year old, a most delicious nourishing and wholesome food, whether stewed, roasted, baked, or boiled; and I make no doubt that it will equally serve in a fricasie, or a ragoust.

I do therefore humbly offer it to publick consideration, that of the hundred and twenty thousand children, already computed, twenty thousand may be reserved for breed, whereof only one fourth part to be males; which is more than we allow to sheep, black cattle, or swine, and my reason is, that these children are seldom the fruits of marriage, a circumstance not much regarded by our savages, therefore, one male will be sufficient to serve four females. That the remaining hundred thousand may, at a year old, be offered in sale to the persons of quality and fortune, through the kingdom, always advising the mother to let them suck plentifully in the last month, so as to render them plump, and fat for a good table. A child will make two dishes at an entertainment for friends, and when the family dines alone, the fore or hind quarter will make a reasonable dish, and seasoned with a little pepper or salt, will be very good boiled on the fourth day, especially in winter.

I have reckoned upon a medium, that a child just born will weigh 12 pounds, and in a solar year, if tolerably nursed, encreaseth to 28 pounds.

I grant this food will be somewhat dear, and therefore very proper for landlords, who, as they have already devoured most of the parents, seem to have the best title to the children.

Infant's flesh will be in season throughout the year, but more plentiful in March, and a little before and after; for we are told by a grave author, an eminent French physician, that fish being a prolifick dyet, there are more children born in Roman Catholick countries about nine months after Lent, the markets will be more glutted than usual, because the number of Popish infants, is at least three to one in this kingdom, and therefore it will have one other collateral advantage, by lessening the number of Papists among us.

I have already computed the charge of nursing a beggar's child (in which list I reckon all cottagers, labourers, and four-fifths of the farmers) to be about two shillings per annum, rags included; and I believe no gentleman would repine to give ten shillings for the carcass of a good fat child, which, as I have said, will make four dishes of excellent nutritive meat, when he hath only some particular friend, or his own family to dine with him. Thus the squire will learn to be a good landlord, and grow popular among his tenants, the mother will have eight shillings neat profit, and be fit for work till she produces another child.

Those who are more thrifty (as I must confess the times require) may flea the carcass; the skin of which, artificially dressed, will make admirable gloves for ladies, and summer boots for fine gentlemen.

As to our City of Dublin, shambles may be appointed for this purpose, in the most convenient parts of it, and butchers we may be assured will not be wanting; although I rather recommend buying the children alive, and dressing them hot from the knife, as we do roasting pigs.

A very worthy person, a true lover of his country, and whose virtues I highly esteem, was lately pleased, in discoursing on this matter, to offer a refinement upon my scheme. He said, that many gentlemen of this kingdom, having of late destroyed their deer, he conceived that the want of venison might be well supply'd by the bodies of young lads and maidens, not exceeding fourteen years of age, nor under twelve; so great a number of both sexes in every country being now ready to starve for want of work and service: And these to be disposed of by their parents if alive, or otherwise by their nearest relations. But with due deference to so excellent a friend, and so deserving a patriot, I cannot be altogether in his sentiments; for as to the males, my American acquaintance assured me from frequent experience, that their flesh was generally tough and lean, like that of our school-boys, by continual exercise, and their taste disagreeable, and to fatten them would not answer the charge. Then as to the females, it would, I think, with humble submission, be a loss to the publick, because they soon would become breeders themselves: And besides, it is not improbable that some scrupulous people might be apt to censure such a practice, (although indeed very unjustly) as a little bordering upon cruelty, which, I confess, hath always been with me the strongest objection against any project, how well soever intended.

But in order to justify my friend, he confessed, that this expedient was put into his head by the famous Salmanaazor, a native of the island Formosa, who came from thence to London, above twenty years ago, and in conversation told my friend, that in his country, when any young person happened to be put to death, the executioner sold the carcass to persons of quality, as a prime dainty; and that, in his time, the body of a plump girl of fifteen, who was crucified for an attempt to poison the Emperor, was sold to his imperial majesty's prime minister of state, and other great mandarins of the court in joints from the gibbet, at four hundred crowns. Neither indeed can I deny, that if the same use were made of several plump young girls in this town, who without one single groat to their fortunes, cannot stir abroad without a chair, and appear at a playhouse and assemblies in foreign fineries which they never will pay for; the kingdom would not be the worse.

Some persons of a desponding spirit are in great concern about that vast number of poor people, who are aged, diseased, or maimed; and I have been desired to employ my thoughts what course may be taken, to ease the nation of so grievous an incumbrance. But I am not in the least pain upon that matter, because it is very well known, that they are every day dying, and rotting, by cold and famine, and filth, and vermin, as fast as can be reasonably expected. And as to the young labourers, they are now in almost as hopeful a condition. They cannot get work, and consequently pine away from want of nourishment, to a degree, that if at any time they are accidentally hired to common labour, they have not strength to perform it, and thus the country and themselves are happily delivered from the evils to come.

I have too long digressed, and therefore shall return to my subject. I think the advantages by the proposal which I have made are obvious and many, as well as of the highest importance.

For first, as I have already observed, it would greatly lessen the number of Papists, with whom we are yearly over-run, being the principal breeders of the nation, as well as our most dangerous enemies, and who stay at home on purpose with a design to deliver the kingdom to the Pretender, hoping to take their advantage by the absence of so many good Protestants, who have chosen rather to leave their country, than stay at home and pay tithes against their conscience to an episcopal curate.

Secondly, The poorer tenants will have something valuable of their own, which by law may be made liable to a distress, and help to pay their landlord's rent, their corn and cattle being already seized, and money a thing unknown.

Thirdly, Whereas the maintainance of an hundred thousand children, from two years old, and upwards, cannot be computed at less than ten shillings a piece per annum, the nation's stock will be thereby encreased fifty thousand pounds per annum, besides the profit of a new dish, introduced to the tables of all gentlemen of fortune in the kingdom, who have any refinement in taste. And the money will circulate among our selves, the goods being entirely of our own growth and manufacture.

Fourthly, The constant breeders, besides the gain of eight shillings sterling per annum by the sale of their children, will be rid of the charge of maintaining them after the first year.

Fifthly, This food would likewise bring great custom to taverns, where the vintners will certainly be so prudent as to procure the best receipts for dressing it to perfection; and consequently have their houses frequented by all the fine gentlemen, who justly value themselves upon their knowledge in good eating; and a skilful cook, who understands how to oblige his guests, will contrive to make it as expensive as they please.

Sixthly, This would be a great inducement to marriage, which all wise nations have either encouraged by rewards, or enforced by laws and penalties. It would encrease the care and tenderness of mothers towards their children, when they were sure of a settlement for life to the poor babes, provided in some sort by the publick, to their annual profit instead of expence. We should soon see an honest emulation among the married women, which of them could bring the fattest child to the market. Men would become as fond of their wives, during the time of their pregnancy, as they are now of their mares in foal, their cows in calf, or sow when they are ready to farrow; nor offer to beat or kick them (as is too frequent a practice) for fear of a miscarriage.

Many other advantages might be enumerated. For instance, the addition of some thousand carcasses in our exportation of barrel'd beef: the propagation of swine's flesh, and improvement in the art of making good bacon, so much wanted among us by the great destruction of pigs, too frequent at our tables; which are no way comparable in taste or magnificence to a well grown, fat yearly child, which roasted whole will make a considerable figure at a Lord Mayor's feast, or any other publick entertainment. But this, and many others, I omit, being studious of brevity.

Supposing that one thousand families in this city, would be constant customers for infants flesh, besides others who might have it at merry meetings, particularly at weddings and christenings, I compute that Dublin would take off annually about twenty thousand carcasses; and the rest of the kingdom (where probably they will be sold somewhat cheaper) the remaining eighty thousand.

I can think of no one objection, that will possibly be raised against this proposal, unless it should be urged, that the number of people will be thereby much lessened in the kingdom. This I freely own, and 'twas indeed one principal design in offering it to the world. I desire the reader will observe, that I calculate my remedy for this one individual Kingdom of Ireland, and for no other that ever was, is, or, I think, ever can be upon Earth. Therefore let no man talk to me of other expedients: Of taxing our absentees at five shillings a pound: Of using neither cloaths, nor houshold furniture, except what is of our own growth and manufacture: Of utterly rejecting the materials and instruments that promote foreign luxury: Of curing the expensiveness of pride, vanity, idleness, and gaming in our women: Of introducing a vein of parsimony, prudence and temperance: Of learning to love our country, wherein we differ even from Laplanders, and the inhabitants of Topinamboo: Of quitting our animosities and factions, nor acting any longer like the Jews, who were murdering one another at the very moment their city was taken: Of being a little cautious not to sell our country and consciences for nothing: Of teaching landlords to have at least one degree of mercy towards their tenants. Lastly, of putting a spirit of honesty, industry, and skill into our shop-keepers, who, if a resolution could now be taken to buy only our native goods, would immediately unite to cheat and exact upon us in the price, the measure, and the goodness, nor could ever yet be brought to make one fair proposal of just dealing, though often and earnestly invited to it.

Therefore I repeat, let no man talk to me of these and the like expedients, 'till he hath at least some glympse of hope, that there will ever be some hearty and sincere attempt to put them into practice.

But, as to my self, having been wearied out for many years with offering vain, idle, visionary thoughts, and at length utterly despairing of success, I fortunately fell upon this proposal, which, as it is wholly new, so it hath something solid and real, of no expence and little trouble, full in our own power, and whereby we can incur no danger in disobliging England. For this kind of commodity will not bear exportation, and flesh being of too tender a consistence, to admit a long continuance in salt, although perhaps I could name a country, which would be glad to eat up our whole nation without it.

After all, I am not so violently bent upon my own opinion, as to reject any offer, proposed by wise men, which shall be found equally innocent, cheap, easy, and effectual. But before something of that kind shall be advanced in contradiction to my scheme, and offering a better, I desire the author or authors will be pleased maturely to consider two points. First, As things now stand, how they will be able to find food and raiment for a hundred thousand useless mouths and backs. And secondly, There being a round million of creatures in humane figure throughout this kingdom, whose whole subsistence put into a common stock, would leave them in debt two million of pounds sterling, adding those who are beggars by profession, to the bulk of farmers, cottagers and labourers, with their wives and children, who are beggars in effect; I desire those politicians who dislike my overture, and may perhaps be so bold to attempt an answer, that they will first ask the parents of these mortals, whether they would not at this day think it a great happiness to have been sold for food at a year old, in the manner I prescribe, and thereby have avoided such a perpetual scene of misfortunes, as they have since gone through, by the oppression of landlords, the impossibility of paying rent without money or trade, the want of common sustenance, with neither house nor cloaths to cover them from the inclemencies of the weather, and the most inevitable prospect of intailing the like, or greater miseries, upon their breed for ever.

I profess, in the sincerity of my heart, that I have not the least personal interest in endeavouring to promote this necessary work, having no other motive than the publick good of my country, by advancing our trade, providing for infants, relieving the poor, and giving some pleasure to the rich. I have no children, by which I can propose to get a single penny; the youngest being nine years old, and my wife past child-bearing.

What is Jonathan Swift's modest proposal? In order to answer this question, tackle the following questions:

1. What does Swift identify as the problem or problems?

2. What solution(s) does he propose?

Now on to the more "weighty" question: What is the actual point in this piece? In order to answer this question, go through the essay and identify the elements of satire that Swift uses. How does identifying these elements help you understand the larger point of Swift's essay? Once you have addressed these questions, discuss them with a classmate.

Jonathan Swift wrote "A Modest Proposal" in an effort to address a critical social/political situation in Ireland in the early 18th-century, a situation that was a reality for his audience. You may not have the same knowledge of the circumstances that gave rise to Swift's satire. Do some research in order to find this information. Does this knowledge change your reading of "A Modest Proposal"? How? Did your research indicate to whom Swift was writing? If not, whom do you think his intended audience was? Audience is always an important consideration in any rhetorical context. Why might it hold extreme significance when one is writing satire?

George Saunders teaches in the MFA program at Syracuse University in New York. He writes for The New Yorker *Magazine, as well as other publications, and he has published several collections of his short stories, novellas, and nonfiction. Known for his satirical voice, Saunders often makes his readers a bit uncomfortable as we examine some of our views through the lens he holds before us. "My Amendment" is a case in point!*

MY AMENDMENT

By George Saunders

As an obscure, middle-aged, heterosexual short-story writer, I am often asked, George, do you have any feelings about Same-Sex Marriage?

To which I answer, Actually, yes, I do.

Like any sane person, I am against Same-Sex Marriage, and in favor of a constitutional amendment to ban it.

To tell the truth, I feel that, in the interest of moral rigor, it is necessary for us to go a step further, which is why I would like to propose a supplementary constitutional amendment.

In the town where I live, I have frequently observed a phenomenon I have come to think of as Samish-Sex Marriage. Take, for example, K, a male friend of mine, of slight build, with a ponytail. K is married to S, a tall, stocky female with extremely short hair, almost a crewcut. Often, while watching K play with his own ponytail as S towers over him, I have wondered, Isn't it odd that this somewhat effeminate man should be married to this somewhat masculine woman? Is K not, on some level, imperfectly expressing a slight latent desire to be married to a man? And is not S, on some level, imperfectly expressing a slight latent desire to be married to a woman?

Then I ask myself, Is this truly what God had in mind?

From *The New Yorker* (2004).

Take the case of L, a female friend with a deep, booming voice. I have often found myself looking askance at her husband, H. Though H is basically pretty masculine, having neither a ponytail nor a tight feminine derrière like K, still I wonder: H, when you are having marital relations with L, and she calls out your name in that deep, booming, nearly male voice, and you continue having marital relations with her (i.e., you are not "turned off"), does this not imply that you, H, are, in fact, still "turned on"? And doesn't this indicate that, on some level, you, H, have a slight latent desire to make love to a man?

Or consider the case of T, a male friend with an extremely small penis. (We attend the same gym.) He is married to O, an average-looking woman who knows how to fix cars. I wonder about O. How does she know so much about cars? Is she not, by tolerating this non-car-fixing, short-penised friend of mine, indicating that, on some level, she wouldn't mind being married to a woman, and is therefore, perhaps, a tiny bit functionally gay?

And what about T? Doesn't the fact that T can stand there in the shower room at our gym, confidently towelling off his tiny unit, while O is at home changing their sparkplugs with alacrity, indicate that it is only a short stroll down a slippery slope before he is completely happy being the "girl" in their relationship, from which it is only a small fey hop down the same slope before T is happily married to another man, perhaps my car mechanic, a handsome Portuguese fellow I shall refer to as J?

Because my feeling is, when God made man and woman He had something very specific in mind. It goes without saying that He did not want men marrying men, or women marrying women, but also what He did not want, in my view, was feminine men marrying masculine women.

Which is why I developed my Manly Scale of Absolute Gender.

Using my Scale, which assigns numerical values according to a set of masculine and feminine characteristics, it is now easy to determine how Manly a man is and how Fem a woman is, and therefore how close to a Samish-Sex Marriage a given marriage is.

Here's how it works. Say we determine that a man is an 8 on the Manly Scale, with 10 being the most Manly of all and 0 basically a Neuter. And say we determine that his fiancée is a -6 on the Manly Scale, with a -10 being the most Fem of all. Calculating the difference between the man's rating and the woman's rating—the Gender Differential—we see that this proposed union is not, in fact, a Samish-Sex Marriage, which I have defined as "any marriage for which the Gender Differential is less than or equal to 10 points."

Friends whom I have identified as being in Samish-Sex Marriages often ask me, George, given that we have scored poorly, what exactly would you have us do about it?

Well, one solution I have proposed is divorce—divorce followed by remarriage to a more suitable partner. K, for example, could marry a voluptuous high-voiced N.F.L. cheerleader, who would more than offset his tight feminine derrière, while his ex-wife, S, might choose to become involved with a lumberjack with very large arms, thereby neutralizing her thick calves and faint mustache.

Another, and of course preferable, solution would be to repair the existing marriage, converting it from a Samish-Sex Marriage to a healthy Normal Marriage, by having the feminine man become more masculine and/or the masculine woman become more feminine.

Often, when I propose this, my friends become surly. How dare I, they ask. What business is it of mine? Do I think it is easy to change in such a profound way?

To which I say, It is not easy to change, but it is possible.

I know, because I have done it.

When young, I had a tendency to speak too quickly, while gesturing too much with my hands. Also, my opinions were unfirm. I was constantly contradicting myself in that fast voice, while gesturing like a girl. Also, I cried often. Things seemed so sad. I had long blond hair, and liked it. My hair was layered and fell down across my shoulders, and, I admit it, I would sometimes slow down when passing a shopwindow to look at it, to look at my hair! I had a strange constant feeling of being happy to be alive. This feeling of infinite possibility sometimes caused me to laugh when alone, or even, on occasion, to literally skip down the street, before pausing in front of a shopwindow and giving my beautiful hair a cavalier toss.

To tell the truth, I do not think I would have scored very high on my Manly Scale, if the Scale had been invented at that time, by me. I suspect I would have scored so Fem on the test that I would have been prohibited from marrying my wife, P, the love of my life. And I think, somewhere in my heart, I knew that.

I knew I was too Fem.

So what did I do about it? Did I complain? Did I whine? Did I expect activist judges to step in on my behalf, manipulating the system to accommodate my peculiarity?

No, I did not.

What I did was I changed. I undertook what I like to think of as a classic American project of self-improvement. I made videos of myself talking, and studied these, and in time succeeded in training myself to speak more slowly, while almost never moving my hands. Now, if you ever meet me, you will observe that I always speak in an extremely slow and manly and almost painfully deliberate way, with my hands either driven deep into my pockets or held stock-still at the ends of my arms, which are bent slightly at the elbows, as if I were ready to respond to the slightest provocation by punching you in the face. As for my opinions, they are very firm. I rarely change them. When I feel like skipping, I absolutely do not skip. As for my long beautiful hair—well, I am lucky, in that I am rapidly going bald. Every month, when I recalculate my ranking on the Manly Scale, I find myself becoming more and more Manly, as my hair gets thinner and my girth increases, thickening my once lithe, almost girlish physique, thus insuring the continuing morality and legality of my marriage to P.

My point is simply this: If I was able to effect these tremendous positive changes in my life, to avoid finding myself in the moral/legal quagmire of a Samish-Sex Marriage, why can't K, S, L, H, T, and O do the same?

I implore any of my readers who find themselves in a Samish-Sex Marriage: Change. If you are a feminine man, become more manly. If you are a masculine woman, become more feminine. If you are a woman and are thick-necked or lumbering, or have ever had the slightest feeling of attraction to a man who is somewhat pale and fey, deny these feelings and, in a spirit of self-correction, try to become more thin-necked and light-footed, while, if you find it helpful, watching videos of naked masculine men, to sort of retrain yourself in the proper mode of attraction. If you are a man and, upon seeing a thick-waisted, athletic young woman walking with a quasi-mannish gait through your local grocery, you imagine yourself in a passionate embrace with her, in your car, a car that is parked just outside, and which is suddenly, in your imagination, full of the smell of her fresh young breath—well, stop thinking that! Are you a man or not?

I, for one, am sick and tired of this creeping national tendency to let certain types of people take advantage of our national good nature by marrying individuals who are essentially of their own gender. If this trend continues, before long our towns and cities will be full of people like K, S, L, H, T, and O, people "asserting their rights" by dating, falling in love with, marrying, and spending the rest of their lives with whomever they please.

I, for one, am not about to stand by and let that happen.

Because then what will we have? A nation ruled by the anarchy of unconstrained desire. A nation of willful human hearts, each lurching this way and that and reaching out for whatever it spontaneously desires, trying desperately to find some comforting temporary shred of warmth in a mostly cold world, totally unconcerned about the external form in which that other, long-desired heart is embodied.

That is not the kind of world in which I wish to live.

I, for one, intend to become ever more firmly male, enjoying my golden years, while watching P become ever more female, each of us vigilant for any hint of ambiguity in the other.

And as our children grow, should they begin to show the slightest hint of some lingering residue of the opposite gender, P and I will lovingly pull them aside and list all the particulars by which we were able to identify their unintentional deficiency.

Then, together, we will devise a suitable correction.

And, in this way, the race will go on.

Collaborate Working with one or two of your classmates, outline and explain the content and structure of George Saunders's piece "My Amendment." What is the problem that Saunders wishes to solve and what solution or solutions does he propose? Be specific in your explanation and provide specific examples. Identify the claims that Saunders makes throughout "My Amendment" and the reasons and evidence that he offers to support those reasons and claims. What is the actual point of Saunders's piece? How do you know? Be prepared to share the key points and your conclusions with the entire class.

Explore Browse the web and/or use the library's resources to find some other examples of contemporary satire (the piece can be an essay, a blog, a story, a meme, a video). Choose one that addresses an issue that matters to you. Bring your choice to class and explain the subject/topic of the piece, how the author uses satire, and why you think the satire is effective.

Compose Read or reread Jonathan Swift's "A Modest Proposal" and Saunders's "My Amendment," noting the specific elements of satire that you find most effective. Then try your hand at satire. *Consider this attempt a draft that you will bring to class to workshop.* Remember that writing satire involves identifying a problem, proposing a solution, and doing so using the conventions of the genre.

Lisa Colletta is Associate Professor of English Language and Literature and Director of the Communication and English Program at the American University of Rome. In her research on satire and humor theory, she investigates how satire and humor can function both as a defense mechanism and a weapon. In this excerpt from her academic article published in The Journal of Popular Culture, *Colletta questions the effectiveness of political satire on television and wonders if, ultimately, it undermines "thoughtful satiric critique and . . . discerning engaged politics."*

POLITICAL SATIRE AND POSTMODERN IRONY IN THE AGE OF STEPHEN COLBERT AND JON STEWART

By Lisa Colletta

Satire is one of the most capacious and most misunderstood literary terms. This may be because it is applied broadly to any art form—in any media—that mocks or sniggers at convention; or it may be that its humor rests on irony, which is a term that is even more misused and misunderstood than the term *satire*. We have Alanis Morissette to thank for most people thinking that rain on your wedding day is ironic, and sports reporters, who claim that it is ironic when basketball players are also good golfers, do not help much either.

Ironically, though, much of the humor in popular culture is ironic, but it is the postmodern irony of cynical knowingness and self-referentiality. Traditionally, irony has been a means to expose the space between what is real and what is appearance, or what is meant and what is said, revealing incoherence and transcending it through the aesthetic form and meaning of a work of art. The irony of postmodernity denies a difference between what is real and what is appearance and even embraces incoherence and lack of meaning. It claims our interpretations of reality impose form and meaning on life: reality is constructed rather than perceived or understood, and it does not exist separately from its construction. Awareness of constructions has replaced awareness of meaning, and postmodern irony replaces unity with multiplicity, meaning with appearance of meaning, depth with surface. A postmodern audience is made conscious of the constructed nature of meaning and of its own participation in the appearance of things, which results in the self-referential irony that characterizes most of our cultural output today. Television, the dominant media of postmodern culture, continually refers to itself, quoting other constructed forms in the form of pastiche. . . . Postmodern irony does

From *The Journal of Popular Culture* 42.5 (2009): 856-74.

not aim to get us to turn off the television, but to entertain us into staying tuned and to be consumers of all cultural product, all the while reassuring us with a wink that we are in on and somehow superior to the giant joke that is being played on us.

The writers of the *The Simpsons* are some of the best tellers of this particular joke. *The Simpsons* are the television family—each episode begins with them elbowing for a position in front of the TV, and the manipulation of Bart and Homer into wanting something they have seen on TV—usually with disastrous results—is a major plot device throughout the series and the point of much of the show's ironic satire. . . . The creators of *The Simpsons* ridicule the seductive and manipulative power of television with both the jaded cynicism of Krusty the Clown and the naive gullibility of Homer. The show's denigration of its own medium keeps us watching because it is extremely funny, and because our desires, the best and the worst, are mediated by television in the same way the characters' desires are; we are seduced by the medium and comforted by the idea that we are aware of the seduction. "Television!" as Homer Simpson put in it one of his moments of ironic clarity, is a "Teacher, mother, secret lover" (*The Simpsons* "Treehouse of Horror V"). This is as true for us as it is for Homer, but the self-reflexive irony allows us to feel superior to him.

This kind of irony is especially evident in the social and political satire we see on television, but in a more subtle form it has come to be the defining aesthetic of politics itself. Politicians perform their roles with a smirk and wink aimed at a television audience, knowing that saying something is true is the equivalent of its being true, that appearing is the same as being. They play a role we all expect them to play while they act in their own self-interest, and the media reports on the competing roles of the performers as if they were the story—not the effects of their political self-interests. Using the narrative and imagery of the most clichéd of television shows, we have had a president, as satirist Stephen Colbert asserts, "who stands for things, not only for things, but on things: things like aircraft carriers and rubble and recently flooded city squares. And that sends a strong message: that no matter what happens to America, she will always rebound—with the most powerfully staged photo ops in the world" ("White House Correspondents' Dinner").

My goal here is not to analyze postmodern politics, per se, but rather to examine the role of satire, particularly television satire, in contemporary political humor. Can the social and political satire of television shows such as *The Daily Show*, *The Colbert Report*, and *The Simpsons* really have any kind of efficacy beyond that of mere entertainment? Or does the smirky, self-referential irony that makes all of these shows so popular actually undermine social and political engagement, creating a disengaged viewer who prefers outsider irreverence to thoughtful satiric critique and ironic, passive democracy to discerning, engaged politics?

In a 1946 article for *Life* magazine, the curmudgeonly trenchant Evelyn Waugh stated,

> Satire is a matter of period. It flourishes in a stable society and presupposes homogeneous moral standards—the early Roman Empire and eighteenth-century Europe. It is aimed at inconsistency and hypocrisy. It exposes polite cruelty and folly by exposing them. It seeks to produce shame. All this has no place in the Century of the Common Man where vice no longer pays lip service to virtue. The artist's only service to the disintegrated society of today is to create little independent systems of order of his own. (304)

Leaving aside Waugh's distaste for "the Common Man" and the complex of associations he meant by this term, his observations about satire are quite true. Not only does satire depend upon a stable set of values from which to judge behavior, it also rests upon engagement, the satirist and the viewer need to feel that something could possibly change.

Satire is defined as a form that holds up human vices and follies to ridicule and scorn. . . . In both Horatian satire, which is somewhat genial and mocks imperfection while finding amusement in it, and Juvenalian satire, which is characterized by invective, insult, and withering attacks, the primary objective is to improve human beings and our institutions. Satire is therefore a hopeful genre; it suggests progress and the betterment of society, and it suggests that the arts can light the path of progress.

However, satire achieves its aim by shocking its audience. . . . In order to shock its audience out of complacency and sentimentality (which is often the companion of convention and hypocrisy) satire is usually aggressive and most often subversive toward power structures and the status quo. In itself, satire is not a comic device—it is a critique—but it uses comedic devices such as parody, exaggeration, slapstick, etc. to get its laughs. Humor is satire's art and its power and what saves it from the banality of mere editorial, but its wit, as Meredith noted, "is warlike" (7).

Most importantly, though, satire's efficacy relies on the ability of the audience to recognize the irony that is at the heart of its humor. Injustice, vice, or polite cruelty have to be recognized as the object of the attack, and they need to be judged against a better moral standard. The satirist may use irony with vicious anger, but it always has a deeper meaning and a social signification beyond that of the humor. If the irony is missed, or the better moral standard is also ironically presented as just another construction, then satire is no longer an effective social critique and may even be misunderstood as an example of the very thing it sets out to critique. . . .

The comic device of exaggeration comes from the traditional rhetorical strategy of showing how an opponent's argument can lead to absurd conclusions if taken far enough. This is the stock-in-trade of Stephen Colbert, whose *Colbert Report* is a symphony of absurdity as he parodies Bill O'Reilly's anti-intellectual rant on Fox Television. For example, taking

O'Reilly's cynical pitting of "ordinary Americans" against "elitist intellectuals" to its ridiculous conclusions, Colbert gives viewers his opinion about books:

> I'm sorry, I've never been a fan of books. I don't trust them. They're all fact, no heart. I mean, they're elitist, telling us what isn't true, or what did or didn't happen. Who's Britannica to tell me the Panama Canal was built in 1914? If I want to say it was built in 1941, that's my right as an American! I'm with the president, let history decide what did or did not happen. ("White House")[1]

The unsettling problem is that O'Reilly himself uses this kind of rhetorical strategy in his noncomedic "news" show, blurring the distinction between absurdity and politics as usual.

The point of Colbert's humor is to mock this fuzzy state of affairs, often inhabiting his O'Reilly persona so perfectly that, for left-leaning viewers, he can be difficult to watch at times. Colbert's satire takes conservative positions and spins them out to their most ludicrous extreme, submitting every topic to the highly charged "elitist thinker vs. common-sense American" debate O'Reilly popularized on Fox. For example, Colbert's comment on school redistricting in Omaha, Nebraska, which was described by some as being racially motivated, turns logic and ethics on its head:

> All the Nebraska legislators are saying is, "We don't see whites, blacks, and Hispanics. We see children, who would be a lot happier sticking with their own kind." These districts will still be equal, but separate. That takes courage. Being the first legislature to re-divide races in the face of opposition could well make them the Rosa Parks of re-segregation. (*Colbert Report*, episode 82)

The sophisticated viewer recognizes the parody of the self-proclaimed "objectivity" of Bill O'Reilly's "No Spin Zone," which is not objective and is all spin and does not refute with facts but with emotional, anecdotal language that appears to appeal to common sense and not identity politics. Colbert ironically spins a potentially racist move as courageous and caring, likening an act of injustice to the truly courageous action of civil rights activist Rosa Parks. However, looking at transcripts from *The O'Reilly Factor* complicates this technique. In an interview with Representative Silverstre Reyes (D-Texas) about putting US troops on the border with Mexico to deter drug trafficking, it is very difficult to see any difference between Colbert's satire and O'Reilly's "news" show. Reyes argues that deploying US troops to patrol both the northern and southern boarders (obliquely addressing the racist undertones of O'Reilly's argument) is a misuse of the armed forces and too expensive, but before he can finish he gets cut off by O'Reilly, who states:

> But I'll tell you what. I've talked to the commanders, and they tell me, "Look, you deploy us down there, we stop the drug traffic dead." We'd save lives because Mexican wetbacks, whatever you want to call them, the coyotes—they're not going to do what they're doing now, so people aren't going to die in the desert.

So we save lives, all right, and we seal it down and make it 100 times harder to come across. (*The O'Reilly Factor*)

The rhetorical strategies of O'Reilly and Colbert are identical: reference to anecdote not facts, appeals to emotion rather than reason, use of "everyman" language and syntax (including a racial slur), and the spinning of a probably racist agenda into something that appears caring and courageous (if we do this Mexicans wont [sic] die). Because O'Reilly's argument is *reductio ad absurdum,* and he is such a parody of himself, it is easy to see why some might have a difficult time identifying the differences between Colbert's satire and O'Reilly's political ranting. The only clues that we are not watching Comedy Central are visual, and O'Reilly would be hilarious if he were not so dangerous.

The distinction between parody and politics is so erased that even the guests on Colbert's show often do not get it, and the interview segments on *The Colbert Report* make for some of the most cringe-making television around. In the largest sense, his satire is against the television medium itself and what it does to the state of political debate on television, and he submits both "liberal" and "conservative" guests to the same ironic treatment. As a result, his irony, like all good post-modern irony, can be seen as confirming whatever angle of vision a viewer brings to the show at the same time it confirms the viewer's cynical reading of all political argument. This raises questions about whether or not his satire is actually efficacious, as the viewer does not have any better standards against which to judge this kind of debate. I am not interested in reading against the grain here, nor am I suggesting that his satire is not committed—I do think Colbert is attacking the conservative agenda—but it does seem that the irony which is necessary for satire to succeed is undercut by the very form of television itself. Irony is not merely a quality belonging to the texts, or the creators of those texts. It requires a reader . . . In other words, if one agrees with him politically, she will get the satire, if one disagrees with him politically, she won't. Or, as I have noticed with so many students when we examine Colbert's comedy in my humor courses, viewers will find his brashness funny but miss the object of his attack entirely. Awareness of irony is essential to understanding satire's point. . . .

Colbert's challenge to cant and spin makes him appealing, and my students, many of whom have conservative political orientations, respond favorably to his in-your-face irreverence (perhaps the same reason viewers like Bill O'Reilly) and laugh at his parody of the news. However, after examining his use of irony and parody and locating the butt of his jokes, a number of students responded with something no comedian wants to hear: "That's not funny." Part of this might be that they miss the irony . . . and part of it might be the mechanics of joke work itself, which, as Freud theorized, requires an emotional distancing from the object of the humorous attack and an identification with the teller of the joke. These ideas suggest that satire might not be all that useful as a political strategy and that humor and satire might not work very well to persuade a viewer to share an interpretive strategy, to use

Fish's terms. Television's goal is to entertain, and in comedy shows it is to make people laugh, but people cannot be counted on to laugh at the "right" things.

Savvy television shows like *The Simpsons*, *The Daily Show*, and *The Colbert Report* satirize the blurring of the real and the virtual, the political and the parodic, but they do it within the same self-reflexive, mediated space of television, and therefore, like all pastiche, the seriousness of their critique is undermined. If the satire is pleasing to audiences, it becomes another mediated gesture to be quoted and referenced. The mainstream media pays close attention to the "fake" news of Stephen Colbert and Jon Stewart, and politicians clamor to get on their shows, and, while this makes for brilliantly funny comedy, it trivializes the seriousness of both the politicians and the satire, turning everything into one big meta-joke.

The media sees its role as merely reporting opposing opinions, and the facts supporting those opinions are no longer the object of investigative or interpretative analysis: Fox News's slogan is, "We report, you decide." This seems to suggest, first, that they are actually reporting information; and, second, that audiences can actually decide anything within a reality that is so heavily mediated. Colbert satirizes the values of a culture in which being a consumer and a product of commercial television appears like real agency and autonomy. He launched his first show with this direct address to viewers:

> This show is not about me. No, this program is dedicated to you, the heroes. And who are the heroes? The people who watch this show, average hard-working Americans. You're not the elites. You're not the country club crowd. I know for a fact my country club would never let you in. You're the folks who say something has to be done. And you're doing something. You're watching TV. (*Colbert Report*, episode 1)

This is deeply serious satire, but it also illustrates the inherent problem of televised social and political satire—if it were truly effective satire it would make audiences turn off their television sets. The best satire attacks the mediated reality of television itself and its manipulation of a consumer audience that confuses passive consumption with agency and action. But, as Rob Wilkie argues, the troubling effect of most political satire on television is that it entertainingly "safeguards the current social relations by the 'fuzzying' of politics . . . its engagement is directed at legitimizing the interests of big business and the strategies of nonengagement" (606). This is further complicated by the fact that the "real" news media is more than ever desirous of being entertaining and taking its cues from Comedy Central. The "fuzzying" of politics and entertainment is the outright goal of most news organizations, and the way in which they "engage" issues, such as the wars in Iraq and the Middle East, abortion, and the environment, "moves further away from producing knowledge [and] aims at producing cynical subjects out of citizens and evacuating the public zone of any serious debate and discussion over collective priorities and needs" (Wilkie 606).

With "news" shows like *The O'Reilly Factor* and *Hannity and Colmes*, what is a satirist to do? If the object of the attack is more absurd than the comedy itself, how can satire make its point? One thing they can do is appear on a "real" news show and ask journalists to do their job, and this is precisely what Jon Stewart did during his now famous performance on *Crossfire*. The satire on *The Daily Show* is broader than on *The Colbert Report*, and where Colbert parodies a type of personality, Stewart mocks the television news media in general. The news segments on his show have names like "The Road to Washington (or as I like to call it, 'I am Ed Helms')," reported, of course, by correspondent Ed Helms, and they mock the fatuousness of television news readers and their reporting. In a segment called "Ashamed to Be Fake News," Rob Corrdry investigates the "real" March 2004 news story about the White House surreptitiously producing news segments that reported favorably on a number of the administration's policy objectives, such as "regime change" in Iraq and Medicare reform, and planting them in the mainstream media. The segments, using actors and featuring "interviews" with senior administration officials in which questions are scripted and answers rehearsed, were broadcast in some of nation's largest television markets, including New York, Los Angeles, Chicago, Dallas, and Atlanta. Stewart reported on the controversy this way:

Jon: This is really a shocking story. Not only did the Whitehouse *pretend* that these were news packages, they went so far to *hire* actors to play journalists.

Rob: I know, Jon. In my 25 years of *The Daily Show* Senior Media Analyst I have never seen anything like this. It's more than a little bit embarrassing.

Jon: In your mind, you feel you're embarrassed for this Whitehouse?

Rob: No, *Jon*, I'm embarrassed for US. We're the ones who are supposed to know the fake news, I saw that Medicare piece and they are kicking our ASS! They created a whole new category of fake news, a hybrid—INFOganda! Yeah, we'll never be able to keep up.

Jon: Rob, did you find any fault with what the Whitehouse did?

Rob: Well, there was one thing, Jon. I'm kinda picking a knit here, but calling their fake news reporter *Karen Ryan*? I know what they're trying to do with the name, its blue collar, but not dirt-poory. I'm sure it *tested* well, but the truth is, real reporters have fake, crazy names. Like "Wolf", and "Gupta", and "Van Susterenenenn . . . ."

Jon: That's it, Rob? That's your only objection? Karen Ryan's name?

Rob: Would it kill them to show us what she looked like? I mean, sounds pretty hot . . .

Jon: Rob, she's fake . . .

Rob: HEY! Fake or real, it's all the same in the dark! BANG! For *The Daily Show*, this is Rob Cor—actually this is Dr. Roberto Van Cord-drensesen . . . . (*The Daily Show*)

The satire here points in so many directions that it is hard to know what to laugh at. The White House's cynical manipulation of the news is almost minor compared to the complacency of a news media that is so preoccupied with ratings and image that it was not vigilant enough to investigate the source of the fake news segments. The blurring of fake/real/fake—a fake news show commenting on a real news story about fake journalists—is so extreme that it is impossible for a viewer to have any reaction except cynical laughter at the "fakeness" of all information. But the laughter is ultimately at the viewer's expense; we are made aware of our inability to distinguish between "infoganda" and knowledge, laugh at it, and keep watching.

Though there is good evidence to suggest that postmodernity has killed irony and satire, I am not willing to say that our culture is no better for having satirists around. All theories of humor essentially come down to incongruity, the sudden recognition that the world is not what we expected it to be. Awareness of incongruity—if it is viewed with enough distance—creates laughter, and as Freud suggested, moves us into an appreciation of aesthetic form rather than to action, which is, of course, the primary criticism of satire's efficacy. However, in a state of suspended activity, we may be forced to see things in a new way and to acknowledge alternative possibilities. This, in turn, could make viewers more tolerant of those who approach things differently, and thus inspire them to action that they have not yet considered.

Notes

Stephen Colbert, White House Correspondents' Association Dinner, April 29, 2006. He also used this bit in his segment on "truthiness" (episode 45, January 31, 2006).

By lack of seriousness, I do not mean that nothing can be funny. Humor, as we are well aware, can be deadly serious and profoundly important.

Tucker Carlson's latest venture is a turn on ABC's reality show, *Dancing With the Stars*. This is so rife with irony, I do not really know where to begin.

Works Cited

The Colbert Report. Comedy Central. Episode 1.

The Colbert Report. Comedy Central. Episode 82.

Colbert, Stephen. *White House Correspondents' Association Dinner*. Transcript. 26 Apr. 2006.

Jan. 2007. hhttp://www.dailykos.com/story-only/2006/4/30/1441/59811i

Crossfire. 15 Oct. 2004. Jan. 2007. CNN. http://www.politicalhumor.about.com/library/bljonstewartcrossfire.htmi

The Daily Show with Jon Stewart. Episode 8114. 17 Mar. 2004. Jan. 2007 http://www.anitasdailyshowpage.tripod.com/transcripts/2004fake.html

Fish, Stanley. "Short People Got No Reason to Live: Reading Irony." *Daedalus* 112 (1998): 175–91.

Freud, Sigmund. *Jokes and their Relation to the Unconscious*. The Standard Edition. Trans. James Strachey. New York: Norton, 1960.

Jameson, Frederic. "Postmodernism and Consumer Society." *The Anti-Aesthetic*. Ed. Hal Foster. Washington: Bay Press, 1986. 27–145.

Meredith, George. "Essay on Comedy." *Comedy*. Ed. Wylie Sypher. Baltimore: Johns Hopkins UP, 1956. 3–60.

O'Reilly, Bill. *The O'Reilly Factor*. 7 Feb. 2003. Jan. 2007. Transcript: http://www.oreilly-sucks.com/reyesvoreilly.htmi

The Simpsons. "Treehouse of Horror V." Fox Television, episode 6, season 6.

Waugh, Evelyn. "Fan-Fare." *The Essays, Articles, and Reviews of Evelyn Waugh*. Ed. Donat Gallagher. Boston: Little, Brown, 1983. 300–304.

Wilkie, Rob. "'W' as a Floating Signifier: Class and Politics after the 'Post.'" *Journal of American Culture* 22.3 (2002): 603–21.

Understanding the terms of a particular discourse or discipline is important to understanding a scholar's arguments. Both "postmodern" and "irony" can be a bit tricky, so you may want to look these terms up in dictionary of literary terms. Lisa Colletta does explain satire in the article. She states the goal of her article, "Political Satire and Postmodern Irony in the Age of Stephen Colbert and Jon Stewart," on page 130. What do you see as significant about this two-part goal? What connections can you identify between her investigation of social/political satire's effectiveness and the various theories of humor you have encountered in your readings? How, according to Colletta, does satire function and what conditions must exist for satire and irony to be effective? What do these conditions reveal about the social aspects of humor or the ethics of humor?

Explicate Colletta's article. Your explication should make clear the writer's main point, supporting arguments, and your reflections on the material. Explication means "unpacking" a text. Your task is first to identify and explain Colletta's arguments and ideas and second to engage critically with them. Critical engagement emerges when you move beyond summary to interpretation.

Working with several of your classmates, identify Lisa Colletta's argument. Identify her supporting reasons and the evidence that she provides to support her reasons and claims. What parts of Colletta's articles do you find the most compelling or persuasive? Why? What seems less persuasive to you? Why? Have someone in your group record your conversation in order share your key points with the class.

Banksy (a pseudonym), a British graffiti artist, painter, filmmaker, and social activist, often incorporates dark humor into his satirical street art.

ART BY BANKSY

BY BANKSY

Let Them Eat Crack (New York 2008)

Ghetto 4 Life (New York 2013)

No Trespassing (San Francisco 2010)

Working with several of your classmates, analyze "Let Them Eat Crack," "Ghetto 4 Life," and "No Trespassing." During your discussion, examine the composition of the art and note the images that Banksy added. What about the placement of the figures? Is the geographical location of each piece relevant to understanding it? Consider the date that it appeared. Do these works contain specific cultural and/or historical references crucial to the message and to the humor? Identify both the humor and the message. Be prepared to share your observations, analysis, and conclusions with the entire class.

Look at the political cartoons in *Funny*. Is Banksy's street art as represented in these examples the same as political cartoons? Explain your answer, using specific elements from "Let Them Eat Crack," "Ghetto 4 Life," "No Trespassing," and the various political cartoons to support your point.

Those who write about Banksy use terms such as "guerilla artist," "subversive," and "secretive" because his street art just seems to appear, and when it does it generates strong reactions. These writers also discuss satire, irony, protest, activism, and rebellion in relation to both this artist and his work. Do some research in order to find out more about Banksy, his art, reactions to it, and debates about it. Using the information you find, write a short paper that includes a brief profile of Banksy and an explanation on how he uses humor/satire in his work.

Jody Baumgartner and Jonathan Morris are Political Scientists at East Carolina University and the editors of Laughing Matters: Humor and American Politics in the Media Age *(2008) and with S. Robert Lichter* Politics Is a Joke!: How TV Comedians Are Remaking Political Life *(2014).*

THE DAILY SHOW EFFECT: CANDIDATE EVALUATIONS, EFFICACY, AND AMERICAN YOUTH

BY JODY BAUMGARTNER AND JONATHAN MORRIS

THE DAILY SHOW AND YOUNG AMERICANS

The Daily Show is a late-night talk show hosted by Jon Stewart. The show airs on cable's Comedy Central at 11:00 p.m., Monday through Thursday; reruns are shown at various other times throughout the day. *The Daily Show* is styled as a fake news program and regularly pokes fun at mainstream news makers, especially politicians. It has become increasingly popular, with ratings in 2004 up by 22% from 2003 ("Jon Stewart Roasts Real News," 2004). The show won two Emmy Awards in 2004 (for outstanding variety, music, or comedy series and outstanding writing for a variety, music or comedy program).

Reflecting this popularity, a wide array of political powerhouses as well as presidential hopefuls have appeared on the show as guests. On September 16, 2003, John Edwards announced his candidacy on Stewart's show, making good on a promise that Stewart would be the first person he told about his presidential intentions. Other presidential hopefuls (Bob Kerrey, Dick Gephardt, Dennis Kucinich, and Joseph Lieberman) appeared in 2003; Howard Dean and Carol Moseley Braun appeared in January 2004; and Democratic candidate John Kerry appeared on August 24, 2004. As a result of the program's prominence, *The Daily Show* has been attracting an increasing amount of attention from journalists and scholars.[1]

There are several characteristics about the audience of *The Daily Show* worth noting. First, they are young. Americans between the ages of 18 and 24 years watch the program more than any other age group. Data from the Pew Research Center (2004b) show

From *American Politics Research* 34.3 (2006): 341-67.

that almost half of those surveyed in this age group (47.7%) watch *The Daily Show* at least occasionally. The percentage declines precipitously as age increases.[2] Second, these same youth are relying less on mainstream political news sources such as network news, newspapers, and newsmagazines (Davis & Owen, 1998; Pew Research Center, 2004b). From 1994 to 2004, the 18- to 24-year-old age group spent 16 fewer minutes on average following news on a daily basis (35 as opposed to 51 minutes). A full 25% reported that they pay no attention at all to hard news. Significantly, only 23% of regular *Daily Show* viewers report that they followed "hard news" closely. Finally, although *The Daily Show* is not intended to be a legitimate news source, over half (54%) of young adults in this age group reported that they got at least some news about the 2004 presidential campaign from comedy programs such as *The Daily Show* and *Saturday Night Live*. Only 15% of Americans over the age of 45 years reported learning something about the campaign from the same sources (Pew Research Center, 2004a).

The picture that emerges from these data is one in which youth are increasingly less likely to follow traditional hard news on a regular basis and, conversely, are more likely than older Americans to get at least some of their news from programs such as *The Daily Show*. Because young people are more impressionable (Sears, 1983) and thus more prone to any adverse effects *The Daily Show* might have, the political effects of *The Daily Show* are important to understand.

THEORY AND HYPOTHESES

Baum's research into the effects of soft news suggests that when candidates appear on talk shows, viewers are likely to evaluate them more positively. But candidate appearances, even during an election season, are relatively rare. What is common, especially on late-night talk shows, is a barrage of jokes based on negative caricatures of candidates (Duerst, Koloen, & Peterson, 2001; Hess, 2001; Niven et al., 2003). *The Daily Show* is particularly harsh in this regard (Jones, 2005; Sarver, 2004). As the result, we expect that *Daily Show* viewers' evaluations of candidates will tend to be more negative.

A variety of factors affect citizens' perceptions and evaluations of candidates. Many of these evaluations center on personal attributes, for example, how well they are liked, how honest they are perceived to be, and whether they are trusted to do the right thing. Political comedy is largely focused on personal traits of public figures rather than policy, and the jokes tend to draw on preexisting negative stereotypes people have of these public figures (Moy, Xenos, & Hess, 2004; Niven et al., 2003; Young, 2004a).

Although it is possible that the barrage of negative jokes simply entertains the audience of *The Daily Show* without consequence, psychology research indicates that messages delivered with humor are both persuasive and memorable (Berg & Lippman, 2001; Lyttle, 2001). On the basis of this rationale, as well as youngsters' susceptibility to persuasion (Sears, 1986), we expect that exposure to *The Daily Show*'s campaign coverage will negatively influence evaluations of the presidential candidates.

Some studies further suggest that media effects tend to be stronger on the evaluations of lesser known candidates (Moy et al., 2004). And although Kerry was fairly well known by the time our experiment was conducted (fall 2004), few people are as well known as incumbent presidents. Therefore, we expect exposure to the show to negatively influence evaluations of the challenger (Kerry) more than President Bush.

> *Hypothesis 1*: Young viewers' evaluations of presidential candidates will become more negative with exposure to campaign coverage on *The Daily Show*.

> *Hypothesis 2*: Young viewers' evaluations of John Kerry will be more negative than those of George W. Bush with exposure to campaign coverage on *The Daily Show*.

Although most existing research on the political effects of late-night humor has focused primarily on candidate evaluations, there is reason to believe that the effects of *The Daily Show* go further. In addition to frequently poking fun at the candidates, *The Daily Show* makes a habit of ridiculing the electoral and political process as a whole (Jones, 2005). This portrayal has the potential to influence how young people perceive the overall effectiveness of the system. Research has illustrated that negatively framed political messages can create a more cynical public (Ansolabehere & Iyengar, 1995; Cappella & Jamieson, 1997), and we expect *The Daily Show* to have a similar effect on young viewers.

Additionally, we expect that the cynicism displayed toward the electoral process will spill over on to the news media. The modern mainstream media have become a widely recognized political institution (Cook, 1998; Sparrow, 1999). Their high visibility and perceived power opens the institution and its practices up to ridicule, which *The Daily Show* takes advantage of frequently. This is implicit in the show's "fake" newscast format but also explicit in its lampooning of mainstream journalists. We contend that the result for young viewers is a more cynical perspective of the news media's ability to fairly and accurately cover politics.

> *Hypothesis 3*: Young viewers' cynicism toward the electoral system will increase with exposure to campaign coverage on *The Daily Show*.

> *Hypothesis 4*: Young viewers' cynicism toward the news media will increase with exposure to campaign coverage on *The Daily Show*.

It could be argued that cynicism is healthy for a representative democracy. A less trusting public is not as likely to be bamboozled by political elites or the media. Recent research, however, has suggested that high levels of cynicism and distrust detract from democratic discourse and overall public interaction (Cappella & Jamieson, 1997; Hetherington, 2005; Putnam, 2000). If our findings on the effects of *The Daily Show* support our hypotheses, it should prompt researchers to revisit the influence of "soft news" on the inattentive public.

RESEARCH DESIGN

To examine the effects of exposure to *The Daily Show* on young adults, we constructed a controlled experiment. Participants were selected on a voluntary basis from introductory-level courses in political science at a medium-sized public university. A common criticism of the use of college students as participants in controlled experiments is that they are unrepresentative of the population as a whole (Sears, 1986), but our concern is with college-aged Americans. Furthermore, the National Annenberg Election Survey (2004) of the audience of *The Daily Show* found that the most likely viewers of the show are of college age. Therefore, our findings are more generalizable to the relevant population. A total of 732 students participated in the experiment and were randomly assigned to one of three experimental conditions.[3]

The first group (n = 245) viewed a video clip of selected coverage of the two major presidential candidates and their campaigns on *The Daily Show*. The clip was a compilation of several short segments on each candidate, lasting a little over 8 minutes in total. This approximates the amount of time that the "fake news" segment of the program devoted to the campaign on a fairly regular basis throughout the campaign season. The second group (n = 198) viewed a video clip of similar length and focus, but the content of this condition was segments from election coverage on *CBS Evening News*.[4] This clip was also composed of segments that focused equally on both candidates. However, unlike the humorous and sarcastic *Daily Show* clip, the *CBS Evening News* clip reflected what is considered mainstream television campaign coverage. Because our aim was to examine the effects of exposure to *The Daily Show* on young adults, the *CBS Evening News* clip provided a baseline for comparison between humorous and traditional television news. The third condition of the experiment contained no video stimulus; this group (n =289) served as the control. The experiment was a posttest-only, control-group design (Campbell & Stanley, 1963). Participants who watched *The Daily Show* or the *CBS Evening News* clip filled out a posttest questionnaire immediately afterward. Control-group participants completed the same questionnaire but watched no news clip. The experiment did not include a pretest.[5]

CONCLUSION

On October 15, 2004, just a few weeks after our experimental analysis was completed, Jon Stewart appeared as a guest on CNN's hard-hitting debate show *Crossfire*. During his appearance, Stewart was quite critical of the influence that shows such as *Crossfire* had on the American public:

> **Stewart:** In many ways, it's funny. And I made a special effort to come on the show today, because I have privately, amongst my friends and also in occasional

newspapers and television shows, mentioned this show [*Crossfire*] as being bad . . . And I wanted to—I felt that wasn't fair and I should come here and tell you that I don't—it's not so much that it's bad, as it's hurting America. So I wanted to come here today and say . . . Stop, stop, stop, stop, stop hurting America. . . . What you do is partisan hackery. . . . You have a responsibility to the public discourse, and you fail miserably.

Tucker Carlson [*Crossfire* cohost]: Wait. I thought you were going to be funny.

Come on. Be funny.

Stewart: No. No. I'm not going to be your monkey.

Jon Stewart is not alone in his criticism of high-octane programs such as *Crossfire*, *The O'Reilly Factor*, or *Hannity and Combs*. Previous research has confirmed that high-conflict programs do negatively influence public support for politicians and political parties, in spite of the fact that the public enjoys watching (Forgette & Morris, 2003; Mutz & Reeves, 2005). Our findings, however, suggest that Jon Stewart should not be so quick to cast stones. Although viewers of *The Daily Show* have slightly higher levels of political knowledge than nonviewers (National Annenberg Election Survey, 2004), there are some detrimental effects as well. Our findings suggest that exposure to *The Daily Show*'s brand of political humor influenced young Americans by lowering support for both presidential candidates and increasing cynicism. The experiment results confirmed a causal connection, and the cross-sectional survey data illustrated that the relationship holds up outside the experimental setting. Our analysis of Pew Research Center national survey data further support these findings.

Our research has several implications. First, we have illustrated that young adults' perceptions of presidential candidates, especially those of lesser known candidates, are diminished as a result of exposure to *The Daily Show*. This latter finding is not unexpected, because attitudes toward President Bush were fairly solidified and were less likely to be affected by humor. But it does have significance for 2008, when there will be no incumbent in the race and a high probability that the sitting vice president will not run. Therefore, the field of presidential candidates is likely to be constituted of individuals who are largely unknown to the public. If young Americans learn about these candidates via Jon Stewart, it is possible that unfavorable perceptions of both parties' nominees could form. This would have the effect of lowering trust in national leaders. Moreover, it may increase the importance of having high name recognition in the primary season, because lesser-known candidates would enjoy less support. Ultimately, negative perceptions of candidates could have participation implications by keeping more youth from the polls.

Second, the evidence presented in this study qualifies previous arguments that soft news adds to democratic discourse (Baum, 2002, 2003a, 2003b, 2005). We do not dispute

Baum's contention that soft news contributes to incidental political learning among the inattentive public. With respect to their effects, however, all variants of soft news are not created equal. In particular, our findings illustrate that *The Daily Show*'s effect on political efficacy is mixed. To begin with, exposure to the show lowered trust in the media and the electoral process. This may be the result of Stewart's tendency to highlight the absurdities of the political world. Relatedly, we found that exposure to *The Daily Show* increased internal efficacy by raising viewers' perception that the complex world of politics was understandable. Stewart's style of humor paints the complexities of politics as a function of the absurdity and incompetence of political elites, thus leading viewers to blame any lack of understanding not on themselves but on those who run the system. In presenting politics as the theater of the absurd, Stewart seemingly simplifies it.

Both of these finding about political efficacy have implications for political participation that need to be explored further. We have demonstrated that there are attitudinal effects to exposure to *The Daily Show*, but what of behavioral effects? Increased internal efficacy might, all other things being equal, contribute to greater participation. Citizens who understand politics are more likely to participate than those who do not. Moreover, the increased cynicism associated with decreased external efficacy may contribute to an actively critical orientation toward politics. This may translate into better citizenship, because a little skepticism toward the political system could be considered healthy for democracy. However, decreased external efficacy may dampen participation among an already cynical audience (young adults) by contributing to a sense of alienation from the political process.[6] And it has been demonstrated that lowered trust can perpetuate a more dysfunctional political system (Hetherington, 2005; Mutz & Reeves, 2005; Putnam, 2000).

Future studies should explore the participation strand by going outside the lab to conduct panel studies of young adults during the course of an election campaign. It would also be beneficial to expand the study to older Americans as well, although our preliminary results indicate that the effects of exposure to *The Daily Show* may be unique to young adults. . . . *The Daily Show*'s popularity and influence during the 2000 and 2004 presidential elections were exceptional, and it is likely to be repeated and mimicked in 2008. Understanding how the attitudes and behavior of young Americans change throughout months of exposure to *The Daily Show* and other similar programming has become increasingly important.

Notes

1. In late 2003, Stewart was on the cover of *Newsweek*, cited as one of the most powerful players in the 2004 presidential election. In early 2004, CBS News noted that "regardless of who winds up on top in the upcoming election, one of the biggest winners so far has been Jon Stewart. He seems to be everywhere" ("Jon Stewart Roasts Real News," 2004).

2. Students participated in the experiment on a voluntary basis. Participants were informed that we were interested in understanding college students' political attitudes and beliefs. Specifically, administrators used a script and told participants, "As part of a research project, we [the administrators of the experiment] are conducting a brief survey of news habits and political attitudes of college students." Participants were told that their participation was strictly voluntary and that their responses on the posttest survey were confidential. For the classes that served as the control group, the survey was then administered. The classes that were randomly assigned to one of the experimental conditions were told, "Before we administer the survey, we would like to show you a brief clip of some television discussion of the ongoing presidential campaign. This clip will last less than 10 minutes."

    The experiment was administered during the height of the 2004 general election campaign, between Monday, September 20, and Thursday, September 23. This was almost 3 weeks after the close of the Republican National Convention and a week before the first debate between John Kerry and George W. Bush.

3. The random assignment of participants was done by classroom rather than by individual. This approach was used because of practical considerations in administering the experiment in an efficient and timely manner. Although the random assignment of entire classes to conditions rather than individuals could lead to significant differences between experimental groups separate from exposure to the stimulus, post hoc differences-of-means tests across each of the classes used in this experiment found no statistically significant differences with regard to the variables of interest at $p < .10$ (Bonferroni post hoc test for multiple-group comparison).

4. Because the major national network news programs follow the same model, any of the three major broadcast providers could have been used. CBS was chosen randomly over NBC and ABC to serve as a representation of this format.

5. Although a classic experimental design includes pretest and posttest surveys, a posttest-only, control-group design does not threaten validity. Participants exposed to the experimental stimuli can be compared with the control group, and significant differences between groups can be legitimately attributed to the manipulation, provided random assignment has taken place. In fact, the lack of a pretest can strengthen the validity of an experiment because the participants are not biased by the introduction of the survey items in a pretest before the stimulus is introduced (Campbell & Stanley, 1963).

6. Here, there is no consensus in the literature. There is a body of work that suggests that lower efficacy (or trust) may actually serve to increase participation (Levi & Stoker, 2000, pp. 486-487).

References

Ansolabehere, S., & Iyengar, S. (1995). *Going negative: How political advertisements shrink and polarize the electorate.* New York: Free Press.

Baum, M. A. (2002). Sex, lies, and war: How soft news brings foreign policy to the inattentive public. *American Political Science Review, 96*, 91-109.

Baum, M. A. (2003a). Soft news and political knowledge: Evidence of absence or absence of evidence? *Political Communication, 20*, 73-190.

Baum, M. A. (2003b). *Soft news goes to war: Public opinion & American foreign policy.* Princeton, NJ: Princeton University Press.

Baum, M. A. (2005). Talking the vote: Why presidential candidates hit the talk show circuit. *American Journal of Political Science, 49*, 213-234.

Berg, E., & Lippman, L. (2001). Does humor in radio advertising affect recognition of novel product brand names? *Journal of General Psychology, 128*, 194-205.

Campbell, D. T., & Stanley, J. C. (1963). *Experimental and quasi-experimental designs for research.* Chicago: Rand McNally.

Cappella, J. N., & Jamieson, K. H. (1997). *Spiral of cynicism: The press and the public good.* New York: Oxford University Press.

Cook, T. E. (1998). *Governing with the news: The news media as a political institution.* Chicago: University of Chicago Press.

Davis, R., & Owen, D. (1998). *New media and American politics.* New York: Oxford University Press.

Duerst, L., Koloen, G., & Peterson, G. (2001, August-September). *It may be funny, but is it true: The political content of late-night talk show monologues.* Paper presented at the annual meeting of the American Political Science Association, San Francisco.

Forgette, R. G., & Morris, J. S. (2003, April). *The state of the (dis)union: The effect of new media coverage of perceptions of congress.* Paper presented at the annual meeting of the Midwest Political Science Association, Chicago.

Hess, V. (2001, August-September). *The role of political comedy in the 2000 election campaign: Examining content and third-person effects.* Paper presented at the annual meeting of the American Political Science Association, San Francisco.

Hetherington, M. J. (2005). *Why trust matters: Declining political trust and the demise of American liberalism.* Princeton, NJ: Princeton University Press.

Jones, J. P. (2005). *Entertaining politics: News political television and civic culture.* Lanham, MD: Rowman & Littlefield.

Lyttle, J. (2001). The effectiveness of humor in persuasion: The case of business ethics training. *Journal of General Psychology, 128*, 206-216.

Moy, P., Xenos, M. A., & Hess, V. K. (2004, May). *Priming effects of late-night comedy*. Paper presented at the annual meeting of the International Communication Association, New Orleans, LA.

Mutz, D. C., & Reeves, B. (2005). The new videomalaise: Effects of televised incivility on political trust. *American Political Science Review, 99*, 1-16.

National Annenberg Election Survey. (2004). *Daily Show viewers knowledgeable about presidential campaigns, National Annenberg Election Survey shows*. Retrieved September 21, 2004, from http://www.naes04.org

Niven, D., Lichter, S. R., & Amundson, D. (2003). The political content of late night comedy. *Press/Politics*, 118-133.

Pew Research Center. (2004b). *Online news audiences larger, more diverse*. Retrieved June 8, 2004, from http://www.people-press.org

Putnam, R. D. (2000). *Bowling alone: The collapse and revival of American community*. New York: Simon & Schuster.

Sarver, D. L. (2004, September). *No laughing matter: Late night television talk shows' coverage of the 2004 democratic presidential primary*. Paper presented at the annual meeting of the American Political Science Association, Chicago.

Sears, D. O. (1983). The persistence of early political predispositions: The roles of attitude object and life stage. In L. Wheeler & P. Shaver (Eds.), *Review of personality and social psychology* (Vol. 4, pp. 79-116). Beverly Hills, CA: Sage.

Sears, D. O. (1986). College sophomores in the laboratory: Influence of a narrow data base on social psychology's view of human nature. *Journal of Personality and Social Psychology, 51*, 515-530.

Sparrow, B. (1999). *Uncertain guardians: The news media as a political institution*. Baltimore: Johns Hopkins University Press.

Young, D. G. (2004a). Late-night comedy in election 2000: Its influence on candidate trait ratings and the moderating effects of political knowledge and partisanship. *Journal of Broadcasting & Electronic Media, 48*, 1-22.

Using the Internet, find more recent demographic information about *The Daily Show with Jon Stewart* than what Baumgartner and Morris provide in their article. Have the demographics remained fairly constant or have they changed? If the latter, what might you speculate about some of Baumgartner and Morris's conclusions?

Baumgartner and Morris note that "a wide array of political powerhouses as well as presidential hopefuls have appeared on the show as guests" on *The Daily Show*, and then name some of these individuals 2003 and 04. Again, using the Internet, make a list of more recent "political powerhouses," and if relevant, "presidential" hopefuls appearing on the show. Then watch a video clip of one or more of these appearances. Write a brief reflection of your reaction to this individual's appearance. Note the subject under discussion, the tone of the conversation, and the overall demeanor of the individual.

Working with several of your classmates, design a survey to gather the following information from your peers:

1. From where they get their primary source of news.

2. Their general feelings about the political process.

3. The name of a current social/political humorist/satirist.

Using the results of this survey, Baumgartner and Morris's findings, and one other reading from this book, as a group prepare a presentation on political humor/satire and American millennials.

Read Lisa Colletta's article "Political Satire and Postmodern Irony in the Age of Stephen Colbert and Jon Stewart," on page 129. Consider what Colletta's piece might add to Baumgartner and Morris's findings, specifically to their concluding points. As you synthesize the ideas and arguments in these two works, look for points of intersection. When you write a synthesis, you create something new. In this new work explain and analyze how shows such as *The Daily Show* or *The Colbert Report* and political humorists/satirists function in our society.

Chris Jones writes on the arts and culture for the Chicago Tribune *in his role as chief theater critic. Although "When Jokes Go Too Far" appeared in the "Arts and Entertainment" section of the* Chicago Tribune, *Chris Jones tackles a serious subject—the use of offensive humor.*

WHEN JOKES GO TOO FAR

BY CHRIS JONES

Oscar hosts are supposed to be irreverent and edgy, otherwise they are instantly accused of boring us silly. So Seth MacFarlane must have been surprised by the rolling backlash from his performance at last week's Academy Awards.

In a gathering storm of protest in forums from *The Atlantic* to the *Los Angeles Times*, the first time Oscar frontman was variously accused of anti-Semitism (for a routine exploiting the old canard that Jews own Hollywood), sexism (for his opening number involving actresses who have revealed their breasts to the cameras) and racism (including for pretending to mix up two African-American actors for comic effect). By the end of the week, the Academy of Motion Picture Arts and Sciences was being pressed to disavow the performance of its own host, although it put out a statement defending him.

MacFarlane was not alone in being on the defensive. Steve Hannah, the Chicago-based CEO of *The Onion*—whose franchise is supposed to be so irreverent and edgy as to make Oscar hosts look like wimps—apologized Monday for what he acknowledged was a tasteless tweet that involved a four-letter word applied to lively 9-year-old Oscar nominee Quvenzhane Wallis.

The anonymous *Onion* offender was chopped up—an irony that did not escape some media observers who noted *The Onion's* in-house tweeter's very tricky job description: Be as offensive as you can until someone actually finds you offensive.

From the *Chicago Tribune* (2013).

Even Jon Stewart, who often out-Onions *The Onion*, issued an apology last week—for making fun of Dick Molpus, a Mississippi politician with a record of fighting for civil rights who just happened to be stuck with a funny name that suggested otherwise . . . to New Yorkers, anyway.

Stewart was as concerned with accuracy as with offense, but all of this would suggest that even the top brand names in comedy are struggling to figure out what's actually offensive nowadays.

After all, eight shows a week in New York and Chicago (and soon in London), *The Book of Mormon* has jokes that lampoon a storied American religion and the naivete of people of faith, and that brings up such taboo topics as African tribal traditions, rape, even children with AIDS. There has been no discernible backlash there, just huge profits. So why do the *South Park* boys get a pass as MacFarlane takes it on the chin?

There's no way to do justice to this issue without first observing that today's social media landscape, where the instant analysis of events like the Oscars is now widely consumed along with the event itself, offers many more opportunities for people to say they were offended.

People have to tweet something. Outrage usually gets attention. Hence, outrage aplenty.

So stipulated. But what did MacFarlane do wrong? They've been discussing that in the comedy studies program at Columbia College. One useful text under discussion is the Gospel According to Molly Ivins, the late newspaper columnist and no shrinking violet when it came to poking fun: "Satire is traditionally the weapon of the powerless against the powerful. I only aim at the powerful."

That's the start of what *The Onion* did wrong: A 9-year-old, even an Oscar nominee, has insufficient power. When that notorious tweet landed in our feeds, it engendered the feeling of leaping to the girl's defense, which killed off whatever humor might have been intended.

That's also a problem with hosting the Oscars—you end up with too much palpable power to operate as a satirist. Especially if you have the kind of glib confidence that comes easily to the seemingly invulnerable MacFarlane.

If you sat in some smoky club watching George Carlin rant about the jerks who run the country, it was cathartic precisely because of the implied inability of the fevered but clearly impotent monologuist to change anything, or land any kind of meaningful blow on the aforementioned leaders.

But at the Academy Awards, even the most naive viewer perceives that the honorees are trapped by contract and convention, forced to smile and grit their teeth as some callow youth of-the-ratings-moment reduces their entire artistic careers to a juvenile catalog of naked body parts.

It's hard to turn pampered celebrities into sympathetic figures, but last Sunday's Academy Awards did a pretty fine job. And that's a large part of why MacFarlane's performance wasn't funny.

Then there's the question of building a relationship.

The Book of Mormon has an entire evening to forge characters and an alternate narrative that is, in its way, quite charming. Second City, which once poked fun at Superman in a wheelchair, also has mastered this imperative. So, when it is writing satirical stories rather than merely tweeting (a whole other skill), has *The Onion*.

In those great *Onion* articles, the outrageous gags are, as they say in the trade, well protected by a clear and credible worldview.

Invent
What is Jones's position on the use of offensive humor? How does he convey his message? As you address this question, consider elements of audience, tone, and use of rhetorical appeals. Find specific examples from the article to illustrate these elements and be prepared to share your response with the class.

Collaborate
Working with a partner or in a small group, identify Jones's key question in "When Jokes Go Too Far." Once you have located that question discuss the answer. Consider the following questions as you flesh out Jones's explanation: Where do issues of power come into play in joking? What makes satire effective? What is the importance of narrative context to humor/satire? Be prepared to share your answers with the entire class.

Bill Carter covers TV for The New York Times, *has written several books, writes for* The New York Times Magazine, *as well as for many other publications.*

IN THE TASTES OF YOUNG MEN, HUMOR IS MOST PRIZED, A SURVEY FINDS

BY BILL CARTER

Comedy Central has a lot riding on, well, comedy. And now research it commissioned about how young men view humor has provided the cable channel with some encouraging conclusions about the preferences of its most important demographic group.

More than music, more than sports, more than "personal style," comedy has become essential to how young men view themselves and others, the research showed.

Stuck in an elevator? Sixty-three percent of young men surveyed said they would choose to be there with Jon Stewart (or some other favorite comic), and only 15 percent said they would prefer that time with Eli Manning (or some other idolized athlete).

Eighty-eight percent of respondents said their sense of humor was crucial to their self-definition, 74 percent said "funny people are more popular," and 58 percent said they sent out funny videos to make what might be called a special impression on someone else.

These sentiments were reflected in an online survey of 2,000 people conducted by Nielsen Entertainment Television. Additional conclusions were formed from the results of so-called buddy groups, run by the research group Sachs Insights, which brought together young men in 19 cities around the country. Comedy Central is studying the results to discern how valuable comedy has become to the generation known as millennials, which it defines as young adults born after the first Reagan inauguration, in 1981.

From *The New York Times* (2012).

"We called them Comedy Natives," said Tanya Giles, the executive vice president for research at Comedy Central's parent, MTV Networks. "Comedy is so central to who they are, the way they connect with other people, the way they get ahead in the world. One big takeaway is that unlike previous generations, humor, and not music, is their No. 1 form of self-expression."

The challenge now, said Michele Ganeless, the president of Comedy Central, "is creating a new business model around all of this."

The channel is well positioned to take advantage. Its ratings are up 10 percent this year among men 18 to 34 years old, its target audience. With an audience that is mostly male and has a median age of 29, Comedy Central is able to charge a premium to advertisers, because young men are by far the hardest viewers to reach.

Jonathan Gray, a professor of media and culture at the University of Wisconsin, said he had a measure of cynicism that "a study by Comedy Central found that comedy matters." But whenever he teaches a course on television and comedy, he said, it is "filled within a matter of minutes," and his students regularly name *South Park*, *The Daily Show* and *The Colbert Report* as shows they like. All are from Comedy Central.

Ms. Giles said Comedy Central's audience "skews 65 percent male." So does most of its talent, with performers like Daniel Tosh of *Tosh.0* and the male sketch comedians in the channel's latest hit, *Key & Peele*.

Young women were included in the wider statistical research, but the channel gathered only young men for its buddy groups, feeding them pizza and asking them to do things like share funny videos, discuss favorite comics, and draw representations of themselves doing funny things.

The channel got back a lot of toilet humor (on a map, the participants marked the 19 cities in the survey with toilet bowls), but also plenty of useful information.

For example, as described by Ms. Giles: "Millennials are comfortable with uncomfortable truths," which she said meant they see just about any subject as fit for humor. They also want comedy with a faster pace. "If you don't get them quick, they can find it somewhere else," she said.

Chanon Cook, the top research executive for Comedy Central, said the results also indicated that "irony has been replaced by absurdity." That is one of many ways she said this generation had separated itself from Generation X, a more dour and cynical group in the Comedy Central analysis, shaped by things like battles over race and class, and growing up as latchkey kids.

Ms. Ganeless said one purpose of the research was "to understand how our audience and technology cross over, so we can be prepared."

Millennials, of course, increasingly say they are distancing themselves from television. Still, the study showed that television easily topped everything else as the main source of comedy.

But the channel also realizes that comedy is popping up on alternate screens, and the men Comedy Central wants to reach are spending more time downloading funny videos. As one buddy group participant put it, "*Tosh.0*, he does what I like to do: watch YouTube videos and make fun of them all day."

Comedy Central is trying to feed these interests. It posted a President Obama sketch from *Key & Peele* on YouTube before the show's premiere; it became the fastest-growing clip in the channel's history, with more than a million views within 48 hours.

It is essential, executives said, for the channel to chase the fans, not vice versa. "Millennials never blame themselves," Ms. Cook, the research executive, said. "They think: what does it say about the brand that you're not everywhere that I am?"

In this article about the value that young men place on humor, you might have noticed the following terms: "millennials," "comedy natives," and "Generation X." Find the passages where these terms appear. How do you understand these terms? What do each of these terms mean within the context of the article? Does their use seem like labeling or stereotyping? Explain your response. If you fall within one of these categories, how do you personally respond to the assertions or assumptions made by the various individuals in the article?

As you read the results of the survey, you may have been struck with the fact that "eighty-eight percent of respondents said their sense of humor was crucial to their self-definition." Read Dana Klein and Nicholas Kuiper' article, "Humor Styles, Peer Relationships, and Bullying in Middle Childhood." Using their research on how children develop and use various styles of humor, write a short 3-4 page essay explaining this relationship between *humor* and *self-definition*. Evidence from Klein and Kuiper's research will help you develop your explanation; however, you will also use other elements of composition in your essay. You may find that you need to define humor or self-definition. Perhaps one of the other pieces that you have read in *Funny* will prove helpful as well as your own personal experiences with and views on humor.

Limor Shifman teaches in the Department of Communication at the Hebrew University of Jerusalem. Her research focuses on media, popular culture, and the social construction of humor. Dafna Lemish, a professor at Southern Illinois University, has published over ten books, and her primary interest is the role media play in the construction of gender identities. My apologies to any blondes who may be reading the following article! However, as Shifman and Lemish make clear in what follows blonde jokes traverse national borders and are found globally, and, as Leon Rappoport, whose "Male Versus Females, Gays versus Straights, and Varieties of Gender Humor" follows, informs us, blonde jokes have a long history.

BLONDEJOKES.COM: THE NEW GENERATION

By Limor Shifman and Dafna Lemish

Question: How does a blonde kill a fish? Answer: She drowns it.

The dumb blonde stereotype has been prominent in American popular-culture for decades. Numerous Hollywood actresses have played the role of the fair-haired, intellectually challenged and sexy women. Famous examples include Marilyn Monroe, Jean Harlow and Jayne Mansfield. The stereotype is still live and kicking in the third millenium, not only in movies (see the 2001 Blockbuster *Legally Blonde*), but also in contemporary advertising and prime time television. Prominent blonde incantations include Phoebe, the challenged blonde from the popular sitcom *Friends* whose identical twin sister is a porn-star, and Kelly Bundy from *Married with Children*, who got progressively more stupid and promiscuous in the course of the series.

One of the main sites for the construction of the dumb blonde stereotype is jokes, which are usually formed either as short stories with a punch line or as riddles. The archetypical blonde has two main features in comic texts. First, she is extremely challenged intellectually: Not only does she lack any formal education, but she also fails to understand simple common sense facts such as where fish live or how (not) to kill them (see joke above). The second prominent feature of the blonde—as framed in jokes—is a combination of sexual allurement and promiscuity. The blonde likes sex and enjoys it, yet her limited intelligence leads men to joyfully take advantage of her.

From *Society* 47 (2010): 19-22.

Although theoretically applicable to both genders, the vast majority of blonde jokes are told about women. This led Shifman and Maapil Varsano to describe such jokes as forms of "specified" sexist humor. Whereas general sexist jokes disparage women as a unified collective, specified sexist jokes mock certain stereotyped feminine groups such as blondes and mothers-in-law. On the surface, the "specified" jokes do not target women in general and might therefore not be regarded as sexist. However, the prototypes appearing in many comic texts—the dumb blonde, the irritating wife and the awful mother-in-law—are always defined by an exaggeration of a traditional feminine stereotype. Thus, the dumb blonde is an extreme version of the "dumb woman" and "sex object" stereotypes prevalent in patriarchal society. According to Greenwood and Isbell's work on "ambivalent sexism," this stereotype may have evolved as the resolution of a dissonance that sexist men experience in relation to sexually attractive women. Such women are appealing, but simultaneously possess the potential for manipulating their sexuality in order to control and even castrate men. Since the blonde is portrayed as dumb, she is not capable of manipulating men and therefore serves as the perfect sexual object. This framing of blonde jokes as sexist has been contested by authors such as Elliot Oring, who claimed that the two values which are highlighted and scorned in the jokes—lack of intelligence and indiscriminate sexual activity—are the antitheses of the values of the modern workaday world. This environment is supposed to be rational, calculated and organized—everything that the blonde is not. The jokes, according to Oring, reinforce these latter values, suggesting that every person who embraces them can be part of the modern workplace.

The "sexy dumb blonde" stereotype—still prevalent in mass media—is also live and thriving nowadays on the Internet. As we shall demonstrate in this paper, contemporary Internet blonde humor incorporates new trends that may lead us to a re-evaluation of the genre and its meaning. As part of our on-going study on humor about gender on the Internet, we identified three such trends: The first relates to the blonde image itself, claiming that stupidity has superseded promiscuity as the main theme of blonde jokes. The second trend deals with the spread of blonde jokes, highlighting the internationalization, or globalization of the blonde joke on the Internet. The third is related to reflexive discourse on the blonde: we describe the emergence of "Meta blonde" jokes—texts that build on the popularity and familiarity of the audience with the blonde joke genre in order to comment and reflect on it, and in so doing, to continue to reinforce it. In what follows, we shall describe these three trends and provide some initial analysis of their meaning.

WHEN DUMB BLONDES BECOME EVEN DUMBER

> The police pull a car over on a country lane and approach the blonde lady driver. "Is there a reason why you're weaving all over the road, madam?" asks the officer. The woman replied, "Oh thank goodness you're here. I almost had an accident. I looked up and there was a tree right in front of me.

I swerved to the left and there was another tree in front of me. I swerved to the right and there was another tree in front of me!" Reaching through the window to the rear view mirror, the officer replied, "Madam, that's your air freshener."

Up till recently, blonde jokes where "double signed," in the sense that they dealt extensively with two features of their butts: attractively/sexual promiscuity and stupidity. However, our investigation of humor about blondes in popular humor websites revealed that of these two characteristic features, Internet humor focuses extensively on stupidity, leaving the promiscuous theme as marginal to this genre.

How can we explain this obliteration of the sexual dimension in contemporary blonde jokes? A possible clue may derive from the comparison of blonde jokes with another type of jokes that is becoming more and more prevalent online—jokes about smart, bitchy castrating women, who use their cleverness to manipulate men. If we accept Greenwood and Isbell's explanation of blonde jokes as motivated by masculine fears of manipulation through sex, we may claim that the obliteration of promiscuity in current Internet humor about blondes might be connected to current masculine anxieties. Perhaps instead of men's traditional fear of women using sex as a manipulative tool, currently they fear women all the more for being manipulative through their smart and "bitchy" qualities. Putting down the blonde for her stupidity rather than her sexiness thus becomes a much stronger disciplinary act for reasserting male-dominance and power. Additionally, we can also explain this trend as a form of adjustment to second and third-waves' feminist recognition of female sexuality, and the sense that laughing at women enjoying sex may be currently less "politically correct." Being stupid, on the other hand, is still universally ridiculed.

THE GLOBALIZATION OF BLONDE JOKES

A commercial airplane is in flight to Chicago, when a blonde woman sitting in economy gets up and moves to an open seat in the first class section. A flight attendant watches her do this, and politely informs the woman that she must return to her seat in the economy class because that's the type of ticket she paid for. The blonde woman replies, "I'm blonde, I'm beautiful, I'm going to Chicago and I'm staying right here." After repeated attempts and no success convicing the woman to return to economy, the flight attendant goes into the cockpit and informs the pilot and co-pilot that there's a blonde bimbo sitting in first class who refuses to go back to her proper seat. The co-pilot goes back to the woman and explains why she needs to move, but once again the woman replies by saying, "I'm blonde, I'm beautiful, I'm going to Chicago and I'm staying right here."

The co-pilot returns to the cockpit and suggests that perhaps they should have the arrival gate call the police and have the woman arrested when they land. The pilot says, "You say she's blonde? I'll handle this. I'm married to a blonde. I speak blonde." He kneels down next to the woman and whispers quietly in her ear, and she says, "Oh, I'm sorry," then quickly moves back to her seat in economy class.

The flight attendant and co-pilot are amazed and ask him what he said to get her to move back to economy without causing any fuss.

"I told her first class isn't going to Chicago."

In parallel to the emergence of the blonde joke in the United States, similar local joke themes emerged around the world. Among these, a joke type that received some academic attention in Christie Davies' work focuses on "Essex girls." Emerging in the UK and gaining popularity in the 1980s and 1990s, Essex girl jokes describe their butts as extremely stupid and promiscuous, adding a subtle class element to the American blonde-joke genre, since Essex girls are identified with working class.

Essex girl jokes—as well as other local variants of the blonde joke—are gradually declining nowadays, leaving the floor to the overwhelmingly successful blonde genre. With the emergence of new global media such as the Internet, humor themes are quick to spread across national and cultural borders. Whereas not all themes of American humor have been globalized (for instance—redneck jokes are still pretty much confined to American websites), jokes about blondes have traveled very well. The blonde, safely seated in the virtual jet, is now flying "first class" across the globe to places in which blonde jokes have never set their (high heeled) feet. Such places include Brazil (in which blonde jokes are replacing jokes about stupid Portuguese), China, Japan and the Arab world. Thus, one can find blonde jokes on the Internet in a wide range of languages, presented on diverse platforms such as blogs, forums and humor-oriented websites.

The vast international expansion of blonde jokes is particularly intriguing in two cases. The first is its successes in countries in which almost all women are fair-haired. For instance, blonde jokes are now becoming prevalent in Scandinavian countries such as Finland and Norway. Thus, one of the first things Finns did with their mobile phones was to use them to send SMS jokes about blondes. A famous ad for mobile services in Helsinki featured a blonde whispering into a Nokia in the supermarket: "How did you know I was here?". Since virtually all women in these countries are blonde, the portray of the blonde in an unusual situation with the smarter *brunet* or *redhead*—a common practice in the genre—is charged with a new meaning.

If in Norway blonde jokes visually describe all women, in places such as China or Japan they describe none of the local women. But the blonde-joke gene has been exported to such places as well. Thus, for instance, the Japanese version of Wikipedia includes an elaborated description of blonde jokes, and Chinese websites and blogs contain dumb blonde jokes (we even found the above joke about the blonde flying "first class" to Chicago in several Chinese blogs, forums and websites). The second intriguing incarnation of global blonde humor is thus the spread of such jokes to places in which blondness is very rare. On its face values, this phenomenon makes little sense: Why should people mock a group that does not exist in their society? A possible explanation might be that blonde jokes in such countries function as indicators for American/Western culture, thus the blonde is seen as inferior since she is not "local." Another possibility is that since the blonde has been globalized through Hollywood and network television series, as well as extensively used in advertizing to promote a capitalist way of life, the image is familiar worldwide. However, this puzzle still requires further analysis and research.

FAKING BLONDE: THE META BLONDE JOKES

"I'm not offended by all these dumb blonde jokes because I know I'm not dumb. I'm also not blond." —Dolly Parton

The dumb blonde genre has become so prevalent in contemporary Internet humor, that it has produced a "meta discourse" about the meaning of the genre, and—maybe more importantly—about the meaning of being blonde:

A young ventriloquist is touring the clubs and one night he's doing a show in a small town in Arkansas. With his dummy on his knee, he starts going through his usual dumb blonde jokes when a blonde woman in the 4th row stands on her chair and starts shouting: "I've heard enough of your stupid blonde jokes. What makes you think you can stereotype women that way? What does the color of a person's hair have to do with her worth as a human being? It's guys like you who keep women like me from being respected at work and in the community and from reaching our full potential as a person. Because you and your kind continue to perpetuate discrimination against not only blondes, but women in general and all in the name of humor!" The embarrassed ventriloquist begins to apologize, and the blonde yells, "You stay out of this, mister! I'm talking to that little shit on your knee."

This joke epitomizes the complex, multifaceted and polysemic qualities of contemporary Internet humor about gender. It is clearly aware of feminist discourse, and is based on an inter-textual play with genres which enables it to be read as a "joke about blonde jokes" rather than about blondes. But the bottom line (or punch line?) is that the dumb blonde, even when parroting feminist discourse, remains a dumb blonde. The old stereotype is preserved and even reinforced. In this manner the meta jokes continue to perpetuate— albeit in a more twisted manner—the very same old dumb-blonde notions we have become so accustomed to in popular culture. Thus, feminist discourse is working against itself in this joke, as it does in many other contemporary Internet texts on gender.

In way of summary, we suggest that while ostensibly a form of light-hearted entertainment, humor constitutes an important vehicle through which distressing and sensitive issues are processed and negotiated. Yet, in ridiculing those who deviate from the "right" mode of behavior, such as blondes in our case, comic texts draw heavily on prevalent ideologies, stereotypes, and cultural codes. Indeed, researchers like ourselves, assume that analyses of comic texts provide us with important insights about what is lurking in the social mind behind the façade of platitudes, conventions, and political correctness used by people in a humorous manner to express what they would never dare to say directly.

Further Reading

Davies, C. 1998. *Jokes and their relation to society*. Berlin: Mouton de Gruyter.

Greenwood, D., & Isbell, L. 2002. Ambivalent sexism and the dumb blonde: men's and women's reactions to sexist jokes. *Psychology of Women Quarterly, 26*(4), 341–350.

Kuipers, G. 2006. *Good humor, bad taste: A sociology of the joke*. Berlin: Mouton de Gruyter.

Oring, E. 2003. *Engaging humor*. Urbana: University of Illinois Press.

Shifman, L., & Maapil Varsano, H. 2007. The clean, the dirty and the ugly: A critical analysis of clean humor websites. *First Monday, 12(2)*. Available at: http://www.firstmonday.org/issues/issue12_2/shifman/index.html

Shifman, L., & Lemish, D. 2008. *Between feminism and fun(ny)mism: Analyzing gender in popular Internet humor*. Paper presented at the International Communication Association Conference (ICA), Montreal.

Shifman, L., & Lemish, D. 2009. *Mars and Venus in virtual space: Post-feminist humor and the Internet*, Paper presented at the International Communication Association Conference (ICA), Chicago.

Summarize Limor Shifman and Dafna Lemish's key points. Once you have completed your summary, use it to explicate "Blondjokes.com: The New Generation." Your explication should make clear their main points, supporting arguments, and your *reflections* on the material. *Explication* means "unpacking" a text. Your task is *first* to identify and explain the Shifman and Lemish's arguments and ideas and *second* to engage critically with them. Critical engagement emerges when you move beyond summary to interpretation.

With a partner or two of your classmates, choose another stereotype that provides fodder for jokes and conduct informal research of your own, what Robert Provine calls "sidewalk science," in order to answer the following three questions:

- Is this joke/stereotype prevalent on the Internet? Make sure you identify the sites you visit.

- What trend or trends can you identify in how the joke is told, where it is told, and by whom?

- What conclusion or conclusions do you draw from your research?

After you have done your research, write a short summary of your findings accompanied by some form of visual presentation (a graph, chart, PowerPoint, Prezi).

Christie Nicholson, a multimedia science journalist, graduated from Columbia University's School of Journalism. She is also a contributing editor at Scientific American. As you read the following article, consider the title and what it reveals about personal, interpersonal, and social aspects of humor.

_____
_____

THE HUMOR GAP

By Christie Nicholson

When comedian Susan Prekel takes to the stage and spots an attractive man in the audience, her heart sinks. "By the end of my gig he's going to find me repulsive. At least as a sexual being," she says.

In more than a decade of performing on the New York City comedy circuit the attractive, tall brunette has been asked out only once after a show. But male comics get swarmed. "They do very well with women. I see it all the time," Prekel says.

Comedians, it turns out, may simply be experiencing an extreme version of the typical romantic interplay between men and women. Although both genders consistently prefer a partner with a sense of humor, there is an intriguing discrepancy in how that preference plays out. Men want someone who will appreciate their jokes, and women want someone who makes them laugh. The complementary nature of these desires is no accident. Researchers suspect humor has deep evolutionary roots—in 1872 Charles Darwin noticed chimps giggling as they played—and many argue that the laws of natural selection can help explain the complex senses of humor we have today.

Men and women use humor and laughter to attract one another and to signal romantic interest—but each gender accomplishes this in a different way. And as a relationship progresses, the way men and women use humor changes; it becomes a means of soothing one another and smoothing over rough patches. In fact, humor is rarely about anything funny at all; rather sharing a laugh can bring people closer together and even predict compatibility over the long haul.

From *Scientific American Mind* 21.2 (2010): 38-45.

Humor in all its forms—sarcastic, witty, anecdotal, ironic, satirical—is as complicated and evolved as language. It can be a weapon used to alienate and a means to communicate interest and intelligence. So at the risk of unweaving a rainbow, it's time to take a serious look at humor.

MAKE ME LAUGH

It was when scientists started watching men and women be funny, in addition to studying what people found funny, that interesting patterns emerged. "The literature prior to the 1990s focused on joke appreciation," says Martin Lampert, humor expert and chair of social sciences at Holy Names University in Oakland, Calif. "This was a contrived situation where subjects were presented with jokes and we documented their reaction." Experiments then started to look at humor production, asking subjects to come up with jokes or studying how people amuse one another in the real world. "This gave us a much more accurate picture of what was happening," Lampert says.

In 1996 Robert R. Provine, professor of psychology at the University of Maryland, analyzed 3,745 personal ads and found that women sought a mate who could make them laugh twice as often as they offered to return the favor. Men, on the other hand, offered humor about a third more than they requested it. These findings were the first big clue that the sexes were approaching humor from different angles.

Ten years later Eric R. Bressler of Westfield State College and Sigal Balshine of Mc-Master University revealed another intriguing gender difference. The psychologists showed 200 people photographs of men and women, each paired with either a funny or a fairly straight autobiographical statement. Women chose the funnier men as potential dates, but men showed no preference for the funny women (as Prekel, the comedian, has been witnessing in the real world). And yet all over the world, both sexes consistently rank a sense of humor as one of the most important traits in a mate—so why the disparity?

"Although both sexes say they want a sense of humor, in our research women interpreted this as 'someone who makes me laugh,' and men wanted 'someone who laughs at my jokes,'" says Rod A. Martin of the University of Western Ontario. In 2006 Martin, along with Bressler and Balshine, asked 127 subjects to choose between pairs of potential partners for either a one-night stand, a date, a short-term relationship, a long-term relationship or friendship. In each pair one partner was described as receptive to the participant's humor but not very funny themselves, and the other partner was described as hilarious but not all that interested in the participant's own witty remarks.

In every context other than friendship, men preferred women who would laugh at their jokes to those who made jokes. Women, however, preferred partners who were funny.

The fact that a man and a woman complement each other when they offer and request humor is striking because laughter is not under our conscious control, Provine points out. And as with many behaviors that occur outside of our awareness, researchers suspect these opposing desires may have a risen because they serve a reproductive purpose.

WHY FUNNY MEN ARE SO ATTRACTIVE

From an evolutionary perspective, the sex that contributes more resources to the development of offspring will likely be the choosier of the two. In all mammals, that choosier sex is the female, because of the burden of pregnancy. So the male must compete for female attention—think of the courtship displays of bucks with their grand antlers. When a female is drawn to an impressive performer, she is unknowingly responding to his genetic health—thereby increasing the likelihood that her offspring will survive.

This evolutionary force is referred to as sexual selection, and psychologist Scott Barry Kaufman of New York University thinks it may explain why humor is so important in early courtship and why men produce the jokes while women appreciate them. "Humor is pretty sexy at first meeting. When you have little else to go on, a witty person who uses humor in a clever, original way is signaling quite a lot of information, including intelligence, creativity, and even aspects of their personality such as playfulness and openness to experience," says Kaufman, who has done studies on the role of creativity in humor.

Supporting this idea are studies that show that humor is a good indicator of intelligence—a highly prized heritable trait. For instance, in 2008 Daniel Howrigan of the University of Colorado at Boulder asked nearly 200 people to create humorous statements and draw funny images. Those who scored higher on a test of general intelligence were also rated by observers as being significantly funnier.

A more subtle test of the sexual selection hypothesis for humor depends on what women want when they are at their most fertile—during ovulation. A large body of research has shown that when considering short-term partners, ovulating women tend to prefer men who have signs of good genes, such as body symmetry, masculine facial features and behavioral dominance. In contrast, when considering long-term partners at any point in their cycle, women show no preference, often choosing men with resources (in this day and age, that means money) and nurturing characteristics—in other words, good dads.

If humor is a sign of creativity and intelligence and hence an indicator of high-quality genes, funny guys should be highly desirable to women when they are ovulating. Indeed, a 2006 study by Geoffrey Miller of the University of New Mexico and Martie Haselton of the University of California, Los Angeles, showed exactly that. Forty-one women read descriptions of creative but poor men and uncreative but wealthy men and rated each man's desirability as a short-term mate. During high fertility, women chose creative men about twice as often as wealthy men for short-term pairing, but no preference emerged for long-term partners—exactly the pattern one would expect.

So if being funny is what it takes to get the girls, then making others guffaw should be a priority for guys. Think back on the class clowns you've known. Were they boys?

And while the boys were clowning, chances are the girls were giggling. Studies of laughter also reveal clues about humor's important, evolved role in courtship, as Provine discovered when he started studying spontaneous conversation in 1993. He had tried studying laughter in the laboratory, but plopping a person in front of a TV with a couple of *Saturday Night Live* episodes did not incite much hilarity. Provine came to the stark realization: laughter is inherently social. So he set out, like a field primatologist to observe human interaction in urban spaces: malls, sidewalks, cafes. He made note of about 1,200 laugh episodes—comments that elicited a laugh from either the speaker or the listener—and figured out which gender laughs when.

The results may not come as a surprise. Women, in general, laugh a lot more than men, according to Provine's data—especially in mixed-sex groups. "Both men and women laugh more at men than at women," Provine observes. This finding aligns with the idea that men are performing humor and women, the "selectors," are appreciating it, but of course there are other possible explanations. Are women simply less discriminating when it comes to humor? Or are men the funnier gender?

CRACKING THE LAUGHTER CODE

Recent research suggests these possibilities are unlikely. Men and women are consistently judged to be equally funny when they go head to head on humor production. For instance, in 2009 Kim Edwards, a Ph.D. student in psychology at the University of Western Ontario, asked men and women to come up with funny captions for single-frame cartoons. Both genders created an equal number of highly rated captions.

In humor appreciation, too, women and men are on equal footing. In 2005 psychiatrist Allan Reiss of Stanford University showed men and women 30 cartoons while scanning their brains. Both genders rated 24 of the cartoons as funny, and when asked to rank them in terms of how funny they were, the genders again agreed. In addition, men and women had very little difference in their response times to the jokes they liked.

Given the sexes' similar capacity for humor production and appreciation, the fact that women laugh more—and men are laughed at more—must have its roots in something other than simply who is being funny. In fact, Provine's data support this idea. too: 80 to 90 percent of the statements that elicited laughter in his field studies were not funny at all. Rather people laughed at banal phrases such as "I'll see you guys later!" or "I think

I'm done." His research also showed that people tend to laugh more when they are speaking as opposed to listening. Many studies have confirmed this finding, and experts believe that when a speaker laughs, it sets his or her audience at ease and facilitates social connections.

Provine found one notable exception to the rule that speakers laugh more than their audience, however: when a man is talking to a woman, the woman laughs more than the man. The difference is sizable: when Provine averaged laughter in two-person pairs, the speakers laughed 46 percent more than the person listening. When a woman was talking to another woman, she laughed 73 percent more than her interlocutor, but when a woman was in conversation with a man she produced 126 percent more laughter. Male speakers laughed less than female speakers, but they still laughed 25 percent more than their listeners when they were talking to other men. But in the specific circumstance where a man was talking to a woman, the men laughed 8 percent less than their partners.

The fact that women laugh so much when they are speaking to men—and they laugh more than men even when the men are doing the talking—suggests that there is some instinct at play. Perhaps it is a refection of the female role as sexual selector, but whatever the roots may be of the female instinct to laugh around men, it works—men find women attractive when they laugh. Perhaps it is because laughter unconsciously signals interest and enjoyment.

Consider that chimpanzees utter laugh like sounds when they are being chased by other chimps, and as with human children, the one being chased is the one who laughs. For chimps playing, the panting laugh is a signal to the chaser that the play is fun and nonthreatening. The enjoyment might come from anticipation, as if the laughter is sending a message: I'm going to keep running, but it's going to be really fun when I get caught. Because women are the ones typically chased in courtship, could there be a link? "I think there's an interesting parallel there," humor expert Martin says. "In both cases, the laughter is a signal of enjoyment and invitation to continue. . . ."

Indeed, studies have shown that laughter is a powerful measurement of the level of attraction between two people. In 1990 psychologists Karl Grammer and Irenaus Eibl-Eibesfeldt of the Ludwig Boltzmann Institute for Urban Ethology in Vienna studied natural conversations in mixed-sex groups and measured the amount of laughter coming from men and women. Later on each individual self-reported how attracted they were to other members of the group. It turns out it is the amount of female laughter that accurately predicts the level of at traction between both partners In other words, a woman laughs a lot when she is attracted to a man or when she senses a man's interest—and that laughter, in turn, might make her more attractive to him or signal that she welcomes his attention.

FUNNY THROUGH THE YEARS

As attraction transitions to a relationship, humor's role changes, but sharing a laugh is no less important. Many agree it is the connection that humor fosters that makes it so good for relationships, especially over the long term. Humor often becomes a private language between two people. A couple's in joke can make a mundane or tense moment hilarious.

But here again, each gender's role is different—and interestingly, in some ways men and women change places. Unlike during courtship, when men are usually the humor producers and women are the appreciators, in long-term relationships it can sometimes be harmful for men to use humor. When women are the humorous partners, however, relationships tend to thrive.

Funny men are not necessarily a curse, of course, but in certain situations male humor might be dangerous. In 1997 psychologists Catherine Cohan of Pennsylvania State University and Thomas Bradbury of the University of California, Los Angeles, analyzed the marriages of 60 couples over an 18-month period, using data from self-reports and audio taped conversations of the couples working through a specific marital issue. They found that in couples who had a major life stressor such as a death in the family or a lost job, the husband's use of humor during problem solving was a warning sign. These couples were more likely to wind up divorced or separated within 18 months than couples with a life stressor where the male did not use humor. This result may be about men knowing how and when to crack the tension with a joke. Timing is key. "Particularly with men's humor we see it used to avoid problems or serious conversations," Martin says. "And if it's used aggressively—in a teasing or put-down way—or at an inappropriate time, it can be detrimental to the relationship."

The idea that male humor might sometimes be bad for a relationship is supported by results from the Coping Humor Scale (CHS) test developed by Martin and psychologist Herbert Lefcourt of the University of Waterloo, which measures how much one uses humor to cope with life stress. They found in 1986 that men who score high on the CHS report less marital satisfaction than their peers who do not use humor as much to cope. They also discovered that men tend to use more disparaging forms of humor, directed at others, when coping with a tough situation. If this is the type of humor men are referring to when they take the CHS, Lefcourt notes, it might explain the lower relationship satisfaction.

Women, on the other hand, have been shown by many studies to often use self-deprecating humor, which may bring relief to a tense situation. . . . And the CHS study found that women who use more humor to cope reported greater marital satisfaction.

A recent physiological study may help explain why. Couples psychologist John Gottman of the Gottman Institute analyzed 130 couples discussing their top three most problematic issues. Starting when they were newlyweds, couples came to Gottman's lab once a year for six years and had private discussions while Gottman measured their physiological responses, such as blood pressure and pulse, with a polygraph and electrocardiogram.

Gottman found that the reduction of the male's heart rate during these intense discussions was critical for a successful marriage (whereas the women's heart rates made no difference). Some men were good at soothing themselves, but the next best way to lower these husbands' heart rates was for their wives to crack a joke to relieve the tension. Couples in which the women deescalated the conflict in this way, according to Gottman, were more likely to have a stable marriage through at least the study's six years, as compared with couples in which the wives did not use humor.

As a relationship progresses, then, a man's humor becomes less important—perhaps even counterproductive in certain situations—whereas a woman's sense of humor becomes a blessing. During courtship, a man's wit attracts a woman, and her appreciative laughter, in turn, is attractive to him. But as commitment increases, the challenge becomes less about landing a mate and more about keeping one around. "Here it is more about sympathy and attunement to the other's feelings and perspectives," Martin says. "The goal is less to entertain and impress and more to reduce interpersonal tensions, convey understanding, save face for oneself and one's partner. Women may be more skilled at these uses of humor."

Of course, in real life men and women inhabit a wide spectrum, with far greater individual variation than is reflected in the trends that show up in the lab. Many people have traits that are the opposite of those normally associated with their sex. But in general, the way men and women use humor betrays its deeper purpose—to help us connect and bond with one another. A genuine laugh is one of the most honest ways to convey: I'm with you.

Invent How do you think the survey findings by Comedy Central that Bill Carter writes about in his article "In the Tastes of Young Men, Humor Is the Most Prized, Survey Finds" relate to the research that Christie Nicholson describes in "The Humor Gap"? Does Nicholson's article explain the survey results? Does the survey illustrate and support some of Nicholson's points? If so, which ones, and how does it do so?

Collaborate With a partner or in a small group, write a brief response to each of the following questions by quoting from, summarizing, and paraphrasing from "The Humor Gap": How do men perceive humor? How do women perceive humor? Why is humor important during courtship? What is the place of humor in long-term relationships (or how should it be used in those relationships?)? Be prepared to share your responses with the entire class.

Tina Fey, actress, comedian, writer, and producer, was the first female head writer of Saturday Night Live. *She has won a number of awards and honors for her writing and acting and as a producer. "Dear Internet" is a chapter from Fey's book,* Bossypants, *about which Janet Maslin wrote in her* New York Times Review. *"Bossypants isn't a memoir. It's a spiky blend of humor, introspection, critical thinking." As several of the writers in* Funny *note humor involves critical thinking and intellectual dexterity.*

DEAR INTERNET

BY TINA FEY

One of my greatest regrets, other than being the Zodiac Killer never learning to tango, is that I don't always have time to answer the wonderful correspondence I receive. When people care enough to write, the only well-mannered thing to do is to return the gift, so please indulge me as I answer some fans here.

From tmz.com

Posted by Sonya in Tx on 4/7/2010, 4:33 P.M.

"When is Tina going to do something about that hideous scar across her cheek??"

Dear Sonya in Tx,

Greetings, Texan friend! (I'm assuming the "Tx" in your screen name stands for Texas and not some rare chromosomal deficiency you have. Hope I'm right about that!)

First of all, my apologies for the delayed response. I was unaware you had written until I went on tmz.com to watch some of their amazing footage of people in L.A. leaving restaurants and I stumbled upon your question.

From *Bossypants* (New York: Reagan Arthur Books, 2011): 163-67.

I'm sure if you and I compare schedules we could find a time to get together and do something about this scar of mine. But the trickier question is *What* am I going to do? I would love to get your advice, actually. I'm assuming you're a physician, because you seem really knowledgeable about how the human body works. What do *you* think I should do about this hideous scar? I guess I could wear a bag on my head, but do I go with linen like the Elephant Man or a simple brown paper like the Unknown Comic? Too many choices, help!

Thank you for your time. You are a credit to Texas and Viking women both.

Yours, Tina

P.S. Great use of double question marks, by the way. It makes you seem young.

———————————————

From Dlisted.com

Posted by Centaurious on Monday, 9/21/2009, 2:08 A.M.

"Tina Fey is an ugly, pear-shaped, bitchy, overrated troll."

Dear Centaurious,

First let me say how inspiring it is that you *have* learned to use a computer.

I hate for our correspondence to be confrontational, but you have offended me deeply. To say I'm an overrated troll, when you have *never even* seen me guard a bridge, is patently unfair. I'll leave it for others to say if I'm the best, but I am certainly one of the most dedicated trolls guarding bridges today. I always ask three questions, at least two of which are riddles.

As for "ugly, pear-shaped, and bitchy"? I prefer the terms "off beat, business class-assed, and exhausted," but I'll take what I can get. There's no such thing as bad press!

Now go to bed, you crazy night owl! You have to be at NASA early in the morning. So they can look for your penis with the Hubble telescope.

Affectionately, Tina

———————————————

From PerezHilton.com

Posted by jerkstore on Wednesday, 1/21/2009, 11:21 P.M.

"In my opinion Tina Fey completely ruined *SNL*. The only reason she's celebrated is because she's a woman and an outspoken liberal. She has not a single funny bone in her body."

Dear jerkstore,

Huzzah for the Truth Teller! Women in this country have been over-celebrated for too long. Just last night there was a story on my local news about a "missing girl," and they must have dedicated seven or eight minutes to "where she was last seen" and "how she might have been abducted by a close family friend," and I thought, "What is this, the News for Chicks?" Then there was some story about Hillary Clinton flying to some country because she's secretary of state. Why do we keep talking about these dumdums? We are a society that constantly celebrates no one but women and it must stop! I want to hear what the men of the world have been up to. What fun new guns have they invented? What are they raping these days? What's Michael Bay's next film going to be?

When I first set out to ruin *SNL*, I didn't think anyone would notice, but I persevered because—like you trying to do a nine piece jigsaw puzzle—it was a labor of love.

I'm not one to toot my own horn, but I feel safe with you, jerkstore, so I'll say it. Everything you ever hated on *SNL* was by me, and anything you ever liked was by someone else who did it against my will.

Sincerely, Tina Fey

P.S. You know who *does* have a funny bone in her body? Your mom every night for a dollar.

From a bodybuilding forum

Posted by SmarterChild, on 2/24/2008, 2:10 P.M.

"I'd stick it in her tail pipe."

Dear SmarterChild,

Thank you so much for your interest. Whether you meant it in a sexual way or merely as an act of aggression, I am grateful. As a "woman of a certain age" in this business, I feel incredibly lucky to still be "catching your eye" "with my anus." You keep me relevant!

Sincerely, Ms. T. Fey

From tmz.com

Posted by Kevin 214 on 11/9/08, 11:38 A.M.

"Tina Fey CHEATED!!!!!! Anyone who has ever seen an old picture of her can see she has had 100% plastic surgery. Her whole face is different. She was ugly then and she is ugly now. She only wished she could ever be as beautiful as Sarah Palin."

Dear Kevin 214,

What can I say? You have an amazing eye. I guess I got caught up in the whole Hollywood thing. I thought I could change a hundred percent of my facial features and as long as I stayed ugly, no one would notice. How foolish I was.

So let's wipe the slate clean. Full disclosure, here is a list of the procedures I've had done. Eye browning, nose lengthening, I get my teeth lightly hennaed each month to give them their amber luster. I've had my lips thinned, and I've had a treatment called Grimmage where two fishing wires are run through my jawline and used to gather the skin until it looks like a fancy pillow.

I've had sebaceous implants (small balls of Restylane placed in random locations to give the appearance of youthful neck acne).

I don't have Botox. Unfortunately I'm allergic. Instead I have monthly injections of Bromodialone, a farm-strength rat poison. This keeps my face in a constant state of irritation and paralysis, which of course is indistinguishable from sexual excitement. My face is longer and thinner than it was twenty years ago, and while some might say that is a natural effect of weight loss and aging, you and I know the truth—I pay a woman to sit on the side of my head twice a week. Madonna and Gwyneth go to her, and we've all had amazing results. Ugh, listen to me, I really have changed! Why did I feel the need to name-drop the fact that I'm friends with Madonna Vickerson and Gwyneth Chung?

Since you're so savvy at spotting plastic surgery, I'm sure you've noticed some of my other famous friends who have "had work done." Bishop Desmond Tutu . . . cheek implants. Supreme Court Judge Ruth Bader Ginsburg? Major tit job. And Sponge Bob SquarePants, gender reassignment.

Keep on helpin' me "keep it real,"

T

Read "Males versus Females, Gays versus Straights, and the Varieties of Gender Humor" by Leon Rappoport and "The Humor Gap" by Christie Nicholson. Drawing on Rappoport's and Nicholson's ideas, explain how you would characterize Tina's Fey's humor in "Dear Internet."

With several of your classmates, discuss Tina Fey's purpose, the strategies she uses to meet that purpose, and her effectiveness in doing so in "Dear Internet." In your discussion you will want to identify her message or messages. Consider the title of this piece. How does it function in relation to her purpose and to the content of the piece? Fey utilizes email correspondences as a way to structure and develop her ideas. Why do you think she made this decision? Think about the complications to "audience" this form invites. What is the tone of "Dear Internet"? As your group discusses this piece, make sure that someone captures your key points to share with the rest of the class.

Leon Rappoport, a social psychologist, taught at Kansas State University for 39 years. He published on a range of topics from the Holocaust, to the psychology of food, to his last book Punchlines, *before his death in 2009. In* Punchlines, *Rappoport examines the possibility that racial, ethnic, and gender humor when performed by the outrageous and controversial comedians of marginalized racial, ethnic, and gender groups reveals the absurdity of intergroup hatred. Ultimately, Rappoport sees this kind of humor as performed by these comedians as contributing to individuals rethinking recognizing their racist, homophobic, or misogynistic views. The excerpt that follows offers context and history for gender humor. As you read it, keep in mind why Rappoport would find it necessary to provide this information to his readers.*

MALES VERSUS FEMALES, GAYS VERSUS STRAIGHTS, AND THE VARIETIES OF GENDER HUMOR

By Leon Rappoport

At least three generalizations about gender humor are usually acknowledged by all authorities on this topic. First, it is virtually universal: if there is any society in the world where men and women do not tell some sort of disparaging stereotype jokes about one another, it is a well-kept secret. Second, men typically tell jokes ridiculing women more frequently than women do about men. Third, women are more likely to laugh at jokes told by men than men are to laugh at jokes told by women. While this last point is less true today than in the past, it helps explain why women in our society have found it more difficult to become comedians and there are fewer of them. . . .

A more immediate question *is* why gender humor is apparently universal. The fundamental answer suggested by common experience as well as all authorities on the subject basically comes down to sex and power. Where sex is concerned, it is not necessary to know anything about Freudian theory (although it helps) to appreciate the fact that wherever there are men and women, there is always some degree of latent or manifest sexual tension between them. Nor do such tensions require close contact with the opposite sex; sometimes the same sex will do, as in gender-segregated situations such as prisons. So it is easy to understand why the tensions associated with sexual needs and desires lend

---

From *Punchlines: The Case for Racial, Ethnic, and Gender Humor* (Westport, CT: Praeger, 2005): 101-17

themselves to the creation of jokes such as: "What are the first words Adam spoke to Eve? 'Stand back! I don't know how big this thing gets.'"

Yet there is much more to gender humor than gross sexual jokes and comedy routines. The universal anxieties and conflicts between men and women extend beyond sexuality to the social power differences that have traditionally separated them. Here we run into a broad range of issues including the social roles prescribed for males and females, the norms specifying acceptable masculine and feminine behaviors, and the developmental processes whereby people acquire a masculine, feminine, or homosexual sense of identity. Distinguishing between jokes that are related to sexuality and jokes that are related to gender power can be difficult because both sexuality and gender power are often involved, but as may be seen in the following oneliners, it depends upon the primary focus of the joke.

> "What's the definition of a perfect woman? One that after you're done screwing, she turns into a six pack and a roast beef sandwich."

> "Why did God invent women? Because sheep can't cook."

Blatantly sexist jokes like these are more concerned with gender stereotypes about power—whose going to provide the food—than about sexuality as such. This point about the traditional male focus on power is perfectly captured in the following one-liner by comedian Elayne Boosler: "When women are depressed they either eat or go shopping. Men invade another country."

The second generalization noted, that men tell more jokes deriding women than women do about men, plainly follows from the historical pattern of male domination. Although sexism has been reduced in contemporary American society to a greater extent than elsewhere, it is still a problem that generates a good deal of ironic feminist humor, as in the joke about a woman who tells her husband that she wants to take a job outside their home. He responds quite seriously and without any awareness of the contradiction: "Stick to your washing, ironing, and cooking. No wife of mine is going to work!" Such unconscious male sexism was discussed by the feminist scholar Elizabeth Janeway, who gave another example of how men often fail to realize sexist contradictions by telling the presumably true story about a woman being interviewed on a radio program. The male host says, "Good morning Mrs. Blank, tell me something about yourself. What does your husband do?"

The well-documented tendency for men to enjoy telling disparaging jokes about women apparently helped to justify their dominance. By evoking stereotypes about the inferiority of women, such jokes provided reassurances of male superiority. The familiar and sometimes overworked analogy is to the way whites employed jokes about blacks in order to justify discrimination. In both cases, of course, when people show excessive pleasure at such humor, it is understood as a way of covering up their feelings of anxiety and insecurity. Many social scientists today believe that as women have been gaining a greater degree of equality with men in our society and entering traditional male occupations, men are becoming more insecure about their status and have accordingly been behaving more aggressively toward women. Sexist humor is a perfect instrument for the symbolic expression of aggression, and as will be noted in the following text, women are aware of this and well able to respond in kind.

The question raised by the third generalization about gender humor that women are more likely to laugh at jokes told by men than men are to laugh at jokes told by women involves both the tradition of male domination and the ways that women have typically been socialized to deal with it. In the first instance, research studies show that regardless of gender, starting in childhood most of us learn to defer to those with greater power or higher status. Where humor is concerned, this means that we have a near automatic tendency to ingratiate ourselves with authority figures by acting as if we appreciate their jokes or humorous remarks. Other things being equal, we are likely to believe, or act as if we believe, that a joke told by a high-status individual is funnier that one told by someone of lower status. This is why common experience confirms studies showing that college students are more likely to laugh at jokes told by professors than by students, nurses are more likely to laugh at jokes told by doctors, and enlisted men are more likely to laugh at jokes told by officers rather than the reverse. Research also shows that because higher status individuals are usually in control of the situation when dealing with others, they are the ones who are more likely to initiate humor. Why? Because they can be confident that their humor will be well received, and if not, then it will do them no harm. But if lower status people initiate humor, they run the risk of drawing attention to themselves in a way that may be seen as inappropriate. Their peers may feel as if they are showing off and their superiors may view them as pushy, and if their joke or remark goes over badly, they are likely to be thought of as fools. So the conventional social science wisdom has it that in most situations, particularly those involving men, most women have been reluctant to run the risk of initiating humor and eager to ingratiate themselves by appearing to appreciate the humor of men.

Another perspective on gender humor is provided by the results of a survey concerning differences between the types of humor preferred by men and women. The main findings were that both men and women tend to dislike jokes about religion, but in social situations, men are much more inclined than women to tell jokes about other people. Women, however, indicated preferences that are in line with some of the observations previously mentioned. They enjoy jokes about themselves to a significantly greater extent than men and view such jokes as a useful means of self-disclosure, a way of telling people about themselves. Typical examples include this line by comedian Wendy Liebman: "I've been on so many blind dates, I should get a free dog." Here is another, from Rita Rudner: "I want to have children but one of my friends told me she was in labor for 36 hours. I don't even want to do anything that feels good for 36 hours."

Nancy Walker's analysis of women's humor emphasizes that such jokes also stand as examples of incongruity theory, except that for women, the incongruity is between traditional sexist behavior standards and their ability to satisfy them. In line with Walker's observation is the fact that women comedians often use routines designed to ridicule sexist stereotypes. This type of incongruity humor was carried to a very successful extreme by Roseanne Barr. She began her career doing stand-up routines disparaging her role as a "normal" housewife. Thus, on housecleaning:

> "The day I worry about cleaning my house is the day Sears comes out with a riding vacuum cleaner."

> And on childrearing: "When my husband comes home at night, if those kids are still alive, hey, I've done my job."

> The critic Sian Mile called Roseanne Barr's stand-up and sitcom work "chainsaw humor," because it directly attacks the traditional roles imposed on women and does so in a way that spares neither men nor women.

More specifically, the four distinctive characteristics of women's humor identified by Regina Barreca include, first, their tendency to dislike slapstick humor and practical jokes where individuals are injured or victimized. Seeing someone slip on a banana peel, get a pie in the face, or suffer some other humiliation is not considered particularly funny. Slapstick humor apparently triggers laughter in men because it evokes their feelings of superiority, whereas in women, it evokes feelings of sympathy. Second, women are more inclined to enjoy humor aimed at ridiculing the pretensions of people in powerful positions. Their jokes tend to be directed upward, against high-status people who seem insensitive to the needs of others, rather than downward. It is rare, for example, to find women telling dialect jokes making fun of immigrants or minorities. Third, women are more inclined to use irony in remarks that appear to be positive, such as when they tell a boyfriend how strong he is because he can crush a beer can with one hand. Fourth, women are more likely than men to use self-critical humor as a means of gaining acceptance and approval. This is a conspicuous feature of the routines employed by women doing stand-up comedy, as well as those performing in TV sitcoms. Two of the best-known sitcom examples still showing in reruns are *I Love Lucy* and *The Mary Tyler Moore Show*. The comedy themes in both of these shows typically centered on embarrassing or awkward situations that the stars would get themselves into. The self-critical themes that have become practically obligatory for women doing stand-up almost always concern their attractiveness to men.

No discussion of gender humor would be complete without consideration of the classic sexist joke targets: mothers-in-law, dumb blonds, Jewish Mothers, and Jewish American Princesses. Jokes about these four groups thus focus on specific categories of women rather than women in general, and although some of the jokes in this area are no longer current, in the past they have all been standard equipment for male comedians. The reasons for this vary, but one thing these four categories of women have in common is familiar, well understood stereotypes.

Jokes about dumb blonds, or more accurately, attractive dumb blonds, apparently can be traced back to stereotypes created by vaudeville and burlesque performers. Many of them found that they could improve their comedy, dance, or magic acts by including buxom women assistants. Dressed in skimpy costumes and often wearing blond wigs, their job was to act sexy and stupid. The stereotype is also probably based on the false notion that beauty and brains do not go together. This idea would surely appeal to many people who might feel inferior to attractive blonds and therefore try to compensate by thinking of them as dumb. Among women who do not meet Barbie Doll standards of attractiveness, dumb blond jokes are bound to be a hit. In any case, such jokes have been a staple of gender humor and are virtually interchangeable with stupid Polish jokes.

Bibliography

Barreca, R. 1991. *They used to call me Snow White . . . but I drifted: Women's strategic use of humor.* New York: Viking Penguin.

Janeway, E. 1975. *Between myth and morning: Women awakening.* New York: William Morrow.

Mile, S. 1992. Roseanne Barr: Canned laughter—containing the subject. In R. Barreca (ed.), *New perspectives on women and comedy.* Philadelphia: Gordon and Breach Science Publishers, 24-38.

Walker, N. 1988. *A very serious thing: Women's humor and American culture.* Minneapolis: University of Minnesota Press.

In his explanation about why gender humor is apparently universal, Rappoport points to sex and power. How does gender power work in jokes? Why, according to Rappoport, is it difficult to tell the difference between jokes "related to sexuality and [those] related to gender power"? Why do you think this distinction matters? To whom and under what circumstances do you think it does or should matter? As you consider your answers, look carefully at the three generalizations about gender humor that Rappoport identifies and his explanations, arguments, and reasons in each category. What evidence does he offer to support his reasons and arguments? Discuss your answers with several of your classmates.

Rappoport uses Regina Barreca's research to present the four characteristics of women's humor. Barreca published her work in 1991 and Rappoport in 2005. Although you cannot conduct a scientifically accurate experiment updating this research, you can informally address some traits identified as characteristics two and four. As support for the fourth characteristic that "[w]omen are more likely than men to use self-critical humor as a means of gaining acceptance and approval," Rappoport points to women doing stand-up comedy and TV sitcoms. Watch a YouTube video of both a female and male comedian preforming stand-up comedy in order to see whether the performances reinforce Barreca's and Rappoport's research and explanations about women's humor in relations to that of men's. You will have to watch the videos more than once. Write a brief 2–3 page report detailing your findings, comparing them to Rappoport's points, and stating your conclusions.

Troy Campbell, a behavioral scientist, is a researcher at Duke University's Fuqua School of Business. Embedded in Troy Campbell's short piece is an argument about the function and place of both humor and comedians in our society. Look for that argument as you read.

WHY WE LOVE LOUIS CK?—HIS PAINFUL HONESTY

By Troy Campbell

Louis CK, possibly the most respected modern comedian, digs deeply, almost uncomfortably into his own neuroses and behavior, often questioning his own and humans' general morality.

The audience cringes as he talks about murder, sexuality, and how he has so many strong noble beliefs but rarely follows them. He jokes about how irrationally mean he is to other drivers, how ungrateful we all are for modern wonders (e.g., flight), and how "maybe" we should allow people with allergies to die. It's dark stuff. With such dark stuff, how has Louis CK become the king of comedy?

A wealth of research by scientists like Boston College's Maya Tamir shows people often desire to take on negative thoughts and feelings. People find meaning in reflecting on negative topics and negative personal issues. Humans are not the pure shallow pleasure seekers we often think of them as. Instead, people find a sense of truth and purpose in pain. However, people also do not like to feel too much pain or threat.

Louis CK provides the best of both worlds. Through the safety of comedy he allows people to consider intense and threatening ideas. In doing so, his performances transform a night out into something special and meaningful.

In an interview, an amateur stand-up comedian once told me that, Louis CK is not my favorite comedian, but he's the one I respect the most because he is just so honest.

In his recent special *Oh My God* Louis CK does not fully touch on his signature style of confronting uncomfortable truths until the last 15 minutes. When watching the first 45 minutes of *Oh My God*, despite its observational funniness, it feels shallow. With this modern king of stand-up comedy, viewers have come to expect more than laughs.

From *The Huffington Post* (2013).

However, in the last 15 minutes of *Oh My God* Louis CK explodes into his signature style, questioning whether he would murder people if it were legal and then spinning further into "a lot of horrible thoughts in a row." And some how this miserableness is a lot more enjoyable.

The theater has always been a place not just for laughs, but for honesty, meaning, and self examination. Louis CK's standup plays out more like a Shakespearian comedy than a traditional stand-up performance hitting on all these notes. He gracefully bounces between lowbrow jokes and deceptively intense social commentary.

And unlike many stand-up comedians, Louis CK does not "baby" his audiences. Instead Louis CK directly brings his audience into the experience. When his audience cringes instead of laughs at one of his *Oh My God* jokes, he reminds them that they had laughed at a joke about letting allergy prone children die. He then tells them: you clapped for dead kids, you're in this with me. If Louis CK keeps hitting the punch lines on such humorous and poetic levels, we all be in this with him for a very long time.

Identify Troy Campbell's argument regarding the function and place of humor and comedians in our society. You may want to identify the assumptions that underlie comparison of Louis CK's stand-up to a "Shakespearian comedy."

If you have not seen Louis CK perform, find a clip of his performance on YouTube. Before watching the clip, write a "Things to Note" list. This list might include the following questions:

- How is this performance social commentary?
- What is the subject of the humor?
- Does meaning emerge in the humor?
- Does Louis CK's performance reinforce or challenge Leon Rappoport's ideas about gender humor? (See "Males versus Females, Gays versus Straights, and the Varieties of Gender Humor.")
- How would you classify Louis CK's humor?

Choose one or more of the questions on the "Thing to Note" list to write up and bring to class so that you can share your analysis with your classmates, and if your classroom is a "smart classroom" and you can share the YouTube video, be prepared to do so.

Building on the "Explore" exercise, write a fully-developed analysis of Louis CK and his humor. In this essay, you should present an argument or your position regarding how you view Louis CK's role *as* humorist. For this paper you may wish to look at Rappoport's book *Punchlines* to help you develop your ideas.

Marcia Clemmitt, a former editor-in-chief of Medicine & Health *and staff writer for* The Scientist, *is a seasoned-journalist who routinely reports on social-policy. The following three readings are part of her larger single-themed, 12,000-word report titled, "Shock Jokes: Should Racist and Misogynistic Speech Be Regulated?"*

_____

_____

ETHNIC HUMOR'S NO JOKE FOR AMATEURS

BY MARCIA CLEMMITT

It gets ugly when aggression overwhelms the humor.

Why did shock-radio host Don Imus call the Rutgers University women's basketball team "nappy-headed hos"? "I was trying to be funny," Imus explained on his April 9 broadcast, several days after the original comment had blown up into a full-fledged national brouhaha over whether racist and sexist jokes have become a blight on American media.

The debate goes on, in the wake of Imus' firing which critics arguing that stereotyping jokes have explosive potential and should be used with caution and, perhaps, not at all. But ethnic humor has a long and robust history, among jokers in public and in private, and few expect to see it abandoned any time soon.

In the 19th and early 20th century, ethnic humor was a staple of stage comedy, but its prevalence receded somewhat as radio brought comedy to the mass media, says Leon Rappoport, professor emeritus of psychology at Kansas State University and author of a recent book on ethnic humor.

The vaudeville stage abounded with "dialect humor," with stereotyped characters like "the operatic Italian" and "the money-grubbing Jew" that audiences easily recognized, Rappoport says. And in the early 20th century, when vaudevillians migrated to radio,

From *CQ Researcher* 17.21 (2007).

the stereotyping humor continued, Fred Allen's radio skits, for example, based their humor on stereotyped characters such as a fast-talking Irishman, a Jewish housewife and numerous others.

Gradually, however, radio comedy "got cleaned up," with ethnic humor mainly expunged, Rappoport says. As a new mass medium, supported by advertisers, radio needed to entice man while offending few, and ethnic jokes—"which can be very aggressive"—risked turning off too many in the unseen listening audience. By the early 1960s, however, ethnic jokes were being heard again in live comedy, by a new breed of edgy comics whose work was based on irony and social criticism, like Lenny Bruce.

Insult humor was briefly banished from public airways, but it returned beginning in the 1970s, says Sheri Parks, associate professor of American studies at the University of Maryland, College Park. Physical comedy and slapstick humor, often fairly violent once abounded in American mass culture, from Charlie Chaplin to the Three Stooges. But when a 1972 U.S. surgeon general's report declared that violence in media leads to real-life violence, comics once again were forced to find non-physically violent ways to make people laugh, says Parks.

And since a key element in much humor is aggression, comics switched from physical to verbal violence—including stereotyping humor, Parks says. Over the past few decades "insult has become the dominant mode of comedy."

There may be a serious problem with raising generations of children exposed on a daily basis to insult humor, television, radio and movies, Parks says. Adults believe when children see comedians and sitcom characters insulting each other aggressively "they know that it's unusual behavior that they shouldn't engage in," she says. "But in fact children look to media for normative behaviors, and when they see or hear something, they just go ahead and do it, too."

Adults like Imus may have a similar problem, according to Arthur Asa Berger, professor of broadcast and electronic communication arts at San Francisco State University and author of books on humor and humor writing. "Humor is a very dangerous thing. There's a lot of aggression in it, and when the aggression overwhelms the humor, we don't excuse" the "hostile" joker, he says.

Some professional comedians employ stereotypes "in a mirthful way," using the context of the joke to convince an audience that "they don't actually mean what they're saying" in a stereotyping joke about a drunken Irishman, for example, says Berger.

Professional humorists are always aware of their role and develop a sense of how far they can go to get a laugh or make a point without crossing the line into speech that the audience will read as hateful rather than funny or insightful, says Berger. "Comedians work very hard to do that," he says. "But when people who aren't humorists start messing around with humor," most don't even realize what the pitfalls are, he says.

When it comes to ethnic humor, most comedians agree that "anything goes as long as it's funny," says Rappoport. Nevertheless, "context and intent matter and there has to be a grain of truth to it," he says. Comics like Richard Pryor, Robin Williams and Chris Rock have joked about ethnic groups, their own and other people's, and "the audience finds itself laughing even if they don't want to," Rappoport says.

But ethnic humor can also spell trouble, if the joker leans too heavily on the ethnic and not enough on the humor, he says. "The thing about the Imus statement is simply that it isn't funny," says Rappoport. In the annals of humor, Imus is "a trivial footnote of somebody who went too far in the wrong context and then got what he deserved."

IS ETHNIC AND RACIAL HUMOR DANGEROUS?

YES: ARTHUR ASA BERGER

Ethnic humor divides as it derides. Societies generally contain many ethnic, racial and religious groups, each of which has distinctive cultural traits, beliefs and values. While ethnic humor may seem to be trivial, it corrodes our sense of community and makes to more difficult for us to live together harmoniously. It focuses on our differences and insults, attacks and humiliates it victims. It is based on stereotyping, which suggests that all members of various ethnic or other groups are the same as far as certain traits deemed "undesirable" by those who use ethnic humor are concerned. This humor can lead to feelings of inferiority and even self-hatred by members of groups attacked by it, while it coarsens and desensitizes those who use it.

Humor is an enigmatic matter that has fascinated our greatest philosophers and thinkers from Aristotle's time to the present. Scholars disagree about why we laugh, but two of the dominant theories about humor—Aristotle's view that it is based upon feelings of superiority and Freud's notion that it involves masked hostility and aggression—apply to ethnic humor.

There is an ethnocentric bias reflected in ethnic humor, a feeling held by those who use this humor that they are superior and that their cultural beliefs and values are the only correct ones. While ethnic humor is widespread—it's found in most countries—it varies considerably from mild teasing to terribly insulting and even vicious humor. Every society seems to find some minority "out-group" to ridicule. But sometimes ethnic humor—about Jews and African-Americans, for example—can easily become anti-Semitic and racist.

People who ridicule Jewish-American "princess" or "dumb Poles" and other ethnic groups think they are just being funny when they tell friends insulting riddles. We might ask "funny to whom?" Such humor isn't amusing to members of the groups that are ridiculed. Those who use ethnic humor feel that they can make fun of ethnic groups with impunity, but in multicultured societies, fortunately, that is no longer the case. The excuse given people who use ethnic humor, "I was trying to be funny," isn't acceptable anymore.

Humor can be liberating and has many benefits, but when it is used to ridicule and insult people, it is harmful to members of the ethnic groups that are victimized by this humor and to society at large. Ethnic humor isn't just a laughing matter.

NO: LEON RAPPOPORT

It is hard to think of any serious harm associated with ethnic humor if you have ever fallen down laughing at a routine by Whoopi Goldberg, Robin Williams or Chris Rock, or heard Jackie Mason's lines about the differences between Jews and gentiles. Yet controversies over humor based on ethnic, racial or gender stereotypes go all the way back to the plays of Aristophanes (circa 430 B.C.), and subsequent writers and performers from Shakespeare through Richard Pryor and Mel Brooks, have been catching flak about it ever since.

Modern social-science studies aimed at settling the harm question have not produced any smoking-gun evidence. The cautious conclusion of 2004 review of experimental research was that exposure to disparagement humor did not reinforce negative images of the targeted group. Relevant field studies have shown that people feel no significant malice when laughing at jokes based on ethnic stereotypes, and common-sense observations support this: Where all the suffering victims of the Polish jokes, dumb-blonde jokes, Jewish-American mother and princess jokes that have come and gone over recent years, not to mention the Lutherans, Catholics and Unitarians regularly worked over in Garrison Keillor's monologues on "A Prairie Home Companion?"

The prominent ethnic-humor scholar Christie Davies (author of three important books on the subject) maintains that laughter at such jokes has little to do with social attitudes but reflects the powerful surge of pleasure we tend to feel from "playing with aggression." And this includes members of the group being ridiculed, who often are most amused by clever takes on the stereotypes they know best. This was clearly true among hundreds of diverse college students who took the class on ethnic humor I taught for several years. They would frequently be particularly carried away with laughter when seeing videos of comedians playing with ironic clichés about their own ethnic, racial or gender group. Like most Americans today, these students grew up in our humor-saturated TV culture and are thus well prepared to maintain a health sense of critical distance while enjoying satire, parody and ridicule—remember Boris and Natasha on "Bullwinkle"?—in the context of ethnic humor.

Part of what holds our increasingly multiethnic society together is our rich stock of ethnic humor. The fact that we can play with our differences, even at the risk of occasionally offending each other, deserves recognition as a matter of pride rather than prejudice.

What points does Clemmitt offer to develop and support the title of her piece, "Ethnic Humor's No Joke for Amateurs"? What information do you find the most effective in explaining ethnic humor's place in American society? Why? What further questions about racial humor arose for you when you read this piece?

In "Ethnic Humor's No Joke for Amateurs," Clemmitt summarizes or paraphrases Associate Professor of American studies, Sheri Parks. Parks points to a 1972 U.S. surgeon general's report linking violence in media to "real-life violence" as one of the reasons comics switched to humor dependent on verbal rather than physical aggression (physical/slapstick comedy). Conduct your own research on media's influence on "real life," looking specifically for studies on depictions of aggressive or insult humor in the media and the effects of these depictions. Use your library's databases or the Internet to locate at least two studies more recent than the 1972 report that Parks references.

In a 2–3 page paper, summarize and synthesize this information and write a concluding paragraph that explains what you find significant about your research. In other words, what conclusions did you draw about how the humor that surrounds us affects how we think about and interact with others?

You have now read three pieces on ethnic humor—one piece, "Ethnic Humor's No Joke for Amateurs," which offers some context for ethnic humor in the United States, and two opinion pieces, by leading scholars in the field of humor studies. Now it's your turn to weigh in on this issue. Write a position paper expressing your stance regarding the place and use of ethnic-racial humor in our society today. You are answering the following question: "Does ethnic and racial humor do more harm than good?"

In your paper, you must include support culled from Clemmitt's, Berger's, or Rappoport's pieces. If you did "Explore" above, you might find that research or several of the other readings in *Funny* helpful (Bailey, Rice, Tapley, Colletta, Baumgartner and Morris).

Jason Bailey is a film editor at Flavorwire and graduate of the Cultural Reporting and Criticism program at New York University's Arthur L. Carter Journalism Institute. His book, Pulp Fiction: The Complete Story of Quentin Tarantino's Masterpiece *was published in 2013, and his writings appear in various publications such as* The Atlantic, Slate, Salon, *and* The Village Voice. *This cultural journalist's treatment of the 1974 film* Blazing Saddles *adds another dimension to the ongoing conversation regarding racial and ethnic humor, its dangers, its complications, and its promise.*

REVISITING MEL BROOKS AND RICHARD PRYOR'S SUBVERSIVELY BRILLIANT RACIAL SATIRE *BLAZING SADDLES*, 40 YEARS LATER

BY JASON BAILEY

For more than two decades now, the term "politically correct" has been, almost exclusively, the go-to refrain for reactionary scum and regressive cultural conservatives, bellowing self-righteously at the civilization's hardheaded refusal to let them share their rape jokes or race gags or "feminazi" screeds in peace. Such complaints usually take a tone of wistful nostalgia, longing for a time when the "Thought Police" weren't on constant patrol (and, thus, white men could pretty much do whatever they damn well pleased), so it's with some care and concern that we take up the topic of one of the great comedy films, *Blazing Saddles*, which turns 40 years old this week. It is a film that, by almost any reasonable standard, is "politically incorrect"; likewise, it is a film that is all but impossible to imagine getting the green light today (from a major studio like Warner Brothers, anyway). But its genius, then and now, was the manner in which director Mel Brooks and his writers turned a broad Western spoof into what was, for its time, a revolutionary satire of race relations.

A bit of background, if (shame on you) you're unfamiliar with the film: *Blazing Saddles* is set in the Old West, in the town of Rock Ridge, which has been targeted by the local railroad. A corrupt politician named Hedley Lamarr (Harvey Korman) wants to get his hands on the town's land before the railroad buys it up, so he figures he can drive out the small-minded locals by appointing Bart (Cleavon Little), a black railroad worker on his way to the hangman's noose, as their sheriff. The town is, to put it mildly, unwelcoming, but after Bart becomes friends with local legend The Waco Kid (Gene Wilder) and tames

---

From the *New York Daily News* (2013).

the savage Mongo (Alex Karras), he joins forces with the townfolk to keep Lamarr's villainous scourges at bay.

Now, some context: In spite of tremendous political and social upheaval, race relations were still barely up for discussion in mainstream cinema. Sidney Poitier had carried the torch for much of the 1960s, but his two most explicitly race-themed pictures, *In the Heat of the Night* and *Guess Who's Coming to Dinner*, were only seven years in the rearview when *Blazing Saddles* was released in February 1974. *Shaft* and *Super Fly* had kicked off the "blaxpoitation" movement in 1971 and 1972, respectively—but those films were geared primarily to a black audience (and they certainly found one). What *Blazing Saddles* brought to the discussion was a film with a black hero, aimed at white audiences, that was primarily about bass-ackwards white racism. It was a movie that laughed with its black protagonist, and laughed at the crackers who got in his way.

And it was a comedy that used what we now carefully refer to as "the n-word." It is used frequently and freely; it is used in casual dialogue and it is used as a punch line. But it's not used for shock value—it is used as it would have been used at the time, and, as Brooks explained, "to show racial prejudice. And we didn't show it from good people, but from bad people who didn't know any better." Still, Brooks was smart enough to know he could both cover his bases and come up with a richer movie by getting an African-American voice on the page, and that was how Richard Pryor got involved.

The film was originally devised as a script called *Tex X*, by a young screenwriter named Andrew Bergman (who later wrote and directed *The Freshman* and *Honeymoon in Vegas*, among others). His idea, in a nutshell, was "H. Rap Brown in the Old West," and the film nearly came together in 1971 with Alan Arkin directing and James Earl Jones in the leading role. But when that project fell apart, the script went into turnaround, which was how it landed on Mel Brooks' desk. Brooks was in a career funk; though he'd won the Oscar for *The Producers*, that award hadn't translated to box office, and his follow-up *The Twelve Chairs* had flopped badly. He wasn't all that interested in directing someone else's script, but his son Max (who would go on to write *World War Z*) had just been born, and he needed a job.

Brooks got the idea of rewriting Bergman's screenplay the way he used to write sketches on *Your Show of Shows*: get a bunch of funny people in a room, get them going, trying to top each other, and just bang it out. He put Bergman in that room, along with a lawyer-turned-writer named Norman Steinberg and his writing partner, a dentist-turned-writer named Alan Uger. But Pryor was the key. He was still a rising young comic (his breakthrough album, *That Nigger's Crazy*, came out three months after *Blazing Saddles*), but his style and voice were firmly in place: he was talking on stage, openly and without boundaries, about matters of race. He was breaking apart stereotypes and assumptions. He was laughing at white people, and white people were laughing along with him.

One would assume that Pryor was mostly responsible for the race-based humor in *Blazing Saddles*, but Brooks has emphasized that it wasn't nearly as simple as that. In recent documentaries about both himself and Pryor, he's said that Pryor's primary interest was in the character of giant simpleton Mongo ("Mongo only pawn in game of life"); elsewhere, he's said, "Pryor wrote the Jewish jokes, the Jews wrote the black jokes." In other words, it wasn't a matter of who wrote what; it was that with Brooks allowing the ship to go anywhere, and a visionary comic voice like Pryor contributing (and, it seems, serving as a kind of permission slip to go wherever the story might take them), anyone could write *anything*.

That "anything goes" spirit resonates throughout *Blazing Saddles*, a comedy that throws everything at you: nonsensical wordplay, Jewish references, wild sight gags (the hangman stringing up a man in a wheelchair, or both a man and the horse he sits atop), leering, historical anachronisms, scatology (the famed "baked beans" scene, which isn't about farts, but the sheer *volume* of them), cheerful vulgarity (a hymn that ends "our town is turning into shit"), genre conventions, celebrity parody (via Madeline Kahn's uproarious Marlene Dietrich vamp), Keystone-style slapstick (there's a pie fight, for God's sake), and breaking the fourth wall—most famously in its climax, which follows the action right off the Warner lot and to a screening of *Blazing Saddles* at Grauman's Chinese.

(Side note: it is by now part of the film's legend that Brooks badly wanted Pryor to play the lead role of Bart, and that he was vetoed by Warner brass, who were worried by both Pryor's minimal film experience and reputation as an unreliable wild man. Poor Cleavon Little, who is very good in the film, will be forevermore compared to the Pryor performance that could have been—a hypothetical that is cruel not only when imagining what he could have done with Pryor-esque bits like that first scene in Rock Ridge, but when noting that it would have paired him with Gene Wilder two years before *Silver Streak*, the first of their four film collaborations.)

Yet the film's primary satirical target, even more than the Panavision Technicolor vistas of the American Western, is racism, and how it is the intellectual property of "simple farmers . . . people of the land. The common clay of the new West. You know . . . morons." As Brooks promises, those who call Bart the n-word are mouth-breathing morons, ignorant hillbillies who share their saloon and town council meetings with cows. Bart, on the other hand, is smart, funny, and handsome, a Gucci saddlebag-sporting cool customer. "What's a dazzling urbanite like you doing in a rustic setting like this?" asks the Waco Kid, not unreasonably; when Bart outsmarts the town by taking himself hostage at his welcoming ceremony, he tells himself, "You are so talented, and they are *so dumb*."

That dichotomy is established early, when Bart is still a railroad worker, and Taggart (Slim Pickens) asks the crew to regale him with "a good ol' nigger work song." Bart and his colleagues respond with a golden-throated rendition of the very white Cole Porter's "I Get a Kick Out of You," which Taggart interrupts with the suggestion of "Camptown Races" (which he incorrectly dubs "Camptown Ladies"). The title prompts puzzled looks and confusion from the crew, so Taggart and his gang perform it *for* the workers, who proceed to watch their supposed betters sing and dance, and barely stifle their laughter.

That dynamic is all the more apparent in *Blazing Saddles'* only genuinely offensive scene, which comes near the end, during the film's raucous takeover of the WB lot. The climactic fight scene spills onto the set of a tux-and-tails musical, where the mincing director and hissing, "sissy" dancers are thrown into the action. It's a wince-inducing scene on its own, but a sharp and valuable contrast to the rest of the film—because this is a scene of just pointing and laughing at a minority. Because it did that wrong, we can fully appreciate what the rest of the movie does so right.

But *Blazing Saddles* doesn't just laugh at racism and leave it at that. Perhaps the most quietly poignant scene in the picture comes after Bart begins to win over the town by taking down Mongo with a *Looney Tunes*-style exploding Candygram (the toughest part, he later explains, was "inventing the Candygram . . . they probably won't give me credit for it"). The sweet little old lady who earlier greeted him with an odious "Up yours, nigger!" brings him a warm pie as a thank you, and they exchange pleasantries. Moments later, she returns with an additional request: "Of course you have the good taste not to mention that I spoke to you?" If, as Brooks said, "the Jews wrote the black jokes," that feels like one that had to have come from Pryor: an acknowledgement, as in the best of his work, that it's all good and well to laugh at this stuff, but there's real pain there too.

Identify the tone of Bailey's piece on *Blazing Saddles*. Is that tone consistent throughout the entire piece? If not, then explain where and why Baily shifts his tone. What do you think is Bailey's main purpose or argument in this piece? What passages best express and/or support that purpose/argument?

Collaborate

Working with a group of your classmates, use a device (smartphone, tablet, laptop, iPad) to find either a video or online interview with Mel Brooks about *Blazing Saddles.* As you listen to or read the interview, note specifically what Brooks says about Richard Pryor's involvement in the film, about Brooks's and/or Pryor's intentions regarding the use of racial humor, and Brooks's larger understanding of how humor works.

Also watch a video clip from the film (ideally one clearly illustrating the use of racial humor).

Then read or revisit Marcia Clemmitt's "Ethnic Humor's No Joke for Amateurs," and the opinion pieces by "Is Ethnic and Racial Humor Dangerous" by Arthur Asa Berger and Leon Rappoport.

Using Bailey's observations and claims and your notes from the Brooks's interviews and the film clips, write an opinion piece as if you were Mel Brooks. In other words, add Brooks's voice to the debate about the danger or efficacy of ethnic and racial humor.

Compose

View *Blazing Saddles* and, in a 3–4 page paper analyze its use of racial humor. As you develop your analysis, consider the historical/social context of the film's production and release date (1974) and identify the specific ethnic/racial issues the film addresses. Bailey calls *Blazing Saddles* "a subversively brilliant racial satire," and other critics also identify it as a satire. Therefore, in your analysis, you must acknowledge this aspect of the film.

David Wall Rice's writings appear in The Washington Post, Vibe, Ebony.com, *and* The Root. *He is an Associate Professor at Morehouse College. Like Troy Campbell in "Why We Love Louis CK?—His Painful Honesty," Rice works on specific assumptions about how humor and comedians can function in society. Although assumptions can be difficult to identify, as you read, look for where Rice's assumptions (stated or unstated) seem to intersect with those of Campbell.*

THE GENIUS OF *CHAPPELLE'S SHOW* 10 YEARS LATER

BY DAVID WALL RICE

"Name your price in the beginning. If it ever gets more expensive than the price you name, get out of there."

> —William David Chappelle III as recounted by his son,
> David Chappelle, on *Inside the Actors Studio*, February 2006

It's easier to go broad than to go narrow when it comes to *Chappelle's Show*. The sketch-serial that first premiered January 22, 2003 has never really been out of rotation. Whether through Comedy Central syndication or clips on their website, the ever-present, half-hour brainchild of Dave Chappelle and co-creator Neal Brennan gives little distance for reflection even though the last patchwork of a show was pushed out way back in 2006. The default, then, is to speak in broad strokes about the cable network behemoth. It broke television-to-DVD sales records and made Dave Chappelle a rich Hollywood oddity, leaving the show at what seemed to be the height of its success.

Chappelle's Show was good, but the show alone was not particularly novel. The clever digs at current times, its commentary on social-political goings-on and scatological humor, were updates of early *Martin* and *In Living Color*. But it was more personally styled, more solidly grounded in the quick wit of Charlie Murphy and the wisdom of Paul Mooney. The show's familiarity and the Chappelle/Brennan cult classic *Half Baked* demonstrated a team capable of solving the Rubik's Cube of new millennium comedy. There were

From *Ebony* (2013).

similarities around content, but the television and motion picture comedy of Chappelle didn't proselytize the way Chris Rock from 1997 to 2000 did over on HBO (*The Chris Rock Show*).

Still, there was an "afflict the comfortable" mentality built into *Chappelle's Show*. Dave and Neal's *Frankenstein* was raw in a way that could grate certain people. It didn't have the cartoon filter of their contemporary, comic-strip cousin, *The Boondocks*. Volatile truths were told that had no deference to social niceties; though there was a healthy respect for their presence, it was their fourth wall. The show was subversive like the best hip-hop artists—Chappelle's peers—were at the time.

The sketches, intro music by the militant hip-hop duo dead prez, cameos by Wayne Brady and John Mayer, and the integration of Chappelle's parents' professorial sensibilities reflected his developing identity. The best of *Chappelle's Show* placed his narratives as devices for insight into modern tropes of culture and context that were far much more accessible and impactful in the everyday than academic journal articles and lectures.

[*Chappelle's Show*] proved important satire until it wasn't satire anymore, so then it stopped. Its greatest fans always knew *Chappelle's Show* was subversively about more than just some jokes.

Chappelle's scathing critiques were tempered with a juvenile silliness, a slippery slope. Silliness was privileged over incisive commentary. Sometimes it threatened to compromise the more sophisticated turns, making them little more than shuffles, i.e., that dude who'd randomly pop up doing the robot in otherwise unrelated skits. Base humor came to define the very popular show, and many saw it as a sell-out move because of an imbalance that stressed puerile sensibilities over revolutionary insights. His Rick James "I'm rich, b*tch" catchphrase trumped skits like the "Racial Draft," "President Black Bush" and so on.

Still, the partnering with mainstream wants and expectations seemed necessary for the important lesson the show's grinding-halt of an ending produced. In 2005 Dave Chappelle dipped from his series production and never returned. The details of his walking away from the show after signing a two-year deal worth a reported $50 million was presented in the media as complicated and weird. But in February 2006, Chappelle quite plainly explained on *The Oprah Winfrey Show*, "I felt like [the show] got me in touch with my inner coon, they stirred him up. When we were doing that [sketch that sparked his departure] and that guy laughed, I felt like they got me."

That level of public self-reflection and commentary makes *Chappelle's Show* particularly watershed in the space of modern culture, beyond the 1.2 million DVDs sold in its first week of release, or the multimillion dollar deal it locked down. Dave proved the show's dead prez bass hum intro music and its social critique was more than rhetorical. It had roots. Ultimately, Dave Chappelle leaving his show was a powerful act of liberation, because it was done unapologetically in front of everyone, Richard Pryor style.

Chappelle's Show remains dope because it was a process, not a goal. It proved important satire until it wasn't satire anymore, so then it stopped. Its greatest fans always knew it was always about more than just some jokes. The show and Dave Chappelle's framing of it was really all about truth telling, the highest art.

In the headnote I asked you to look for similarities between Rice's assumptions about how humor and comedians function in society and those of Campbell in "Why We Love Louis CK—His Painful Honesty." What are those assumptions, and where do they intersect with those of Campbell?

Rice refers to a variety of comedians, writers, actors, TV shows, and movies, and he also assumes his readers know the circumstances surrounding Chappelle's departure from *Chappelle's Show*. Using the Internet find information on the individuals, shows, and movies to which Rice refers, even if you are familiar with most of these references. In addition, find the complete story of why Chappelle left his show at the height of its success. Once you have filled in these gaps or refamiliarized yourself with these references, reread Rice's essay. Then write two or three paragraphs describing and comparing your two readings experiences. What conclusions can you draw about how one should read or approach an article like Rice's with so many references? What conclusions can you draw about Rice's understanding of his audience?

Watch several episodes of *Chappelle's Show* and then choose one to analyze as an example of "important satire" to quote Rice. In a 3-4 page essay, identify the social issue that the show addresses, describe how it addresses that issue, point out the elements of satire in the show, and, finally, evaluate its effectiveness as satire.

Dave Barry identifies himself as a professional humorist. In addition to writing a nationally syndicated humor column for The Miami Herald *(1983-2005), he has written more than 30 books (fiction, nonfiction, young adult), and won a Pulitzer Prize for commentary. "Technology," a chapter from* I'll Mature When I'm Dead: Dave Barry's Amazing Tales of Adulthood, *opens with a nostalgic look at the "good old days" before moving to the current reality of technological connectedness.*

TECHNOLOGY

BY DAVE BARRY

There was a time when the human race did not have technology. This time was called "the 1950s." I was a child then, and it was horrible. There were only three TV channels, and at any given moment at least two of them were showing men playing the accordion in black and white. There was no remote control, so if you wanted to change the channel, you had to yell at your little brother, "Phil! Change the channel!" (In those days people named their children "Phil.")

Your household had one telephone, which weighed eleven pounds and could be used as a murder weapon. It was permanently tethered to the living-room wall, and you had to dial it by manually turning a little wheel, and if you got a long-distance call, you'd yell, "It's long distance!" in the same urgent tone you would use to yell "Fire!" Everybody would come sprinting into the living room, because in the 1950s long distance was more exciting than sex. In fact there *was* no sex in the 1950s, that I know of.

There were automobiles, but they lacked many of the features that automobiles have today, such as a working motor. In the Barry household, we had a series of cars named (these were all real Barry cars) the "Rambler," the "Minx," the "Metropolitan," and the "Valiant." You could rely on these cars—rain or shine, hot or cold—to not start. The "Metropolitan," in particular, was no more capable of internal combustion than of producing a litter of puppies.

From *I'll Mature When I'm Dead: Dave Barry's Amazing Tales of Adulthood* (New York: Berkley Books, 2012): 55-64.

There also were computers in those days, but they filled entire rooms and weighed many tons. An ill-advised effort by IBM to market one of these in the "laptop" configuration was abandoned when the first test user was converted into what the medical examiner's report described as "basically a human pizza twelve feet in diameter."

This pre-technology era was especially brutal for young people. We had no Wii. Mainly what we had to play with was rocks, which we had to throw at each other by hand. What few toys we had were lame, like the Slinky, which did basically one thing: go down stairs. And it did that only in the TV commercials, which apparently were filmed on a planet with much more gravity. Here on the Earth, the Slinky went down maybe two steps, then fell over on its side, twitched, and died, like a snake having a heart attack.

We also had the Wheel-0. This was a toy that, by federal law, was issued to every American boy and girl who was alive during the Eisenhower administration. The Wheel-0 consisted of a red wheel and a wire frame:

> The wheel stuck to the frame because of magnetism, which was a new and much more exciting force back then. To play with your Wheel-0, you tilted the frame so the wheel rolled down, then up, then down, then up, and so on. Before you knew it, two minutes had flown by, and it was time to go outside and throw rocks.

The most technologically advanced toy I had was the Erector Set, which was a box containing hundreds of metal pieces, gears, bolts, nuts, washers, etc., along with instructions showing how to assemble these into projects such as a miniature Ferris wheel that actually rotated. This required many hours of effort, but I found that if I followed the instructions carefully, I learned something important: I could never, ever, make an object that looked anything like the miniature Ferris wheel in the instruction book. What

I produced looked more like a tragic miniature building collapse. That is why I became an English major.

We have come a long way since the 1950s. Today we have technology up the wazoo,[1] and we use it constantly in our every day lives. Consider, for example, my typical morning routine:

> For openers, I sleep next to an alarm clock that is accurate to something like one jillionth of a second. This is because it receives wireless signals from the official U.S. atomic clock, which as its name suggests is a clock made out of atoms, making it very small and difficult to wind. Half the time the government scientists can't even find it. ("Dang! I think I sucked the atomic clock up my nose again!") But it's very accurate, so when I go to bed at night and set my alarm clock for 7 A.M., I know for a fact that in the morning I will be awakened at precisely 5:43 A.M., because that is when my dog, Lucy, decides that it's time to go out.

Lucy is also part of the high-tech revolution: She contains a tiny implanted microchip, which can identify her if she runs off, which is not an unlikely scenario given that she has the IQ of a radish. Actually, that's not fair. If you feed and care for a radish, it will have the sense to stay with you. Whereas Lucy would leave in a heartbeat with anybody. A machete-wielding lunatic could come to our house, hack us to tiny pieces, then whistle to Lucy, and she would cheerfully follow him away, especially if he was holding her squeaky toy.

So anyway, at 5:43 A.M. sharp, according to the U.S. atomic clock, Lucy and I head out to the backyard so she can initiate the complex process of finding an acceptable place to poop. I think that while they're implanting chips in dogs, they should implant one in the dog's brain, assuming they can find it, that would allow you to make your dog poop by remote control. As it is, I have to wait while Lucy sniffs, one by one, every single odor molecule in our yard before settling on the exact spot where she has pooped 1,378 consecutive times.

In the old low-tech days, I would spend this idle backyard time standing around scratching myself with both hands. But now, thanks to technology, I scratch with just the one hand, while using the other one to be productive on my cell phone. With this amazing device, I can send and receive e-mail and text messages, surf the Internet, pay my bills, book flights, play games, take pictures, listen to music, watch TV shows—in short almost anything except reliably make or receive telephone calls. For some reason, cellular telephones lack that capability. It's as if they made a washing machine that mowed your lawn and made daiquiris, but if you put your actual clothes into it, they burst into flames.

1 I mean this literally. Medical researchers at UCLA recently fitted a fifty-seven-year-old man with a working artificial wazoo.

But my point is that while Lucy is inhaling her way around the yard, I am using cell-phone technology to get things done. I am reading e-mails offering to sell me male-enhancement products so powerful that I will need a wheelbarrow to cart my privates around. I am also reading e-mails from available women on other continents who are hoping to strike up a friendship with me that could blossom into a deeper relationship with the promise—someday—of exchanging intimate personal financial data.

I can also use my phone to go to Facebook and Twitter to read messages and "tweets" from a vast network of people I do not really know, updating me on their random neural firings on such issues as what they are eating. In the old pre-technology days, it would have been almost impossible to replicate Facebook or Twitter. The closest you could get would be to mail dozens of postcards a day to everybody you knew, each with a brief message about yourself like: "Finally got that haircut I've been putting off." Or: "Just had a caramel frappuccino. Yum!"

The people receiving these postcards would have naturally assumed that you were a moron with a narcissism disorder. But today, thanks to Facebook and Twitter, you are seen as a person engaging in "social networking." As the technology improves, we'll reach the point when you don't even need a phone to socially network. You'll have some kind of device implanted in your brain so you can receive other people's brain waves directly as they occur. You will know *everything* about them. You will know when they *fart*.

Speaking of which: When Lucy finally decides, after much deliberation and a minimum of eight full clockwise rotations of her body, to poop on exactly the same spot for the 1,379th consecutive time, we head into the house. The sun isn't even up yet, and I have already, using handheld technology with just one hand, wasted more time than my father did in an entire day.

And I am just getting started. In the kitchen, I turn on a TV set that has hundreds[2] of channels devoted to every conceivable subject including celebrity bunion removal. I tune in to one of the literally dozens of news shows, all of which feature a format of 55 percent celebrities promoting things, 30 percent e-mails from viewers, and 15 percent YouTube videos showing bears jumping on trampolines. While I'm catching up on these developments, I turn on the programmable coffeemaker, which I hope that someday, perhaps by attending community college, I will learn to program. Then I take a breakfast "sausage" made of processed tofu from the freezer and pop it into the microwave oven, which in seconds converts it from a frozen, unappetizing gray cylinder into a piping hot unappetizing gray cylinder. It performs this culinary miracle by bombarding the frozen tofu with atomic radiation—the very same deadly force that, back in the 1950s, caused insects to mutate into savage monster killers the

---

2 This week: David Hasselhoff.

size of Charles Barkley, now harnessed by modem technology for peaceful breakfast purposes.

OK, that might not be 100 percent technically accurate. The truth is, I don't really know how my microwave oven works. I also don't know how my cell phone works, or my TV, or my computer, or my iPod, or my OPS, or my camera that puts nineteen thousand pictures inside a tiny piece of plastic, which is obviously NOT PHYSICALLY POSSIBLE, but there it is. Basically all I know about these devices is how to turn them on, and if they stop working, I know I should turn them off and then turn them back on, because usually this makes them resume working. If it doesn't, I know I need to buy a new device, because nobody in the entire world knows how to fix a broken one.

Don't get me wrong: I love technology. I don't want to go back to the days when people had to churn their own butter and make their own sausage by going out to the barn and personally slaughtering tofus. But it bothers me that I depend on so many things that operate on principles I do not remotely understand, and which might not even be real.

Take "digital" technology. At some point (I think during the Clinton administration) all media-photographs, TV, movies, music, oven thermometers, pornography, doorbells, etc.—became "Digital." If you ask a technical expert what this means, he or she will answer that the information is, quote, "broken down into ones and zeros." Which sounds good, doesn't it? Ones and zeros! Those are digits, all right!

But here's the problem. Say you're watching a TV show. Say it's *24*, starring Kiefer Sutherland as Jack Bauer, the angst-ridden lone-wolf federal agent who protects America from terrorism by sooner or later causing the violent death of pretty much everybody he meets. If you study this show carefully, you will notice something curious: *Jack Bauer never goes to the bathroom.* That's why he's so ridden with angst.

But the other curious thing you will notice is that no matter how close you get to the TV screen—even if you get one inch away and examine the picture (I have done this) with a magnifying glass, so that any given one of Jack Bauer's nostrils is the size of the Lincoln Tunnel—you *cannot see any ones or zeros.* They're lying to us about that.

Why is this? My theory—and bear in mind that I have won several journalism awards— is that the "experts" don't really know how any of this technology works either. All they know is that it arrives here in boxes from China. I don't know where the Chinese are getting it, but I do know that they're not making it themselves. I have been to China, and if the Chinese had any grasp of technology, they would have better toilets.

So the bottom line is that we have become totally dependent in our daily lives on technology that nobody understands and that could be coming from (this is speculation) space. What if all this technology is some kind of sneak alien invasion force? What if one day all these devices rose up and attacked us? What if, for example, all the Bluetooth phone earpieces in the world suddenly sprouted drill bits and bored into people's brains?

OK, that particular example would actually be fine. But you see my point, don't you? If so, could you send me an e-mail or tweet explaining it?

No, seriously, my point is that technology is a blessing, but it is also a serious potential threat to humanity in general. Somebody needs to look into this. I'd do it myself, but right now I can't. My atomic-clock alarm is going off, signaling that it's 7 A.M., which means it's time for me to go back to bed.

Invent

What do you think is the point of "Technology," by Dave Barry? What passages do you consider most effectively convey this point? Why? Explain your answers to a classmate. Working with this classmate, discuss *how* Barry conveys his message. Consider the following questions as you look at the various techniques and strategies that Barry uses to make his points: Does he use irony? Understatement? Hyperbole? What about tone? Is it consistent throughout the piece? If not, where does it shift and why? Are these shifts effective? Distracting? At whom does he poke fun? Why? Be prepared to share your ideas with the entire class.

Collaborate

Choose several of your classmates with whom to work. Begin your conversation by describing how and how often each of you uses technology daily. Have someone in your group record your conversation. Working from these notes create a visual representation—a chart, graph, table—of this information. Once you have created this visual, put it in conversation with Dave Barry's piece, "Technology," by pulling a quote from the text that you think captures the data on the chart, graph, or table. Think about your visual as an illustration of Barry's text or conversely Barry's text as an explanation for your chart. Be prepared to explain your choice to the class.

Compose

Write your own creative nonfiction piece about your relationship with technology. Before you begin reread "Technology" and note what makes this piece successful. Note Barry's inclusion of specific details, descriptions, narration, and, of course, humor!

Oxford Dictionary designated selfie the 2013 Word of the Year. According to Oxford a selfie is "a photograph that one has taken of oneself, typically one taken with a smartphone or webcam and uploaded to a social media website," and the research conducted by the dictionary's editors showed a 17,000% increase in the frequency of the word selfie between November 2012 and November 2013 (Oxford.com). "Short Imagined Monologues" is a regular column on McSweeny's Internet Tendency, an online humor site. Each author of the monologue writes from the point of a real or fictitious character, and in so doing offers observations about and insights into a particular topic.

SELFIE'S WORD OF THE YEAR ACCEPTANCE SPEECH

By Rachel Callman

OMFG. For real, I just can't even right now! I mean, it makes total sense, but Word of The Year? That's such an honor. This really means a lot to me—#nofilter. Especially because there were some great words this year. I mean, I did this the hard way though, with dedication and God. Not all of us can say that. I'm looking at you, Twerk.

But Tweeps? You were on my level the whole way up. I partially have my Tweeps to thank for WINNING this thing. Without all of you ignoring your friends and family and just focusing on getting that one perfect, tweet-ready shot of just yourself, where would I be? Probably in a garbage bag instead of a hashtag, amiright?

All kidding aside, it really is amazing to be up here tonight, looking down at company I never thought I'd be in, like GIF, he's in the audience and he literally cannot sit still. It really is amazing. And though it might not seem like it, because some have called me a hero, I really am humble.

They do have a point though. See, it was just a few years ago people would spend hours getting ready to go out, just to go to a dark club where no one would see how perfectly their lip gloss matched the bra under their see-through shirt. What did this lead to? It lead to America's number one killer: depression. And I single-handedly pulled these

From *McSweeny's* (2013).

souls out of their despair and literally gave them a reason to get dressed in the morning. A reason to put on gym clothes. A reason to pucker up and get their duck on, for crying out loud. (*Dodges a wine glass.*) Oh come on, I'm sorry Facebook, but don't get your Depends in a twist. Times are changing and you aren't really keeping up. But hey, I will admit that you were an original at one point, so no hard feelings, #followforfollow man.

Let's move on, I have quite a few thank yous to dole out and I already hear the muzak starting up.

I'd like go back for a minute and thank online dating sites, who really helped me break on the scene back when I was known just as Bathroom Selfie. Laugh all you want. I came up from the bottom. Holler back, Drake. So all of you shirtless men out there, thank you so much for taking all of that time trying to get the perfect angle in the bathroom mirror, where it looks like one might almost just barely see your naughty bits.

And traffic, boredom, working out, loneliness, I know you all get a bad rap, but we're cool. You've really been supportive too.

But of course, I've saved the best for last, my dear Instagram. (*Holds hands over heart.*) In. Sta. Gram. OMFG. You. If I needed a soulmate, it would be you. Every meaningful #throwbackthursday I have is with you, my friend. If it weren't for you and our late nights with the Kardashians and Rihanna, I don't even know where I would be. I mean, probably still here, but a word needs biffles. #Instalove to you all.

Oh, looks like I really have gone over the time limit. Just real quick, digital cameras, smart phones, photobooth—you guys rock! If I could just ask the escorts to step out of the frame really quickly, need to get a shot of myself up here. Perfect #picoftheday. Thanks!

Can we read Rachel Callman's "Selfie's Word of the Year Acceptance Speech" as more than a mere entertainment—as some humorous piece of writing? If so, what do you see as its value? Does it provide insights into the influence of social media in today's society? If so, what are those insights? What specific passages or phrases do you find funny *and* also revealing? What specific elements does Callman use in "Selfie's Word of the Year Acceptance Speech" that you have encountered in other readings in *Funny*? How would you characterize her use of humor?

Rachel Callman's piece appeared on *Timothy McSweeney's Internet Tendency*, a daily humor website (http://www.mcsweeneys.net/tendency). Visit and explore the website. Find information about its creator, function, submission guidelines, and audience. Read several selections from the various categories and choose a representative sample to bring to class. Based on these samples and the information you found about the website, what general conclusions can you draw about humor? About its social function? What kinds of humor did you run across on this website?

In some ways, Callman's piece updates or complements Dave Barry's "Technology." If you have not done so, read "Technology" and write a 3-4 page essay analyzing how each writer conveys his or her message. In this analysis, you should address the following elements: tone, rhetorical context, audience, purpose. Your essay should indicate that you understand each writer's message and whether you find their presentation of that message effective.

MAJOR ASSIGNMENTS

MAJOR ASSIGNMENT #1:
EXPLAINING THE CONCEPT OF HUMOR

BACKGROUND

Thinkers as far back as Plato have been fascinated by humor and its complex nature. Humor can be simultaneously very personal and idiosyncratic, culturally specific and, because of the Internet and social media, transcultural. As you have discovered in your reading, scholars in many fields study the various aspects of humor, and as they do so, they introduce and explain concepts in order to convey their information, support their arguments, clarify their analyses, and communicate their purpose. We encounter concepts all the time. Sometimes we pause to think critically about them. Humor is a concept—something abstract, like love, justice, nationalism. *Funny* asks you to think critically about this concept in all its expansiveness.

ASSIGNMENT

Write a paper explaining the concept of humor. Writers have many options regarding how to convey their message to readers. However, because concepts are critical to how we understand almost any subject, writers must explain them fully and clearly, and more importantly, **they must convey why the explanation matters**. As you consider your approach to this assignment, revisit the readings in this book, your class notes, and any written assignments related to the topic. This material provides a good starting place for you to explain the concept of humor.

QUESTIONS FOR RESEARCH AND INVENTION

1. What most intrigues you about humor?

2. What aspects seem most important to you and which do you want to stress?

3. What information do you think most people already know about humor?

4. What faulty assumptions might people have about humor?

5. What terms or theories might you need to include and define?

GENERAL TIPS ABOUT EXPLAINING A CONCEPT

*   Remember your "task" is twofold: to help your readers understand and care about the concept. Therefore, as you develop your paper, keep the second goal in mind by checking to see if you make this subject interesting. Do you present the material in a way that your readers will want to know about it? Do you make your observations, explanations, and commentary relevant to your readers? In other words, can you answer their "So what?" question?

*   Definition: Defining terms, jargon, or theories is a critical aspect of explaining a concept. Think carefully about what strategies of definition you will use. Will you use sentence definitions, extended definitions, historical definitions, some or all of these methods? Your instructor will be a good source of guidance here, as will be your peers and your campus writing center.

*   Illustration/examples: The examples that you choose should best represent the specific point you wish to clarify, and these examples should also be relevant to your overall purpose, helping readers understand and care about the concept.

*   Sources: Your instructor may or may not require research for this assignment; however, a successful explanation of a concept almost always includes information from other sources. Writers incorporate this information through summaries, paraphrases, and direct quotations, using proper in-text documentation.

MAJOR ASSIGNMENT #2:
ANALYSIS OF THE RHETORIC OF HUMOR

BACKGROUND

In *Funny* you have read a lot about humor and how it "works" in our world. Many individuals, from the Roman orators Cicero and Quintilian to our modern day satirists Jon Stewart and Stephen Colbert, recognize humor's persuasive power. Humor can influence how we think and or can evoke a reaction in us, which is precisely why Plato viewed humor with suspicion. However, as many of the writers in this book argue or demonstrate through the use of humor in their own writing, this same potential to influence thinking and actions is what makes humor so attractive to cultural critics, satirists, advertisers, and anyone hoping to solidify power (and "make friends and influence others"). Furthermore, we live in a society permeated by humor. Therefore, becoming astute readers of the rhetoric of humor proves a crucial skill in recognizing, respecting, and realizing its persuasive power.

ASSIGNMENT

Choose a humorous text and write a rhetorical analysis of it. *Text* in this context can mean written, visual, audio (song), print/digital. **Your task is to analyze how the writer uses humor in the text and to determine if he or she does so effectively.** Your instructor may not require research for this assignment. However, you may find the essays on satire as well as the introduction helpful as you develop your analysis.

QUESTIONS FOR RESEARCH AND INVENTION

1. Why did you choose this text?

2. What elements of the text are specific to humor?

3. Can you situate the humor or comedy within one more of the theories of humor?

GENERAL TIPS FOR WRITING A RHETORICAL ANALYSIS PAPER

- Identify the context for the text. In order to write a successful rhetorical analysis, you may need to situate the text in its larger cultural or social environment (as would be the case if you were writing on Swift's "A Modest Proposal").

- Consider the issue of audience. To whom is the text directed? Is there a "created" or implied audience?

- Consider the writer. As you address the idea of or real writer, you will consider a crucial element of rhetorical analysis—ethos. Ethos deals with the credibility of the author, to his or her positioning of him or herself in relation to readers/audience, and to the writers' presumptions about shared assumptions and values.

- Identify the writer's/creator's overall rhetorical choices (consider his/her use of appeals [ethos, logos, pathos] specific claims, organization, argument strategies, types of evidence, tone, and style).

Your instructor will provide further guidance to help you determine which of the suggestions will be the most helpful for your specific choice.

MAJOR ASSIGNMENT #3:
TAKING A STAND ON THE SOCIAL VALUE OF HUMOR
AND/OR ITS ETHICAL USE

BACKGROUND

Regardless of the approach that the individual writers take on the subject of humor or to any of its related topics—comedy, laughter, jokes—all agree on the social aspect of humor. However, not all agree on what that social aspect is or how it should function. In addition, disagreement also exists on the ethical or responsible uses of humor. Questions arise about who can tell what jokes and to whom. Issues of censorship and taste also prove relevant when considering both the social value and ethical use of humor. As you read the various perspectives on the social value or ethics of humor, what were your reactions? Did you find that you wanted to talk back to a specific writer? Did you have an "aha" moment?

ASSIGNMENT

For this assignment you will make clear your views regarding the social value of humor and/or the ethics of humor. In other words, you will decide whether you agree with the scholars, cultural critics, writers, and others who insist that humor holds an important and valued place in our society. You may, instead, decide whether you agree with the view that those who "use" humor must do so ethically and responsibly. **The purpose of this paper is to present your position—your argument—effectively supported by all relevant strategies of argument.**

QUESTIONS FOR RESEARCH AND INVENTION

1. Did you agree or disagree with a specific writer?

    •   You may agree with some points that a writer makes and disagree with others that he or she makes, thus partially agreeing with his or her major claim.

2. With what points did you agree/disagree?

    •   Identifying points over which you are undecided might also prove helpful as these may be the ones that push you to think the most critically about your position.

3. Can you identify and restate arguments that oppose yours?

    •   A strong paper will include evidence that you understand "the other side."

    •   Conveying the opposing argument clearly and fairly enhances your ethos (credibility) as a writer.

4. What do you see as the most important supporting points (sub-arguments) to your position?

5. What evidence will you use to support your thesis and your sub-arguments?

GENERAL TIPS FOR TAKING A STAND

- A sophisticated and skilled writer may not claim an either/or position in a taking a stand paper. In other words, you may make your position clear while simultaneously presenting the complex nature of the subject. Not every issue allows a definitive for or against position. However, your instructor may wish for a clear position paper and will provide instructions to you if this is the case.

- You can support your thesis and sub-arguments in a variety of ways throughout this paper: sound reasoning (inductive and deductive) and logic, evidence (examples, illustrations, outside sources).

- The essays, stories, articles, blogs, and other pieces in *Funny* will provide ample support for this assignment. However, you may wish to do additional research by reading other works by the writers in this book or the longer works from which some of the excerpts come. In addition, your instructor may require that you conduct research using your library databases.

MAJOR ASSIGNMENT #4:
BIO-CRITICAL ESSAY ON COMEDIAN, COMIC, HUMORIST

BACKGROUND

The study of humor inevitably involves the study of the comedians—the comics—the individuals, who make us laugh. Humorists, satirists, and comedians write plays, poetry, and stories rife with satire, irony, bawdiness, and just plain hilariousness, or enduring satirical essays. Humor and laughter, as so many of the writers in *Funny* have pointed out, are social and serve a social function. Comics/humorists, then, play an important role in society. These "funny" men and women also perform their comedy, acting as cultural critics and keen observers of humanity—commenting on our foibles and flaws as well as our triumphs and joys.

ASSIGNMENT

Research a past or current comedian, comic, satirist, or humorist and write a bio-critical essay consisting of biography and critical analysis. You may choose someone who writes comedy or satire or whose use of irony is notable or a stand-up comic, talk show host, political humorist, TV comedy writer. **You will identify and analyze this individuals' contribution to the field of humor and his or her cultural significance.**

The first step is to find out and write about the biographical details of this individual's life and the cultural/historical context in which he or she performed or performs/wrote or writes. In addition to this biographical and cultural/historical information, you will identify the cultural or social issues that he or she addresses through his or her humor.

QUESTIONS FOR RESEARCH AND INVENTION

For analysis

1. What did this individual's presence add to his or her comedy niche?

2. Was or is he or she a major influence on other comedians/humorists?

3. Did this individual change a comedy genre (written, performative, cinematic)?

4. Has this comedian/humorist, through his or her comedy (written or performative) helped shift the way people think about a social issue(s)?

RESEARCH

Although your instructor may provide specific instructions regarding research for this assignment, consulting scholarly reference works for biographical and historical information will prove helpful. The Internet also offers a wealth of resources such as online interviews (videos and texts) and clips of comedy performances. The filmography at the end of this book offers suggestions for documentaries on comedians. In addition to these sources, academic and scholarly research exists on many comedians/humorists, past and present.

KEY ELEMENTS OF THIS ASSIGNMENT

- Biography

- Cultural/social/historical context (when the individual lived/lives, wrote/writes, performed/performs)

- Cultural/social topics the individual addresses

- Contribution to the field of humor

- Cultural significance

GENERAL TIPS FOR EFFECTIVE RESEARCH

- Find sources that help you provide all the information necessary to fully develop your topic: Do you have all the biographical details of this individual's life? Have you looked at more than one source? Do you find conflicting accounts? How do you reconcile those accounts in your "telling" of this person's life?

- Find sources that help you contextualize your topic: What do you need to know about the social and cultural aspects of humor? What do you need to know about the various kinds of humor? Are controversies regarding "political correctness" relevant to your topic? Are controversies regarding race and humor, gender and humor, sexuality and humor relevant?

- Find sources that help you support your analysis/observations/explanations: Will your sources provide specific examples that develop your analysis? Does your research provide varied and ample evidence to make your analysis and observations relevant to your audience?

MAJOR ASSIGNMENT #5:
RESEARCHING, EXPLORING, ANALYZING A TOPIC ON HUMOR

BACKGROUND

The study of humor involves many different approaches from a variety of disciplines. Someone studying humor can focus on its health benefits, or its social aspect, or the efficacy of satire to influence individuals' thinking, or the relationship between humor and gender, or the ethics of humor. Perhaps you had never thought about the multiple topics related to humor until reading many of the pieces in this book. Perhaps as you read, one the topics surprised or intrigued you, and you want to find out more about it, or conversely, perhaps one of them resonated with you, and you want to dig more deeply into that aspect of humor.

ASSIGNMENT

For this assignment, you will become a humor studies scholar. You will research, explore, and analyze a topic, an aspect, of humor and convey the significance of your analysis. **Your research and analysis will lead you beyond merely reporting on your subject; instead, you will present an exploratory argument. In other words, this paper will have a controlling idea (thesis) that makes clear the topic, the critical issues involved, and the implications of your exploration and analysis.** Your class notes and any previous written assignments pertaining to your topic will provide an excellent place to begin your research.

QUESTIONS FOR RESEARCH AND INVENTION

Narrowing your topic

1. Which readings did you find the most interesting, compelling? Why?

   • Do you want to know more about how humor and laughter affect our overall health and mental well-being?

   • Does humor's place in politics and political campaigns seem important to you?

   • Are you intrigued by the notion that comedians, humorists, and satirists can use stereotypes in order to collapse and subvert those stereotypes?

2. What subcategories might exist within this topic?

3. What do you already know about this topic?

For analysis

1. What are the various elements of this topic?

   - Are there processes involved?

   - Controversies?

   - Key figures?

2. What concepts do you need to introduce and explain?

   - Do you need to explain the theories of humor?

   - Is it important that your readers understand the difference between laughter and humor?

3. What is significant about your analysis?

   - What has your analysis added to both your readers' and your own understanding of the topic?

   - How has your research and analysis answered your readers "So what?" question?

GENERAL TIPS FOR EFFECTIVE RESEARCH

- Find sources that help you provide all the information necessary to fully develop your topic: Many of the readings in *Funny* contain bibliographical information, either in the form of a works cited page or footnotes, so these are a good place to begin your research.

- Find sources that help you contextualize your topic: Do you need to find sources that provide historical context or information about past or current debates on the topic?

- Find sources that help you support your analysis/observations/explanations: Will your sources provide specific examples that develop your analysis? Does your research provide varied and ample evidence to make your analysis and observations relevant to your audience?

- Using online sources: Your instructor will provide guidelines for using and checking the credibility of online sources. The Internet offers a wealth of resources such as online interviews (videos and texts) and clips of comedy performances.

MAJOR ASSIGNMENT #6: COLLABORATIVE MULTI-MODAL ESSAY: CREATING SOMETHING FUNNY

BACKGROUND

Whatever perspective you take on how humor functions in our world, you do know what makes you laugh. The various ideas expressed by the writers, humorists, bloggers, columnists, cultural critics, researchers, and scholars in this book move us beyond our personal views of humor and help us see it as multifaceted and as anything but simple. Hopefully, these readings have encouraged you to think critically about why you find something funny and why someone else might or might not find that same thing funny. Now you will have the opportunity to flex your comedy muscle—to put some of these theories to work—to think beyond your own sense of humor and to create something funny.

ASSIGNMENT

This collaborative assignment is multi-modal which means that you will compose in and use different modes (physical, digital, visual, audio). In addition to the final original production piece, this assignment will include a critical essay.

For this assignment, you will be part of a team of writers that will create and present an original humorous production in a medium of your choice (see below for suggestions). Your team will design this project using the theories, approaches, and perspectives of the various writers, humorists, and scholars that you have encountered in *Funny*, your class notes, in-class activities, research and any previous writing assignments. **Your final project must contain original humorous material and generally convey a coherent sense of purpose (goal).**

THE CRITICAL ESSAY

The purpose of this essay is twofold: 1) to demonstrate your understanding of humor; 2) to explain the humor in your final production. In order to meet these goals, your team will explain the following in the essay and will draw on the various readings in *Funny* to contextualize and support your explanations.

- Explain why you chose this project.
- Identify what you hoped to accomplish with the humor.
- Explain the choices you made as you composed the humor.
- Explain what you did to connect to your audience.

- Explain each person's contribution to the project.
- Explain any "creative" differences and how you negotiated these differences.

You are not limited to these six areas, but you must address each of them.

TIPS FOR WRITING THE ESSAY

- Do not merely address each of the areas; instead, write a compelling narrative about how your team conceived of, developed, and brought this project to fruition.

- Your introduction provides the context for the rest of your essay.

- Have a clear focus.

- Provide transitions both inside and between paragraphs.

- Use the organization and structure that most effectively convey your creative process and best explains the choices that you made regarding the kinds of humor you used and how you delivered that humor.

SUGGESTIONS FOR HUMOROUS PRODUCTION

- Design and compose humorous content for a website such as *FunnyorDie*, *Cracked*, *CollegeHumor*, or the LOL feed on *BuzzFeed*.
- Design and write original content for a digital media satirical news sources such as *The Onion*.
- Create, produce, and film a
  - sketch comedy (e.g., Key & Peele, *Inside Amy Schumer*, *Saturday Night Live*)
  - segment for a satirical television news program (e.g., *The Daily Show*, *The Colbert Report*)
  - parody of TV genre (talk show, reality show, soap opera)
  - trailer for a "new" comedy film
- Create, produce, and perform live
  - any of the above (except the trailer)
  - a stand-up routine (the material written by your team of comedy writers)

Your instructor will provide guidance regarding the media production resources available to you.

FILMOGRAPHY

FEATURED FILMS
POLITICAL SATIRE

Dr. Strangelove or: How I Learned to Stop Worrying and Love the Bomb
Wag the Dog
Thank You for Smoking
Bulworth
The Campaign
The Dictator
Head of State

ZEITGEIST SHAPING MOVIES: "DUMB SMART MOVIES"

Animal House
Ghostbusters
Groundhog Day

COMEDY-DRAMA

The Big Lebowski
Life is Beautiful
Crimes and Misdemeanors
Silver Linings Playbook
Real Women Have Curves

Tortilla Soup
Burn after Reading
Being John Malkovich
The Royal Tenenbaums

DARK HUMOR

M*A*S*H*
Fargo
Prizzi's Honor
Harold and Maude
Nurse Betty

DOCUMENTARIES

Fahrenheit 9/11
Sicko
Religulous

DOCUMENTARIES: COMEDIANS AND COMEDY

Comedian
This film follows Jerry Seinfield's return to stand-up comedy after the end of his television sitcom. 2002.

Looking for Lenny
This film looks at the pioneer of stand-up comedy and addresses issues of censorship, obscenity, free speech, and challenging social boundaries. 2011.

Mr. Warmth: The Don Rickles Project
In addition to interviews with Rickles's contemporaries this 2007 documentary includes commentary from more contemporary comedians. Known for his caustic wit, Rickles did not shy away from social taboos.

Joan Rivers: A Piece of Work
Made in 2011, this film shows Rivers's tenacity in a business dominated by males.

Why We Laugh: Black Comedians on Black Comedy
Made in 2011, this documentary chronicles the history of black comedy since 1901.

American: The Bill Hicks Story
This film is a 2009 study of this counterculture satirist.

Richard Pryor: Omit the Logic
This 2013 documentary chronicles the life and career of Pryor and addresses his personal tragedies as well as exploring his battles over censorship, his status as a black comedian, and what he "meant" to white and black audiences.

Make 'Em Laugh: The Funny Business of America
This 2008 PBS documentary, originally aired as six one-hour episodes hosted by Billy Crystal and narrated by Amy Sedaris. Part performance, biography, and history, this documentary includes interviews with comedians, writers, producers, and historians. It reveals how American comedians/comedy confront political, race, and gender issues as well as providing a historical look at humor's place in America.

When Comedy Was King 1960; DVD.
A feature-length documentary devoted to the great clowns of silent comedy, Charlie Chaplin, Harry Langdon, Buster Keaton, and Stan Laurel and Oliver Hardy.

ACKNOWLEDGMENTS

Amies, Toby. "The Art of the Perfect Prank." From bbc.com, March 30, 2001. Reprinted with permission of BBC News.

Anderson, Nick. *Houston Chronicle*, 2012. Copyright © Nick Anderson. Used with permission.

Bailey, Jason. "Revisiting Mel Brooks and Richard Pryor's Subversively Brilliant Racial Satire *Blazing Saddles*, 40 Years Later." From *Flavorwire.com*. Reprinted with permission.

Barry, Dave. "Technology." From *I'll Mature When I'm Dead: Dave Barry's Amazing Tales of Adulthood*. Published by Berkley Books, 2012. Copyright © 2010 by Dave Barry. Reprinted with permission.

Baumgartner, Jody and Jonathan Morris "*The Daily Show* Effect: Candidate Evaluations, Efficacy, and American Youth." Reprinted with permission from *American Politics Research*, Vol. 34.3, pp 341-67. Copyright © 2006 Sage Publications.

Bergson, Henri. "The Comic in General—The Comic Element in Forms and Movements—Expansive Force of the Comic." From *Laughter: An Essay on the Meaning of the Comic*. Trans. Cloudsley Brereton and Fred Rothwell. 1911. Reprinted from Project Guttenberg.

Callman, Rachel, "Selfie's Word of the Year Acceptance Speech" Published at McSweeney's.net in *Short Imagined Monologues* on November 21, 2013. Used with permission of the author.

Campbell, Troy. "Why We Love Louis CK?—His Painful Honesty" Reprinted from *The Huffington Post*.

Carter, Bill. "In the Tastes of Young Men, Humor Is Most Prized, A Survey Finds." From *The New York Times*. Reprinted with permission.

Clemmitt, Marcia. "Ethnic Humor's No Joke for Amateurs." Reprinted with permission from *CQ Researcher*, Vol.17.21. Copyright © 2007 Sage Publications.

Colletta, Lisa. "Political Satire and Postmodern Irony in the Age of Stephen Colbert and Jon Stewart." From *The Journal of Popular Culture*, Vol. 42.5 (2009): 856-74. Reprinted with permission of John Wiley & Sons, Inc.

Ellis, Iain. "Political Humor and Its Diss-Content." Reprinted from *Pop Matters* with permission of Iain Ellis.

Fey, Tina. "Dear Internet." From *Bossypants*, published by Reagan Arthur Books, 2011. Copyright © 2011 by Little Stranger, Inc. All rights reserved.

Funt, Peter. "The Jokes on Whom?" From *New York Times Sunday Review*. Reprinted with permission.

Gorman, James. "Scientists Hint at Why Laughter Feels So Good." From *The New York Times*. Reprinted with permission.

Harding, Luke and Kim Willsher. "Anger as Papers Reprint Cartoons of Muhammad." Reprinted from *The Guardian*.

"Health Care Savvy: Heart Benefits of a Hearty Laugh" Reprinted from *Consumer Reports*.

Jones, Chris. "When Jokes Go too Far." Reprinted with permission from the *Chicago Tribune*.

Keyes, Allison. "Political Humor's Hysterical History." Reprinted with permission from *National Public Radio*.

Klein, Dana and Nicholas Kuiper. "Humor Styles, Peer Relationships, and Bullying in Middle Childhood." Reprinted from *Humor*, Vol. 9.4 (2006): 383-404.

Lefcourt, Herbert M. "Early Conceptions of Humor in Religion, Medicine, Philosophy, and Psychology." From *Humor: The Psychology of Living Buoyantly*. Copyright © 2001 Kluwer Academic/Plenum Publishers. Reprinted with permission.

Luckovich, Mike. Cartoon appeared in the *Atlanta Journal-Constitution*, September 26, 2013. Copyright © 2013 Mike Luckovich. Used with permission.

MacAdam, Alison, "For Cartoonists Who Cover Obama: Four More Ears." From *National Public* Radio. Reprinted with permission.

Martin, Rod A. "Humor and Mental Health." Reprinted from *The Psychology of Humor: An Integrative Approach*. Copyright © 2007, with permission of Elsevier.

Matson, R. J. Copyright © 2013 RJ Matson. All rights reserved.

Morreall, John. "The Social Value of Humor." From *Taking Laughter Seriously* and published by SUNY Press,1983. Reprinted with permission.

Nicholson, Christie. "The Humor Gap." From *Scientific American Mind*, Vol. 21.2 (2010): 38 45. Reprinted with permission.

Provine, Robert. "A Big Mystery: Why Do We Laugh?" From msnbc.com, May 27, 1999. Reprinted with permission of NBC News.

Rappoport, Leon. "Males versus Females, Gays versus Straights, and the Varieties of Gender Humor." From *Punchlines: The Case for Racial, Ethnic, and Gender Humor*. Reprinted with permission of Praeger, 2005.

Reynolds, Gretchen. "Laughter as a Form of Exercise." From *New York Times Magazine*. Reprinted with permission.

Rice, David Wall. "The Genius of 'Chappelle's Show' 10 Years Later." From ebony.com.

Sack, Steve. Copyright © 2012 Steve Sack. All rights reserved.

Saunders, George. "My Amendment." Reprinted with permission from *The New Yorker*.

Shapiro, Ari. "Not Just for Laughs: Why Humor Can Be a Powerful Campaign Tool" Reprinted with permission from *National Public Radio*.

Shifman, Limor and Dafna Lemish. "Blondejokes.com: The New Generation." Reprinted from *Society*, Vol. 47 (2010):19-22.

Swift, Jonathan. *A Modest Proposal*, 1729. Reprinted from Project Guttenberg.

Tapley, Robin. "The Value of Humor." From *The Journal of Value Inquiry*, Vol. 40 (2006): 421 31. Reprinted with permission of Springer.

Watterson, Bill. Copyright © 1989 Bill Watterson and Universal Press Syndicate. All rights reserved.

Weyant, Christopher. Copyright © Christopher Weyant. All rights reserved.